HTML5 Canvas Cookbook

Over 80 recipes to revolutionize the web experience with HTML5 Canvas

Eric Rowell

BIRMINGHAM - MUMBAI

HTML5 Canvas Cookbook

First published: November 2011

Production Reference: 1171111

Published by Packt Publishing Ltd.
Livery Place
35 Livery Street
Birmingham B3 2PB, UK.

ISBN 978-1-84969-136-9

www.packtpub.com

Cover Image by Sujay Gawand (sujay0000@gmail.com)

Credits

Author
Eric Rowell

Reviewers
Kevin Roast
Rokesh Jankie
Ian Pollock
Denis Samoilov
Alika Jain

Acquisition Editor
Wilson D'souza

Development Editor
Maitreya Bhakal

Technical Editor
Sakina Kaydawala

Project Coordinator
Shubhanjan Chatterjee

Proofreader
Joanna McMahon

Indexer
Monica Ajmera Mehta

Graphics
Valentina D'silva

Production Coordinator
Shantanu Zagade

Cover Work
Shantanu Zagade

About the Author

Eric Rowell is a professional frontend web developer and entrepreneur who is fascinated with the web industry, business, technology, and how they fit together. He's the founder and chief editor of `http://www.Html5CanvasTutorials.com`, an HTML5 canvas resource that's designed to complement the recipes in this book, and is also the creator of the KineticJS library, a lightweight JavaScript library that extends the 2D context by enabling canvas interactivity for desktop and mobile applications. When he's not building software, he loves spending time with his beautiful wife, Andie, and his spunky little dog, Koda. If you're feeling social, you can follow him on Twitter at `@ericdrowell`.

About the Reviewers

Kevin Roast is a frontend software developer with 12 years professional experience and a lifelong interest in computers and computer graphics. He has developed web software for several companies including his current employer Alfresco Software Ltd. He is very excited by the prospect of the HTML5 standardization of the Web, the progress of web-browser software in recent years and the bright future of HTML5 canvas development. He was co-author of a book called *Professional Alfresco: Practical Solutions for Enterprise Content Management*.

Rokesh Jankie graduated in 1998 with a Masters degree in Computer Science from Leiden University, The Netherlands. His field of specialization was Algorithms and NP-complete problems. Scheduling problems can be NP-complete and that's the area which he focused on. After that he started working for Leiden University, ORTEC Consultants, Ponte Vecchio and then Qualogy. At Qualogy, he used what he experienced so far to set up a product. Qualogy works in the field of Oracle and Java technology. With the current set of technologies, interesting products can be delivered, for example QAFE (see `http://www.qafe.com` for more info).

The company he works for now specializes in Oracle and Java technology. As the Head of the product development department his focus is on the future of web application development. They are using modern technologies (HTML5, Google APIs, GWT, Java) and have close contact with some excellent people at Google to make things work.

I'm very honored and grateful that I was contacted to review this book and to Shubhanjan Chatterjee for giving me the opportunity. It feels good to be part of the next big thing on the Web (HTML5) in this way. The future of web applications looks very promising.

Ian Pollock is an artist and educator. He holds a Master of Fine Arts in New Genre, and is currently completing a Master of Education in Instructional Design.

Since 1998, Ian has been teaching undergraduate and graduate classes in the US and the Middle East in media fine arts, web and graphic design, photography, as well as audio and video production.

His other experience includes building industry advisory boards, facilitating quality assurance procedures in academic programs, and coordinating system-wide learning objectives and curriculum alignment for courses across 11 campuses.

He currently advises as the director for education and social engagement at Illume Magazine Foundation.

His interests include digital media, fine art, citizen journalism, activism, social learning strategies, connectivist learning, social capacity building, web design and development, ux/uix, video and audio production, government 2.0, education 2.0, and curriculum development.

Ian currently teaches at the University of San Francisco and the CSU Eastbay.

I would like to extend my gratitude to Robert Frager, Ramona Manhein, and Kemal Guler, and all my loving friends, without whose care and support it would be difficult to accomplish anything in this world. I would also like to thank my students, who have forced me to become a deeper thinker and a more caring educator, and whose enthusiasm for art and technology inspires me every day.

Denis Samoilov is a web developer at HeBS Digital. Denis lives in Tallinn, Estonia with his girlfriend Natasha. He got involved in web development and design about ten years ago working on small projects. After finishing high school he decided to study Informatics in Tallinn Technical University. For two years, he has been working as SQA engineer, after that he tried himself as web designer, but found that web development is more interesting area for him.

I would like to thank my girlfriend Natasha for her support on those busy evenings and always being able to put a smile on my face, my colleagues Vladimir Sobolev for invaluable advices and Tim Sklyarov for providing designs of the most interesting award wining and challenging projects, Shubhanjan Chatterjee for providing me opportunity to review this book, also I would like to thank my parents, because without them I wouldn't be where I am today.

Alika Jain has extensive experience in the design and development of web applications for industries. She is skilled in frontend programming.

She has sound knowledge of technologies including HTML, XHTML, CSS, jQuery, JavaScript, and the Creative Adobe Suite.

I couldn't do this without the support of my family, but it is two special people's time to shine—Gulshan Modi (my father) and Parveen Jain (my husband).

www.PacktPub.com

Support files, eBooks, discount offers and more

You might want to visit www.PacktPub.com for support files and downloads related to your book.

Did you know that Packt offers eBook versions of every book published, with PDF and ePub files available? You can upgrade to the eBook version at www.PacktPub.com and as a print book customer, you are entitled to a discount on the eBook copy. Get in touch with us at service@packtpub.com for more details.

At www.PacktPub.com, you can also read a collection of free technical articles, sign up for a range of free newsletters and receive exclusive discounts and offers on Packt books and eBooks.

http://PacktLib.PacktPub.com

Do you need instant solutions to your IT questions? PacktLib is Packt's online digital book library. Here, you can access, read and search across Packt's entire library of books.

Why Subscribe?

- Fully searchable across every book published by Packt
- Copy and paste, print and bookmark content
- On demand and accessible via web browser

Free Access for Packt account holders

If you have an account with Packt at www.PacktPub.com, you can use this to access PacktLib today and view nine entirely free books. Simply use your login credentials for immediate access.

Table of Contents

Preface

The HTML5 canvas is revolutionizing graphics and visualizations on the Web. Powered by JavaScript, the HTML5 Canvas API enables web developers to create visualizations and animations right in the browser without Flash. Although the HTML5 Canvas is quickly becoming the standard for online graphics and interactivity, many developers fail to exercise all of the features that this powerful technology has to offer.

The **HTML5 Canvas Cookbook** begins by covering the basics of the HTML5 Canvas API and then progresses by providing advanced techniques for handling features not directly supported by the API such as animation and canvas interactivity. It winds up by providing detailed templates for a few of the most common HTML5 canvas applications—data visualization, game development, and 3D modeling. It will acquaint you with interesting topics such as fractals, animation, physics, color models, and matrix mathematics.

By the end of this book, you will have a solid understanding of the HTML5 canvas API and a toolbox of techniques for creating any type of HTML5 canvas application, limited only by the extent of your imagination.

What this book covers

Chapter 1, Getting Started with Paths and Text, begins by covering the basics of sub-path drawing and then moves on to more advanced path drawing techniques by exploring algorithms to draw zigzags and spirals. Next, the chapter dives into text drawing and then completes with an exploration of fractals.

Chapter 2, Shape Drawing and Composites, begins by covering the basics of shape drawing and also shows you how to use color fills, gradient fills, and patterns. Next, the chapter takes an in-depth look at transparencies and composite operations, and then provides recipes for drawing more complex shapes such as clouds, gears, flowers, card suits, and even a full vector-style jet complete with layers and shading.

Chapter 3, Working with Images and Videos, covers the basics of image and video handling, shows you how to copy-and-paste sections of the canvas, and covers different types of pixel manipulation. The chapter also shows you how to convert images into data URLs, save a canvas drawing as an image, and load a canvas with a data URL. Finally, the chapter ends with a pixilated image focus algorithm that can be used to focus and blur images dynamically with pixel manipulation.

Chapter 4, Mastering Transformations, explores what's possible with canvas transformations, including translations, scaling, rotations, mirror transforms, and free-form transformations. In addition, the chapter also explores the canvas state stack in detail.

Chapter 5, Bringing the Canvas to Life with Animation, begins by constructing an `Animation` class to handle an animation stage, and shows you how to create a linear motion, a quadratic motion, and an oscillating motion. Next, it covers some more complex animations such as the oscillation of a soap bubble, a swinging pendulum, and rotating mechanical gears. Finally, the chapter ends with a recipe for creating your own particle physics simulator, and also provides a recipe for creating hundreds of microscopic organisms inside the canvas to stress performance.

Chapter 6, Interacting with the Canvas: Attaching Event Listeners to Shapes and Regions, begins by constructing an `Events` class which extends the canvas API by providing a means for attaching event listeners to shapes and regions on the canvas. Next, the chapter covers techniques for getting the canvas mouse coordinates, detecting region events, detecting image events, detecting mobile touch events, and drag-and-drop. The chapter ends by providing a recipe for creating an image magnifier and another recipe for creating a drawing application.

Chapter 7, Creating Graphs and Charts, provides production-ready graph and chart classes, including a pie chart, a bar chart, an equation grapher, and a line chart.

Chapter 8, Saving the World with Game Development, gets you started with canvas game development by showing you how to create an entire side-scroller game called Canvas Hero. The chapter shows you how to create sprite sheets, create levels and boundary maps, create classes to handle the hero, the bad guys, the level, and the hero's health, and also shows you how to structure the game engine using an MVC (model view controller) design pattern.

Chapter 9, Introducing WebGL, begins by constructing a WebGL wrapper class to simplify the WebGL API. The chapter introduces WebGL by showing you how to create a 3D plane and a rotating cube, and also shows you how to add textures and lighting to your models. The chapter ends by showing you how to create an entire 3D world that you can explore in first person.

Appendices A, B, and *C* discuss other special topics such as canvas support detection, security, canvas vs. CSS3 transitions and animations, and the performance of canvas applications on mobile devices.

What you need for this book

All you need to get started with HTML5 canvas is a modern browser such as Google Chrome, Firefox, Safari, Opera, or IE9, and a simple text editor such as notepad.

Who this book is for

This book is geared towards web developers who are familiar with HTML and JavaScript. It is written for both beginners and seasoned HTML5 developers with a good working knowledge of JavaScript.

What is HTML5 Canvas

Canvas was originally created by Apple in 2004 to implement Dashboard widgets and to power graphics in the Safari browser, and was later adopted by Firefox, Opera, and Google Chrome. Today, canvas is a part of the new HTML5 specification for next generation web technologies.

The HTML5 canvas is an HTML tag that you can embed inside an HTML document for the purpose of drawing graphics with JavaScript. Since the HTML5 canvas is a bitmap, every pixel drawn onto the canvas overrides pixels beneath it.

Here is the base template for all of the 2D HTML5 Canvas recipes for this book:

```
<!DOCTYPE HTML>
<html>
    <head>
        <script>
            window.onload = function(){
                var canvas = document.getElementById("myCanvas");
                var context = canvas.getContext("2d");

                // draw stuff here
            };
        </script>
    </head>
    <body>
        <canvas id="myCanvas" width="578" height="200">
        </canvas>
    </body>
</html>
```

Notice that the canvas element is embedded inside the body of the HTML document, and is defined with an `id`, a `width`, and a `height`. JavaScript uses the `id` to reference the canvas tag, and the `width` and `height` are used to define the size of the drawing area. Once the canvas tag has been accessed with `document.getElementById()`, we can then define a 2D context with:

```
var context = canvas.getContext("2d");
```

Although most of this book covers the 2D context, the final chapter, *Chapter 9*, uses a 3D context to render 3D graphics with WebGL.

Conventions

In this book, you will find a number of styles of text that distinguish between different kinds of information. Here are some examples of these styles, and an explanation of their meaning.

Code words in text are shown as follows: "Define the `Events` constructor."

A block of code is set as follows:

```
var Events = function(canvasId){
    this.canvas = document.getElementById(canvasId);
    this.context = this.canvas.getContext("2d");
    this.stage = undefined;
    this.listening = false;
};
```

When we wish to draw your attention to a particular part of a code block, the relevant lines or items are set in bold:

```
var Events = function(canvasId){
    this.canvas = document.getElementById(canvasId);
    this.context = this.canvas.getContext("2d");
    this.stage = undefined;
    this.listening = false;
};
```

New terms and **important words** are shown in bold. Words that you see on the screen, in menus or dialog boxes for example, appear in the text like this: "It writes out the text **Hello Logo!** at the origin."

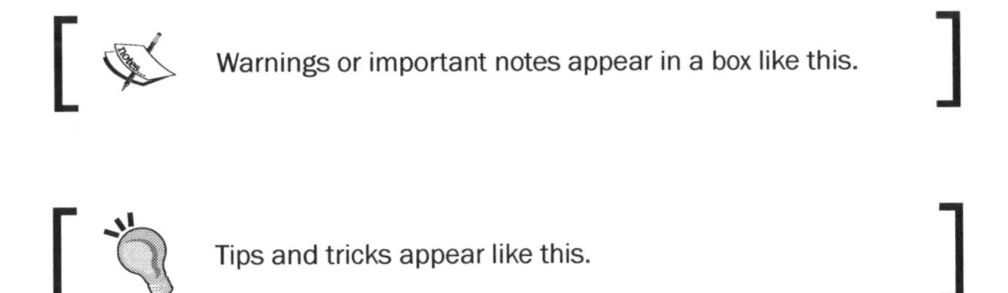

Warnings or important notes appear in a box like this.

Tips and tricks appear like this.

Reader feedback

Feedback from our readers is always welcome. Let us know what you think about this book—what you liked or may have disliked. Reader feedback is important for us to develop titles that you really get the most out of.

To send us general feedback, simply send an e-mail to feedback@packtpub.com, and mention the book title via the subject of your message.

If there is a book that you need and would like to see us publish, please send us a note in the **SUGGEST A TITLE** form on www.packtpub.com or e-mail suggest@packtpub.com.

If there is a topic that you have expertise in and you are interested in either writing or contributing to a book, see our author guide on www.packtpub.com/authors.

Customer support

Now that you are the proud owner of a Packt book, we have a number of things to help you to get the most from your purchase.

Downloading the example code for this book

You can run the demos and download the resources for this book from www.html5canvastutorials.com/cookbook, or you can download the example code files for all Packt books you have purchased from your account at http://www.PacktPub.com. If you purchased this book elsewhere, you can visit http://www.PacktPub.com/support and register to have the files e-mailed directly to you.

Errata

Although we have taken every care to ensure the accuracy of our content, mistakes do happen. If you find a mistake in one of our books—maybe a mistake in the text or the code—we would be grateful if you would report this to us. By doing so, you can save other readers from frustration and help us improve subsequent versions of this book. If you find any errata, please report them by visiting `http://www.packtpub.com/support`, selecting your book, clicking on the **errata submission form** link, and entering the details of your errata. Once your errata are verified, your submission will be accepted and the errata will be uploaded on our website, or added to any list of existing errata, under the Errata section of that title. Any existing errata can be viewed by selecting your title from `http://www.packtpub.com/support`.

Piracy

Piracy of copyright material on the Internet is an ongoing problem across all media. At Packt, we take the protection of our copyright and licenses very seriously. If you come across any illegal copies of our works, in any form, on the Internet, please provide us with the location address or website name immediately so that we can pursue a remedy.

Please contact us at `copyright@packtpub.com` with a link to the suspected pirated material.

We appreciate your help in protecting our authors, and our ability to bring you valuable content.

Questions

You can contact us at `questions@packtpub.com` if you are having a problem with any aspect of the book, and we will do our best to address it.

1
Getting Started with Paths and Text

In this chapter, we will cover:

- Drawing a line
- Drawing an arc
- Drawing a Quadratic curve
- Drawing a Bezier curve
- Drawing a zigzag
- Drawing a spiral
- Working with text
- Drawing 3D text with shadows
- Unlocking the power of fractals: Drawing a haunted tree

Introduction

This chapter is designed to demonstrate the fundamental capabilities of the HTML5 canvas by providing a series of progressively complex tasks. The HTML5 canvas API provides the basic tools necessary to draw and style different types of sub paths including lines, arcs, Quadratic curves, and Bezier curves, as well as a means for creating paths by connecting sub paths. The API also provides great support for text drawing with several styling properties. Let's get started!

Drawing a line

When learning how to draw with the HTML5 canvas for the first time, most people are interested in drawing the most basic and rudimentary element of the canvas. This recipe will show you how to do just that by drawing a simple straight line.

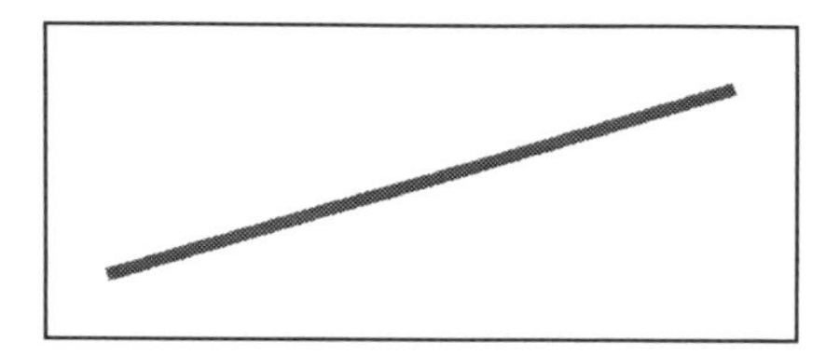

How to do it...

Follow these steps to draw a diagonal line:

1. Define a 2D canvas context and set the line style:

```
window.onload = function(){
  // get the canvas DOM element by its ID
     var canvas = document.getElementById("myCanvas");
  // declare a 2-d context using the getContext() method of the
  // canvas object
     var context = canvas.getContext("2d");

  // set the line width to 10 pixels
     context.lineWidth = 10;
  // set the line color to blue
     context.strokeStyle = "blue";
```

2. Position the canvas context and draw the line:

```
  // position the drawing cursor
     context.moveTo(50, canvas.height - 50);
  // draw the line
     context.lineTo(canvas.width - 50, 50);
  // make the line visible with the stroke color
     context.stroke();
};
```

3. Embed the canvas tag inside the body of the HTML document:

```
<canvas id="myCanvas" width="600" height="250" style="border:1px
solid black;">
</canvas>
```

Downloading the example code

You can run the demos and download the resources for this book from `www.html5canvastutorials.com/cookbook` or you can download the example code files for all Packt books you have purchased from your account at `http://www.PacktPub.com`. If you purchased this book elsewhere, you can visit `http://www.PacktPub.com/support` and register to have the files e-mailed directly to you.

How it works...

As you can see from the preceding code, we need to wait for the page to load before trying to access the canvas tag by its ID. We can accomplish this with the `window.onload` initializer. Once the page loads, we can access the canvas DOM element with `document.getElementById()` and we can define a 2D `canvas` context by passing `2d` into the `getContext()` method of the canvas object. As we will see in the last two chapters, we can also define 3D contexts by passing in other contexts such as `webgl`, `experimental-webgl`, and others.

When drawing a particular element, such as a path, sub path, or shape, it's important to understand that styles can be set at any time, either before or after the element is drawn, but that the style must be applied immediately after the element is drawn for it to take effect, We can set the width of our line with the `lineWidth` property, and we can set the line color with the `strokeStyle` property. Think of this behavior like the steps that we would take if we were to draw something onto a piece of paper. Before we started to draw, we would choose a colored marker (`strokeStyle`) with a certain tip thickness (`lineWidth`).

Now that we have our marker in hand, so to speak, we can position it onto the canvas using the `moveTo()` method:

```
context.moveTo(x,y);
```

Think of the canvas context as a drawing cursor. The `moveTo()` method creates a new sub path for the given point. The coordinates in the top-left corner of the canvas are (0,0), and the coordinates in the bottom-right corner are (canvas width, canvas height).

Once we have positioned our drawing cursor, we can draw the line using the `lineTo()` method by defining the coordinates of the line's end point:

```
context.lineTo(x,y);
```

Finally, to make the line visible, we can use the `stroke()` method. Unless, otherwise specified, the default stroke color is black.

To summarize, here's the typical drawing procedure we should follow when drawing lines with the HTML5 canvas API:

1. Style your line (like choosing a colored marker with a specific tip thickness).
2. Position the canvas context using `moveTo()` (like placing the marker onto a piece of paper).
3. Draw the line with `lineTo()`.
4. Make the line visible using `stroke()`.

There's more...

HTML5 canvas lines can also have one of three varying line caps, including **butt**, **round**, and **square**. The line cap style can be set using the `lineCap` property of the canvas context. Unless otherwise specified, the line cap style is defaulted to butt. The following diagram shows three lines, each with varying line cap styles. The top line is using the default butt line cap, the middle line is using the round line cap, and the bottom line is using a square line cap:

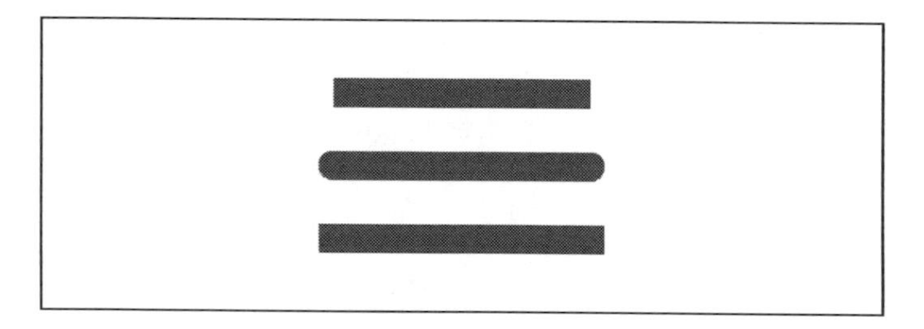

Notice that the middle and bottom lines are slightly longer than the top line, even though all of the line widths are equal. This is because the round line cap and the square line cap increase the length of a line by an amount equal to the width of the line. For example, if our line is 200 px long and 10 px wide, and we use a round or square line cap style, the resulting line will be 210 px long because each cap adds 5 px to the line length.

See also...

- *Drawing a zigzag*
- *Putting it all together: Drawing a jet* in *Chapter 2*

Drawing an arc

When drawing with the HTML5 canvas, it's sometimes necessary to draw perfect arcs. If you're interested in drawing happy rainbows, smiley faces, or diagrams, this recipe would be a good start for your endeavor.

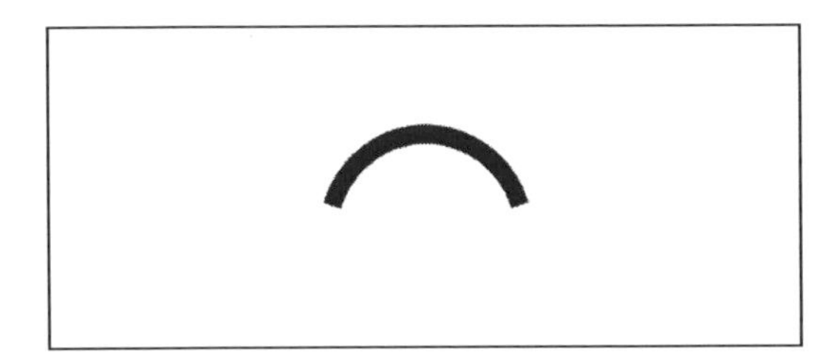

How to do it...

Follow these steps to draw a simple arc:

1. Define a 2D canvas context and set the arc style:

```
window.onload = function(){
    var canvas = document.getElementById("myCanvas");
    var context = canvas.getContext("2d");
    context.lineWidth = 15;
    context.strokeStyle = "black"; // line color
```

2. Draw the arc:

```
context.arc(canvas.width / 2, canvas.height / 2 + 40, 80, 1.1 *
Math.PI, 1.9 * Math.PI, false);
    context.stroke();
};
```

3. Embed the canvas tag inside the body of the HTML document:

```
<canvas id="myCanvas" width="600" height="250" style="border:1px
solid black;">
</canvas>
```

How it works...

We can create an HTML5 arc with the `arc()` method which is defined by a section of the circumference of an imaginary circle. Take a look at the following diagram:

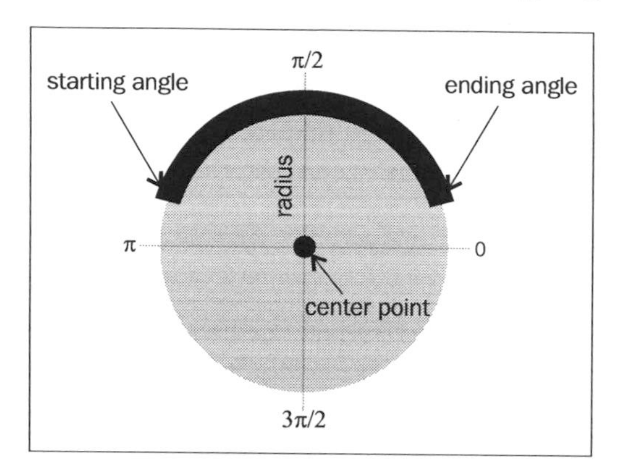

The imaginary circle is defined by a center point and a radius. The circumference section is defined by a starting angle, an ending angle, and whether or not the arc is drawn counter-clockwise:

```
context.arc(centerX,centerY, radius, startingAngle,
      endingAngle,counterclockwise);
```

Notice that the angles start with 0π at the right of the circle and move clockwise to $3\pi/2$, π, $\pi/2$, and then back to 0. For this recipe, we've used 1.1π as the starting angle and 1.9π as the ending angle. This means that the starting angle is just slightly above center on the left side of the imaginary circle, and the ending angle is just slightly above center on the right side of the imaginary circle.

There's more...

The values for the starting angle and the ending angle do not necessarily have to lie within 0π and 2π. In fact, the starting angle and ending angle can be any real number because the angles can overlap themselves as they travel around the circle.

For example, let's say that we define our starting angle as 3π. This is equivalent to one full revolution around the circle (2π) and another half revolution around the circle (1π). In other words, 3π is equivalent to 1π. As another example, - 3π is also equivalent to 1π because the angle travels one and a half revolutions counter-clockwise around the circle, ending up at 1π.

Another method for creating arcs with the HTML5 canvas is to make use of the `arcTo()` method. The resulting arc from the `arcTo()` method is defined by the context point, a control point, an ending point, and a radius:

```
context.arcTo(controlPointX1, controlPointY1, endingPointX,
endingPointY, radius);
```

Unlike the `arc()` method, which positions an arc by its center point, the `arcTo()` method is dependent on the context point, similar to the `lineTo()` method. The `arcTo()` method is most commonly used when creating rounded corners for paths or shapes.

See also...

- *Drawing a circle in Chapter 2*
- *Animating mechanical gears* in *Chapter 5*
- *Animating a clock in Chapter 5*

Drawing a Quadratic curve

In this recipe, we'll learn how to draw a Quadratic curve. Quadratic curves provide much more flexibility and natural curvatures compared to its cousin, the arc, and are an excellent tool for creating custom shapes.

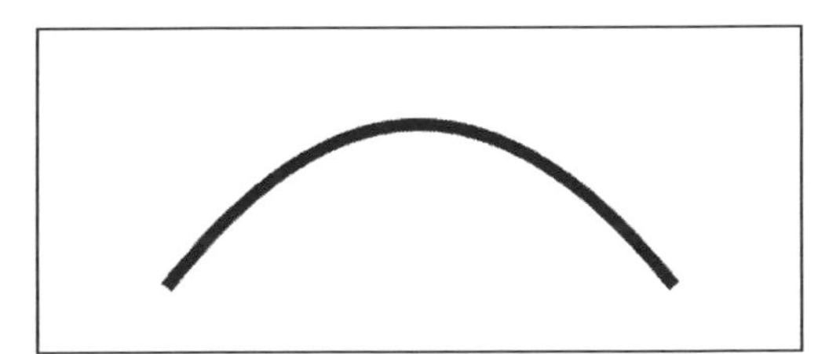

How to do it...

Follow these steps to draw a Quadratic curve:

1. Define a 2D canvas context and set the curve style:

```
window.onload = function(){
    var canvas = document.getElementById("myCanvas");
    var context = canvas.getContext("2d");

    context.lineWidth = 10;
    context.strokeStyle = "black"; // line color
```

2. Position the canvas context and draw the Quadratic curve:

```
context.moveTo(100, canvas.height - 50);
    context.quadraticCurveTo(canvas.width / 2, -50, canvas.width
- 100, canvas.height - 50);
    context.stroke();
};
```

3. Embed the canvas tag inside the body of the HTML document:

```
<canvas id="myCanvas" width="600" height="250" style="border:1px
solid black;">
</canvas>
```

How it works...

HTML5 Quadratic curves are defined by the context point, a control point, and an ending point:

```
  context.quadraticCurveTo(controlX, controlY, endingPointX,
endingPointY);
```

Take a look at the following diagram:

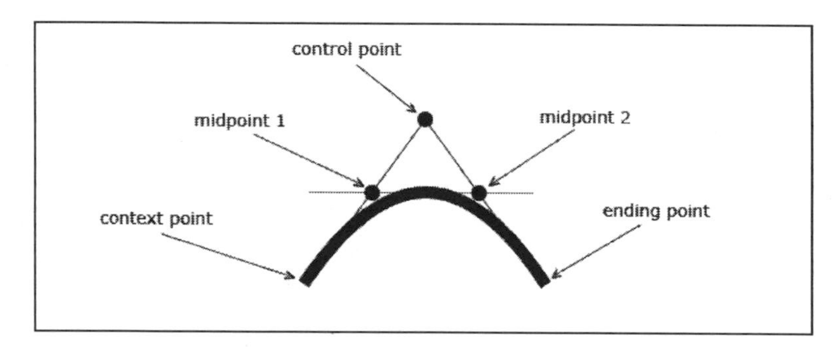

The curvature of a Quadratic curve is defined by three characteristic tangents. The first part of the curve is tangential to an imaginary line that starts with the context point and ends with the control point. The peak of the curve is tangential to an imaginary line that starts with midpoint 1 and ends with midpoint 2. Finally, the last part of the curve is tangential to an imaginary line that starts with the control point and ends with the ending point.

See also...

- *Putting it all together: Drawing a jet*, in *Chapter 2*
- *Unlocking the power of fractals: Drawing a haunted tree*

Drawing a Bezier curve

If Quadratic curves don't meet your needs, the Bezier curve might do the trick. Also known as cubic curves, the Bezier curve is the most advanced curvature available with the HTML5 canvas API.

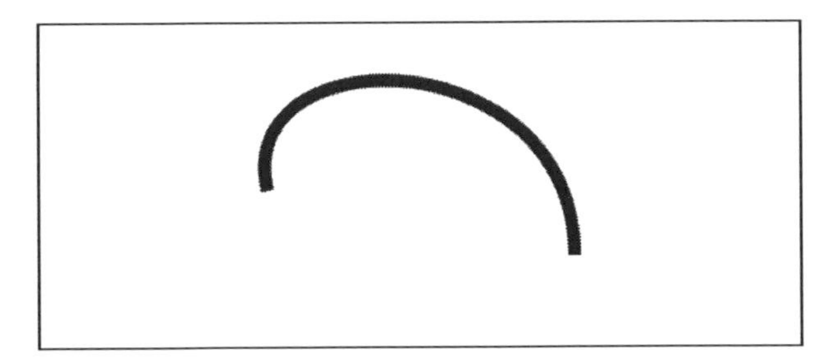

How to do it...

Follow these steps to draw an arbitrary Bezier curve:

1. Define a 2D canvas context and set the curve style:

```
window.onload = function(){
    var canvas = document.getElementById("myCanvas");
    var context = canvas.getContext("2d");

    context.lineWidth = 10;
    context.strokeStyle = "black"; // line color
    context.moveTo(180, 130);
```

2. Position the canvas context and draw the Bezier curve:

```
context.bezierCurveTo(150, 10, 420, 10, 420, 180);
    context.stroke();
};
```

3. Embed the canvas tag inside the body of the HTML document:

```
<canvas id="myCanvas" width="600" height="250" style="border:1px
solid black;">
</canvas>
```

How it works...

HTML5 canvas Bezier curves are defined by the context point, two control points, and an ending point. The additional control point gives us much more control over its curvature compared to Quadratic curves:

```
context.bezierCurveTo(controlPointX1, controlPointY1,
    controlPointX2, controlPointY2,
    endingPointX, endingPointY);
```

Take a look at the following diagram:

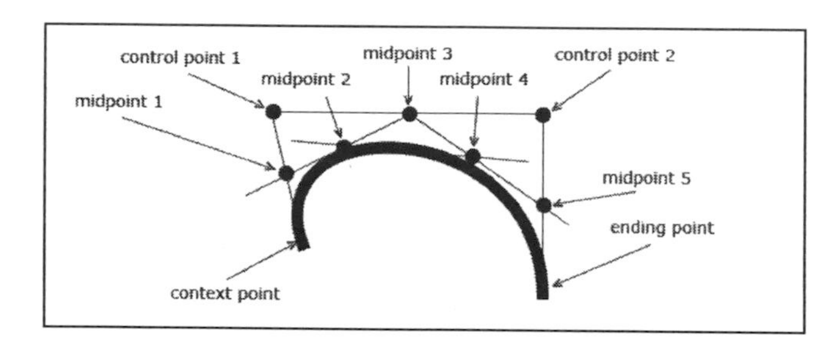

Unlike Quadratic curves, which are defined by three characteristic tangents, the Bezier curve is defined by five characteristic tangents. The first part of the curve is tangential to an imaginary line that starts with the context point and ends with the first control point. The next part of the curve is tangential to the imaginary line that starts with midpoint 1 and ends with midpoint 3. The peak of the curve is tangential to the imaginary line that starts with midpoint 2 and ends with midpoint 4. The fourth part of the curve is tangential to the imaginary line that starts with midpoint 3 and ends with midpoint 5. Finally, the last part of the curve is tangential to the imaginary line that starts with the second control point and ends with the ending point.

See also...

- *Randomizing shape properties: Drawing a field of flowers* in *Chapter 2*
- *Putting it all together: Drawing a jet* in *Chapter 2*

Drawing a zigzag

In this recipe, we'll introduce path drawing by iteratively connecting line subpaths to draw a zigzag path.

How to do it...

Follow these steps to draw a zigzag path:

1. Define a 2D canvas context and initialize the zigzag parameters:

```
window.onload = function(){
    var canvas = document.getElementById("myCanvas");
    var context = canvas.getContext("2d");

    var startX = 85;
    var startY = 70;
    var zigzagSpacing = 60;
```

2. Define the zigzag style and begin the path:

```
context.lineWidth = 10;
    context.strokeStyle = "#0096FF"; // blue-ish color
    context.beginPath();
    context.moveTo(startX, startY);
```

3. Draw seven connecting zigzag lines and then make the zigzag path visible with `stroke()`:

```
// draw seven lines
    for (var n = 0; n < 7; n++) {
        var x = startX + ((n + 1) * zigzagSpacing);
        var y;

        if (n % 2 == 0) { // if n is even...
            y = startY + 100;
        }
        else { // if n is odd...
            y = startY;
        }
```

```
            context.lineTo(x, y);
        }

        context.stroke();
    };
```

4. Embed the canvas tag inside the body of the HTML document:

```
<canvas id="myCanvas" width="600" height="250" style="border:1px
solid black;">
</canvas>
```

How it works...

To draw a zigzag, we can connect alternating diagonal lines to form a path. Programmatically, this can be achieved by setting up a loop that draws diagonal lines moving upwards and to the right on odd iterations, and downwards and to the right on even iterations.

The key thing to pay attention to in this recipe is the `beginPath()` method. This method essentially declares that a path is being drawn, such that the end of each line sub path defines the beginning of the next sub path. Without using the `beginPath()` method, we would have to tediously position the canvas context using `moveTo()` for each line segment while ensuring that the ending points of the previous line segment match the starting point of the current line segment. As we will see in the next chapter, the `beginPath()` method is also a required step for creating shapes.

Line join styles

Notice how the connection between each line segment comes to a sharp point. This is because the line join style of the HTML5 canvas path is defaulted to **miter**. Alternatively, we could also set the line join style to **round** or **bevel** with the `lineJoin` property of the canvas context.

If your line segments are fairly thin and don't connect at steep angles, it can be somewhat difficult to distinguish different line join styles. Typically, different line join styles are more noticeable when the path thickness exceeds 5 px and the angle between line sub paths is relatively small.

Drawing a spiral

Caution, this recipe may induce hypnosis. In this recipe, we'll draw a spiral by connecting a series of short lines to form a spiral path.

How to do it...

Follow these steps to draw a centered spiral:

1. Define a 2D canvas context and initialize the spiral parameters:

```
window.onload = function(){
    var canvas = document.getElementById("myCanvas");
    var context = canvas.getContext("2d");

    var radius = 0;
    var angle = 0;
```

2. Set the spiral style:

```
context.lineWidth = 10;
    context.strokeStyle = "#0096FF"; // blue-ish color
    context.beginPath();
    context.moveTo(canvas.width / 2, canvas.height / 2);
```

3. Rotate about the center of the canvas three times (50 iterations per full revolution) while increasing the radius by 0.75 for each iteration and draw a line segment to the current point from the previous point with `lineTo()`. Finally, make the spiral visible with `stroke()`:

```
for (var n = 0; n < 150; n++) {
        radius += 0.75;
        // make a complete circle every 50 iterations
        angle += (Math.PI * 2) / 50;
        var x = canvas.width / 2 + radius * Math.cos(angle);
        var y = canvas.height / 2 + radius * Math.sin(angle);
        context.lineTo(x, y);
    }

    context.stroke();
};
```

4. Embed the canvas tag inside the body of the HTML document:

```
<canvas id="myCanvas" width="600" height="250" style="border:1px
solid black;">
</canvas>
```

How it works...

To draw a spiral with HTML5 canvas, we can place our drawing cursor in the center of the canvas, iteratively increase the radius and angle about the center, and then draw a super short line from the previous point to the current point. Another way to think about it is to imagine yourself as a kid standing on a sidewalk with a piece of colored chalk. Bend down and put the chalk on the sidewalk, and then start turning in a circle (not too fast, though, unless you want to get dizzy and fall over). As you spin around, move the piece of chalk outward away from you. After a few revolutions, you'll have drawn a neat little spiral.

Working with text

Almost all applications require some sort of text to effectively communicate something to the user. This recipe will show you how to draw a simple text string with an optimistic welcoming.

Hello World!

How to do it...

Follow these steps to write text on the canvas:

1. Define a 2D canvas context and set the text style:

```
window.onload = function(){
    var canvas = document.getElementById("myCanvas");
    var context = canvas.getContext("2d");

    context.font = "40pt Calibri";
    context.fillStyle = "black";
```

2. Horizontally and vertically align the text, and then draw it:

```
// align text horizontally center
    context.textAlign = "center";
    // align text vertically center
    context.textBaseline = "middle";
    context.fillText("Hello World!", canvas.width / 2, 120);
};
```

3. Embed the canvas tag inside the body of the HTML document:

```
<canvas id="myCanvas" width="600" height="250" style="border:1px
solid black;">
</canvas>
```

How it works...

To draw text with the HTML5 canvas, we can define the font style and size with the `font` property, the font color with the `fillStyle` property, the horizontal text alignment with the `textAlign` property, and the vertical text alignment with the `textBaseline` property. The `textAlign` property can be set to `left`, `center`, or `right`, and the `textBaseline` property can be set to `top`, `hanging`, `middle`, `alphabetic`, `ideographic`, or `bottom`. Unless otherwise specified, the `textAlign` property is defaulted to `left`, and the `textBaseline` property is defaulted to alphabetic.

There's more...

In addition to `fillText()`, the HTML5 canvas API also supports `strokeText()`:

```
context.strokeText("Hello World!", x, y);
```

This method will color the perimeter of the text instead of filling it. To set both the fill and stroke for HTML canvas text, you can use both the `fillText()` and the `strokeText()` methods together. It's good practice to use the `fillText()` method before the `strokeText()` method in order to render the stroke thickness correctly.

See also...

- *Drawing 3D text with shadows*
- *Creating a mirror transform in Chapter 4*
- *Drawing a simple logo and randomizing its position, rotation, and scale in Chapter 4*

Drawing 3D text with shadows

If 2D text doesn't get you jazzed, you might consider drawing 3D text instead. Although the HTML5 canvas API doesn't directly provide us with a means for creating 3D text, we can certainly create a custom `draw3dText()` method using the existing API.

How to do it...

Follow these steps to create 3D text:

1. Set the canvas context and the text style:

   ```
   window.onload = function(){
     canvas = document.getElementById("myCanvas");
     context = canvas.getContext("2d");

     context.font = "40pt Calibri";
     context.fillStyle = "black";
   ```

2. Align and draw the 3D text:

   ```
   // align text horizontally center
       context.textAlign = "center";
       // align text vertically center
       context.textBaseline = "middle";
       draw3dText(context, "Hello 3D World!", canvas.width / 2, 120,
   5);
   };
   ```

3. Define the `draw3dText()` function that draws multiple text layers and adds a shadow:

   ```
   function draw3dText(context, text, x, y, textDepth){
       var n;

       // draw bottom layers
   ```

```
        for (n = 0; n < textDepth; n++) {
            context.fillText(text, x - n, y - n);
        }

        // draw top layer with shadow casting over
        // bottom layers
        context.fillStyle = "#5E97FF";
        context.shadowColor = "black";
        context.shadowBlur = 10;
        context.shadowOffsetX = textDepth + 2;
        context.shadowOffsetY = textDepth + 2;
        context.fillText(text, x - n, y - n);
    }
```

4. Embed the canvas tag inside the body of the HTML document:

```
<canvas id="myCanvas" width="600" height="250" style="border:1px
solid black;">
</canvas>
```

How it works...

To draw 3D text with the HTML5 canvas, we can stack multiple layers of the same text on top of one another to create the illusion of depth. In this recipe, we've set the text depth to five, which means that our custom `draw3dText()` method layers five instances of "Hello 3D World!" on top of one another. We can color these layers black to create the illusion of darkness beneath our text.

Next, we can add a colored top layer to portray a forward-facing surface. Finally, we can apply a soft shadow beneath the text by setting the `shadowColor`, `shadowBlur`, `shadowOffsetX`, and `shadowOffsetY` properties of the canvas context. As we'll see in later recipes, these properties aren't limited to text and can also be applied to sub paths, paths, and shapes.

Unlocking the power of fractals: Drawing a haunted tree

First thing's first—what are fractals? If you don't already know, fractals are the awesome result when you mix mathematics with art, and can be found in all sorts of patterns that make up life. Algorithmically, a fractal is based on an equation that undergoes recursion. In this recipe, we'll create an organic-looking tree by drawing a trunk which forks into two branches, and then draw two more branches that stem from the branches we just drew. After twelve iterations, we'll end up with an elaborate, seemingly chaotic mesh of branches and twigs.

How to do it...

Follow these steps to draw a tree using fractals:

1. Create a recursive function that draws a single branch that forks out into two branches, and then recursively calls itself to draw another two branches from the end points of the forked branches:

```
function drawBranches(context, startX, startY, trunkWidth, level){
    if (level < 12) {
        var changeX = 100 / (level + 1);
        var changeY = 200 / (level + 1);

        var topRightX = startX + Math.random() * changeX;
        var topRightY = startY - Math.random() * changeY;

        var topLeftX = startX - Math.random() * changeX;
        var topLeftY = startY - Math.random() * changeY;
```

```
        // draw right branch
        context.beginPath();
        context.moveTo(startX + trunkWidth / 4, startY);
        context.quadraticCurveTo(startX + trunkWidth / 4, startY
- trunkWidth, topRightX, topRightY);
        context.lineWidth = trunkWidth;
        context.lineCap = "round";
        context.stroke();

        // draw left branch
        context.beginPath();
        context.moveTo(startX - trunkWidth / 4, startY);
        context.quadraticCurveTo(startX - trunkWidth / 4, startY -
        trunkWidth, topLeftX, topLeftY);
        context.lineWidth = trunkWidth;
        context.lineCap = "round";
        context.stroke();

        drawBranches(context, topRightX, topRightY, trunkWidth *
0.7, level + 1);
        drawBranches(context, topLeftX, topLeftY, trunkWidth *
0.7, level + 1);
    }
}
```

2. Initialize the canvas context and begin drawing the tree fractal by calling `drawBranches()`:

```
window.onload = function(){
    canvas = document.getElementById("myCanvas");
    context = canvas.getContext("2d");

    drawBranches(context, canvas.width / 2, canvas.height, 50, 0);
};
```

3. Embed the canvas tag inside the body of the HTML document:

```
<canvas id="myCanvas" width="600" height="500" style="border:1px
solid black;">
</canvas>
```

How it works...

To create a tree using fractals, we need to design the recursive function that defines the mathematical nature of a tree. If you take a moment and study a tree (they are quite beautiful if you think about it), you'll notice that each branch forks into smaller branches. In turn, those branches fork into even smaller branches, and so on. This means that our recursive function should draw a single branch that forks into two branches, and then recursively calls itself to draw another two branches that stem from the two branches we just drew.

Now that we have a plan for creating our fractal, we can implement it using the HTML5 canvas API. The easiest way to draw a branch that forks into two branches is by drawing two Quadratic curves that bend outwards from one another.

If we were to use the exact same drawing procedure for each iteration, our tree would be perfectly symmetrical and quite uninteresting. To help make our tree look more natural, we can introduce random variables that offset the ending points of each branch.

There's more...

The fun thing about this recipe is that every tree is different. If you code this one up for yourself and continuously refresh your browser, you'll see that every tree formation is completely unique. You might also be interested in tweaking the branch-drawing algorithm to create different kinds of trees, or even draw leaves at the tips of the smallest branches.

Some other great examples of fractals can be found in sea shells, snowflakes, feathers, plant life, crystals, mountains, rivers, and lightning.

2
Shape Drawing and Composites

In this chapter, we will cover:

- Drawing a rectangle
- Drawing a circle
- Working with custom shapes and fill styles
- Fun with Bezier curves: drawing a cloud
- Drawing transparent shapes
- Working with the context state stack to save and restore styles
- Working with composite operations
- Creating patterns with loops: drawing a gear
- Randomizing shape properties: drawing a field of flowers
- Creating custom shape functions: playing card suits
- Putting it all together: drawing a jet

Introduction

In Chapter 1, Getting Started with Paths and Text, we learned how to draw sub paths such as lines, arcs, Quadratic curves, and Bezier curves, and then we learned how to connect them together to form paths. In this chapter, we'll focus on basic and advanced shape drawing techniques such as drawing rectangles and circles, drawing custom shapes, filling shapes, working with composites, and drawing pictures. Let's get started!

Drawing a rectangle

In this recipe, we'll learn how to draw the only built-in shape provided by the HTML5 canvas API, a rectangle. As unexciting as a rectangle might seem, many applications use them in one way or another, so you might as well get acquainted.

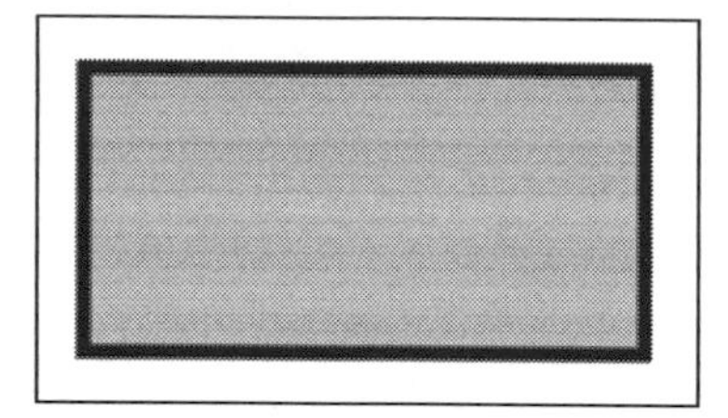

How to do it...

Follow these steps to draw a simple rectangle centered on the canvas:

1. Define a 2D canvas context:

```
window.onload = function(){
    var canvas = document.getElementById("myCanvas");
    var context = canvas.getContext("2d");
```

2. Draw a rectangle using the `rect()` method, set the color fill with the `fillStyle` property, and then fill the shape with the `fill()` method:

```
    context.rect(canvas.width / 2 - 100, canvas.height / 2 - 50,
200, 100);
    context.fillStyle = "#8ED6FF";
    context.fill();
    context.lineWidth = 5;
    context.strokeStyle = "black";
    context.stroke();
};
```

3. Embed the canvas tag inside the body of the HTML document:

```
<canvas id="myCanvas" width="600" height="250" style="border:1px
solid black;">
</canvas>
```

How it works...

As you can see from the preceding code, we can draw a simple rectangle by using the `rect()` method:

```
context.rect(x,y,width,height);
```

The `rect()` method draws a rectangle at the position `x,y`, and defines its size with `width` and `height`. Another key thing to pay attention to in this recipe is the usage of `fillStyle` and `fill()`. Similar to `strokeStyle` and `stroke()`, we can assign a fill color using the `fillStyle` method and fill the shape using `fill()`.

Notice that we used `fill()` before `stroke()`. If we were to stroke a shape before filling it, the fill style would actually overlay half of the stroke style, effectively halving the line width style set with `lineWidth`. As a result, it's good practice to use `fill()` before using `stroke()`.

There's more...

In addition to the `rect()` method, there are two additional methods that we can use to draw a rectangle and also apply styling with one line of code, the `fillRect()` method and the `strokeRect()` method.

The fillRect() method

If we intend to fill a rectangle after drawing it with `rect()`, we might consider both drawing the rectangle and filling it with a single method using `fillRect()`:

```
context.fillRect(x,y,width,height);
```

The `fillRect()` method is equivalent to using the `rect()` method followed by `fill()`. When using this method, you'll need to define the fill style prior to calling it.

The strokeRect() method

In addition to the `fillRect()` method, we can draw a rectangle and stroke it with a single method using the `strokeRect()` method:

```
context.strokeRect(x,y,width,height);
```

The `strokeRect()` method is equivalent to using the `rect()` method followed by `stroke()`. Similar to `fillRect()`, you'll need to define the stroke style prior to calling this method.

Unfortunately, the HTML5 canvas API does not support a method that both fills and strokes a rectangle. Personally, I like to use the `rect()` method and apply stroke styles and fills as needed using `stroke()` and `fill()` because it's more consistent with custom shape drawing. However, if you're wanting to apply both a stroke and fill to a rectangle while using one of these short-hand methods, it's good practice to use `fillRect()` followed by `stroke()`. If you were to use `strokeRect()` followed by `fill()`, you would overlay the stroke style by the fill, halving the stroke line width.

See also...

- *Creating a linear motion* in *Chapter 5*
- *Detecting region events* in *Chapter 6*
- *Creating a bar chart* in *Chapter 7*

Drawing a circle

Although the HTML5 canvas API doesn't support a circle method, we can certainly create one by drawing a fully enclosed arc.

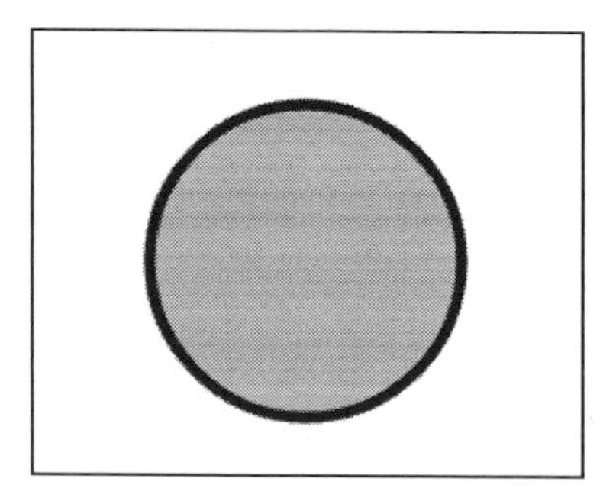

How to do it...

Follow these steps to draw a circle centered on the canvas:

1. Define a 2D canvas context:

```
window.onload = function(){
    var canvas = document.getElementById("myCanvas");
    var context = canvas.getContext("2d");
```

2. Create a circle using the `arc()` method, set the color fill using the `fillStyle` property, and then fill the shape with the `fill()` method:

```
    context.arc(canvas.width / 2, canvas.height / 2, 70, 0, 2 *
Math.PI, false);
    context.fillStyle = "#8ED6FF";
    context.fill();
    context.lineWidth = 5;
    context.strokeStyle = "black";
    context.stroke();
};
```

3. Embed the canvas tag inside the body of the HTML document:

```
<canvas id="myCanvas" width="600" height="250" style="border:1px
solid black;">
</canvas>
```

How it works...

As you might recall from Chapter 1, we can create an arc using the `arc()` method which draws a section of a circle defined by a starting angle and an ending angle. If, however, we define the difference between the starting angle and ending angle as 360 degrees (2π), we will have effectively drawn a complete circle:

```
context.arc(centerX, centerY, radius, 0, 2 * Math.PI, false);
```

See also...

- *Creating patterns with loops: drawing a gear*
- *Transforming a circle into an oval* in *Chapter 4*
- *Swinging a pendulum* in *Chapter 5*
- *Simulating particle physics* in *Chapter 5*
- *Animating a clock* in *Chapter 5*
- *Detecting region events* in *Chapter 6*
- *Creating a pie chart* in *Chapter 7*

Working with custom shapes and fill styles

In this recipe, we'll draw four triangles and then fill each one with a different fill style. The fill styles available with the HTML5 canvas API are color fills, linear gradients, radial gradients, and patterns.

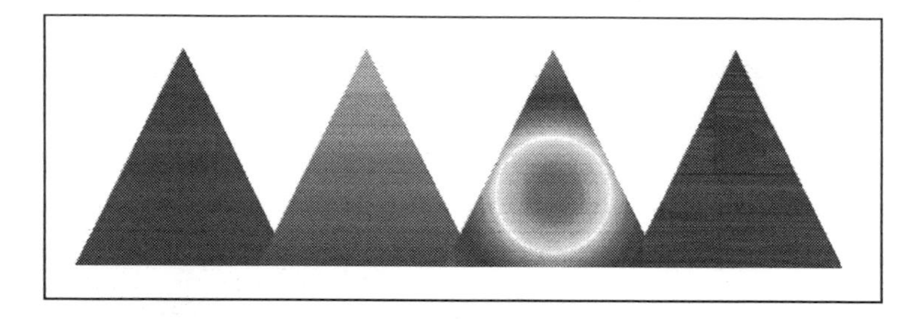

How to do it...

Follow these steps to draw four triangles, one with a color fill, one with a linear gradient fill, one with a radial gradient fill, and one with a pattern fill:

1. Create a simple function that draws a triangle:

```
function drawTriangle(context, x, y, triangleWidth,
triangleHeight, fillStyle){
    context.beginPath();
    context.moveTo(x, y);
    context.lineTo(x + triangleWidth / 2, y + triangleHeight);
    context.lineTo(x - triangleWidth / 2, y + triangleHeight);
    context.closePath();
    context.fillStyle = fillStyle;
    context.fill();
}
```

2. Define a 2D canvas context and set the height, width, and y position of our triangles:

```
window.onload = function(){
    var canvas = document.getElementById("myCanvas");
    var context = canvas.getContext("2d");

    var grd;
    var triangleWidth = 150;
    var triangleHeight = 150;
    var triangleY = canvas.height / 2 - triangleWidth / 2;
```

3. Draw a triangle using a color fill:

```
    // color fill (left)
    drawTriangle(context, canvas.width * 1 / 5, triangleY,
triangleWidth, triangleHeight, "blue");
```

4. Draw a triangle using a linear gradient fill:

```
    // linear gradient fill (second from left)
    grd = context.createLinearGradient(canvas.width * 2 / 5,
triangleY, canvas.width * 2 / 5, triangleY + triangleHeight);
    grd.addColorStop(0, "#8ED6FF"); // light blue
    grd.addColorStop(1, "#004CB3"); // dark blue
    drawTriangle(context, canvas.width * 2 / 5, triangleY,
triangleWidth, triangleHeight, grd);
```

5. Draw a triangle using a radial gradient fill:

```
    // radial gradient fill (second from right)
    var centerX = (canvas.width * 3 / 5 +
    (canvas.width * 3 / 5 - triangleWidth / 2) +
    (canvas.width * 3 / 5 + triangleWidth / 2)) / 3;

    var centerY = (triangleY +
    (triangleY + triangleHeight) +
    (triangleY + triangleHeight)) / 3;

    grd = context.createRadialGradient(centerX, centerY, 10,
centerX, centerY, 100);
    grd.addColorStop(0, "red");
    grd.addColorStop(0.17, "orange");
    grd.addColorStop(0.33, "yellow");
    grd.addColorStop(0.5, "green");
    grd.addColorStop(0.666, "blue");
    grd.addColorStop(1, "violet");
    drawTriangle(context, canvas.width * 3 / 5, triangleY,
triangleWidth, triangleHeight, grd);
```

6. Draw a triangle using a pattern fill:

```
    // pattern fill (right)
    var imageObj - new Image();
    imageObj.onload = function(){
        var pattern = context.createPattern(imageObj, "repeat");
        drawTriangle(context, canvas.width * 4 / 5, triangleY,
triangleWidth, triangleHeight, pattern);
    };
    imageObj.src = "wood-pattern.png";
};
```

7. Embed the canvas tag inside the body of the HTML document:

```
<canvas id="myCanvas" width="600" height="250" style="border:1px
solid black;">
</canvas>
```

How it works...

As you might recall from Chapter 1, we can start a new path with the `beginPath()` method, place our drawing cursor using `moveTo()`, and then draw consecutive sub paths to form a path. We can add one more step to this procedure by closing our path with the `closePath()` method of the canvas context to create a shape:

```
context.closePath();
```

This method essentially tells the canvas context to complete the current path by connecting the last point in the path with the start point of the path.

In the `drawTriangle()` method, we can begin a new path using `beginPath()`, position the drawing cursor using `moveTo()`, draw two sides of the triangle using `lineTo()`, and then complete the third side of the triangle with `closePath()`.

As you can see from the preceding screenshot, the second triangle from the left is filled with a linear gradient. Linear gradients can be created with the `createLinearGradient()` method of the canvas context, which is defined by a start point and an end point:

```
var grd=context.createLinearGradient(startX,startY,endX,endY);
```

Next, we can set the colors of the gradient using the `addColorStop()` method which assigns a color value at an offset position along the gradient line from 0 to 1:

```
grd.addColorStop(offset,color);
```

Colors assigned with an offset value of 0 will be positioned at the starting point of the linear gradient, and colors assigned with an offset value of 1 will be positioned at the end point of the linear gradient. In this example, we've positioned a light blue color at the top of the triangle and a dark blue color at the bottom of the triangle.

Next up, let's cover radial gradients. The second triangle from the right is filled with a radial gradient composed of six different colors. Radial gradients can be created using the `createRadialGradient()` method of the canvas context, which requires a starting point, a start radius, an end point, and an end radius:

```
var grd=context.createRadialGradient(startX,startY,

   startRadius,endX,endY,endRadius);
```

Radial gradients are defined by two imaginary circles. The first imaginary circle is defined by `startX`, `startY`, and `startRadius`. The second imaginary circle is defined by `endX`, `endY`, and `endRadius`. Similarly to linear gradients, we can position colors along the radial gradient line using the `addColorStop()` method of the canvas context.

Finally, the fourth type of fill style available with the HTML5 canvas API is patterns. We can create a `pattern` object using the `createPattern()` method of the canvas context, which requires an `image` object and a repeat option:

```
var pattern=context.createPattern(imageObj, repeatOption);
```

The `repeatOption` can take one of the four options, `repeat`, `repeat-x`, `repeat-y`, and `no-repeat`. Unless otherwise specified, the `repeatOption` is defaulted to `repeat`. We'll cover images more in depth in *Chapter 3, Working with Images and Videos*.

See also...

- *Putting it all together: drawing a jet*

Fun with Bezier curves: drawing a cloud

In this recipe, we will learn how to draw a custom shape by connecting a series of Bezier curve sub paths to create a fluffy cloud.

How to do it...

Follow these steps to draw a fluffy cloud in the center of the canvas:

1. Define a 2D canvas context:

```
window.onload = function(){
    var canvas = document.getElementById("myCanvas");
    var context = canvas.getContext("2d");
```

2. Draw a cloud by connecting six Bezier curves:

```
    var startX = 200;
    var startY = 100;

  // draw cloud shape
    context.beginPath();
    context.moveTo(startX, startY);
    context.bezierCurveTo(startX - 40, startY + 20, startX - 40,
startY + 70, startX + 60, startY + 70);
    context.bezierCurveTo(startX + 80, startY + 100, startX + 150,
startY + 100, startX + 170, startY + 70);
    context.bezierCurveTo(startX + 250, startY + 70, startX + 250,
startY + 40, startX + 220, startY + 20);
    context.bezierCurveTo(startX + 260, startY - 40, startX + 200,
startY - 50, startX + 170, startY - 30);
    context.bezierCurveTo(startX + 150, startY - 75, startX + 80,
startY - 60, startX + 80, startY - 30);
    context.bezierCurveTo(startX + 30, startY - 75, startX - 20,
startY - 60, startX, startY);
    context.closePath();
```

3. Define a radial gradient with the `createRadialGradient()` method and fill the shape with the gradient:

```
  //add a radial gradient
    var grdCenterX = 260;
    var grdCenterY = 80;
    var grd = context.createRadialGradient(grdCenterX, grdCenterY,
10, grdCenterX, grdCenterY, 200);
    grd.addColorStop(0, "#8ED6FF"); // light blue
    grd.addColorStop(1, "#004CB3"); // dark blue
    context.fillStyle = grd;
    context.fill();
```

4. Set the line width and stroke the cloud:

```
  // set the line width and stroke color
    context.lineWidth = 5;
    context.strokeStyle = "#0000ff";
    context.stroke();
};
```

5. Embed the canvas tag inside the body of the HTML document:

```
<canvas id="myCanvas" width="600" height="250" style="border:1px
solid black;">
</canvas>
```

How it works...

To draw a fluffy cloud using the HTML5 canvas API, we can connect several Bezier curves to form the perimeter of the cloud shape. To create the illusion of a bulbous surface, we can create a radial gradient using the `createRadialGradient()` method, set the gradient colors and offsets using the `addColorStop()` method, set the radial gradient as the fill style using `fillStyle`, and then apply the gradient using `fill()`.

Drawing transparent shapes

For applications that require shape layering, it's often desirable to work with transparencies. In this recipe, we will learn how to set shape transparencies using the global alpha composite.

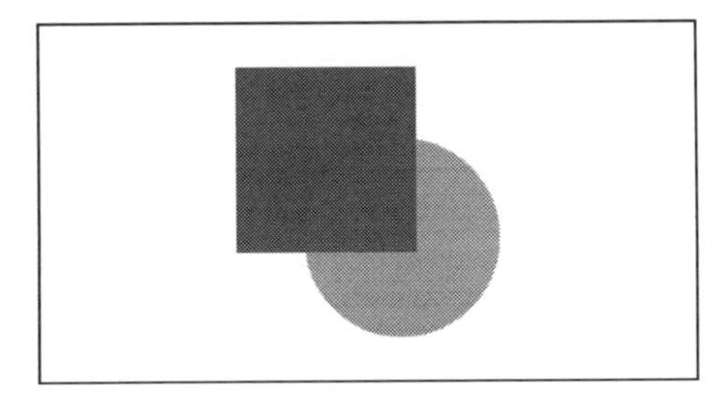

How to do it...

Follow these steps to draw a transparent circle on top of an opaque square:

1. Define a 2D canvas context:

```
window.onload = function(){
    var canvas = document.getElementById("myCanvas");
    var context = canvas.getContext("2d");
```

2. Draw a rectangle:

```
    // draw rectangle
    context.beginPath();
    context.rect(240, 30, 130, 130);
    context.fillStyle = "blue";
    context.fill();
```

3. Set the global alpha of the canvas using the `globalAlpha` property and draw a circle:

```
        // draw circle
        context.globalAlpha = 0.5; // set global alpha
        context.beginPath();
        context.arc(359, 150, 70, 0, 2 * Math.PI, false);
        context.fillStyle = "red";
        context.fill();
    };
```

4. Embed the canvas tag inside the body of the HTML document:

```
<canvas id="myCanvas" width="600" height="250" style="border:1px
solid black;">
</canvas>
```

How it works...

To set the opacity of a shape using the HTML5 canvas API, we can use the `globalAlpha` property:

```
context.globalAlpha=[value]
```

The `globalAlpha` property accepts any real number between 0 and 1. We can set the `globalAlpha` property to `1` to make shapes fully opaque, and we can set the `globalAlpha` property to `0` to make shapes fully transparent.

Working with the context state stack to save and restore styles

When creating more complex HTML5 canvas applications, you'll find yourself needing a way to revert back to previous style combinations so that you don't have to set and reset dozens of style properties at different points in the drawing process. Fortunately, the HTML5 canvas API provides us with access to the context state stack which allows us to save and restore context states. In this recipe, we'll demonstrate how the state stack works by saving the context state, setting the global alpha, drawing a transparent circle, restoring the state stack to the state before we set the global alpha, and then drawing an opaque square. Let's take a look!

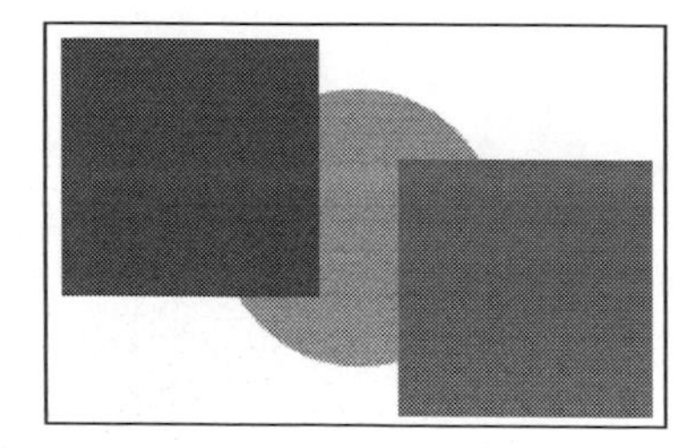

Getting ready...

Before we cover the canvas state stack, it's imperative that you understand how a stack data structure works (if you already do, you can skip to the *How it works* section).

A stack data structure is a last in, first out (LIFO) structure. Stacks have three major operations – **push**, **pop**, and **stack top**. When an element is pushed onto the stack, it gets added to the top of the stack. When the stack is popped, the top element is removed from the stack. The *stack top* operation simply returns the element at the top of the stack.

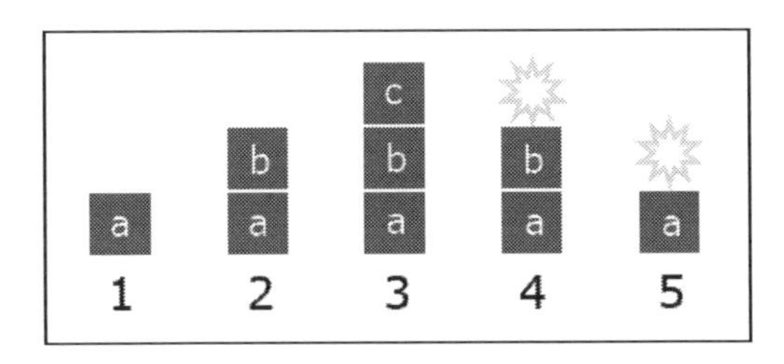

Take a look at the preceding diagram, which represents the state of a stack throughout multiple actions. In step 1, we start out with a stack containing one element, element "a". In step 2, the "b" element is pushed onto the stack. In step 3, the "c" element is pushed onto the stack. In step 4, we pop the stack, which removes the last element pushed onto the stack. Since element "c" was at the top of the stack, it's the element that's removed. In step 5, we again pop the stack, which removes the last element pushed onto the stack. Since element "b" was at the top of the stack, it's the element that's removed.

As we will see in the next section, stacks are a wonderful data structure for saving states as they change over time, and then restoring them by popping the stack.

How to do it...

Follow these steps to draw an opaque square on top of a transparent circle:

1. Define a 2D canvas context:

```
window.onload = function(){
    var canvas = document.getElementById("myCanvas");
    var context = canvas.getContext("2d");
```

2. Draw a rectangle:

```
    // draw rectangle
    context.beginPath();
    context.rect(150, 30, 130, 130);
    context.fillStyle = "blue";
    context.fill();
```

3. Save the context state with `save()`, set the global alpha of the canvas using the `globalAlpha` property, draw a circle, and then restore the canvas state with `restore()`:

```
    // wrap circle drawing code with save-restore combination
    context.save();
    context.globalAlpha = 0.5; // set global alpha
    context.beginPath();
    context.arc(canvas.width / 2, canvas.height / 2, 70, 0, 2 *
Math.PI, false);
    context.fillStyle = "red";
    context.fill();
    context.restore();
```

4. Draw another rectangle (which will be opaque) to show that the context state has been restored to the state before the global alpha property was set:

```
    // draw another rectangle
    context.beginPath();
    context.rect(canvas.width - (150 + 130), canvas.height - (30 +
130), 130, 130);
    context.fillStyle = "green";
    context.fill();
};
```

5. Embed the canvas tag inside the body of the HTML document:

```
<canvas id="myCanvas" width="600" height="250" style="border:1px
solid black;">
</canvas>
```

How it works...

As you can see in the preceding code, by wrapping the circle drawing code with a save-restore combination, we are essentially encapsulating any styles that we use between the `save()` method and the `restore()` method such that they don't affect the shapes drawn afterwards. Save-restore combinations can be thought of as a way to induce style scoping, similar to the way that a function induces variable scope in JavaScript. Although you might be saying "Well that sounds like a complicated way to set the globalAlpha back to 1!" Hold on partner. In the real world, you'll typically be dealing with lots of different combinations of styles for different sections of code. In this type of scenario, save-restore combinations are a life-saver. Writing complex HTML5 canvas applications without save-restore combinations is a lot like building a complex web application with one big block of JavaScript code using nothing but global variables. Yikes!

There's more...

As we'll see in *Chapter 4, Mastering Transformations*, another common usage of the state stack is to save and restore transformation states.

See also...

- *Handling multiple transforms with the state stack* in *Chapter 4*

Working with composite operations

In this recipe, we'll explore composite operations by creating a table of each variation. Composite operations are particularly useful for creating complex shapes, drawing shapes underneath other shapes instead of on top of them, and creating other interesting effects.

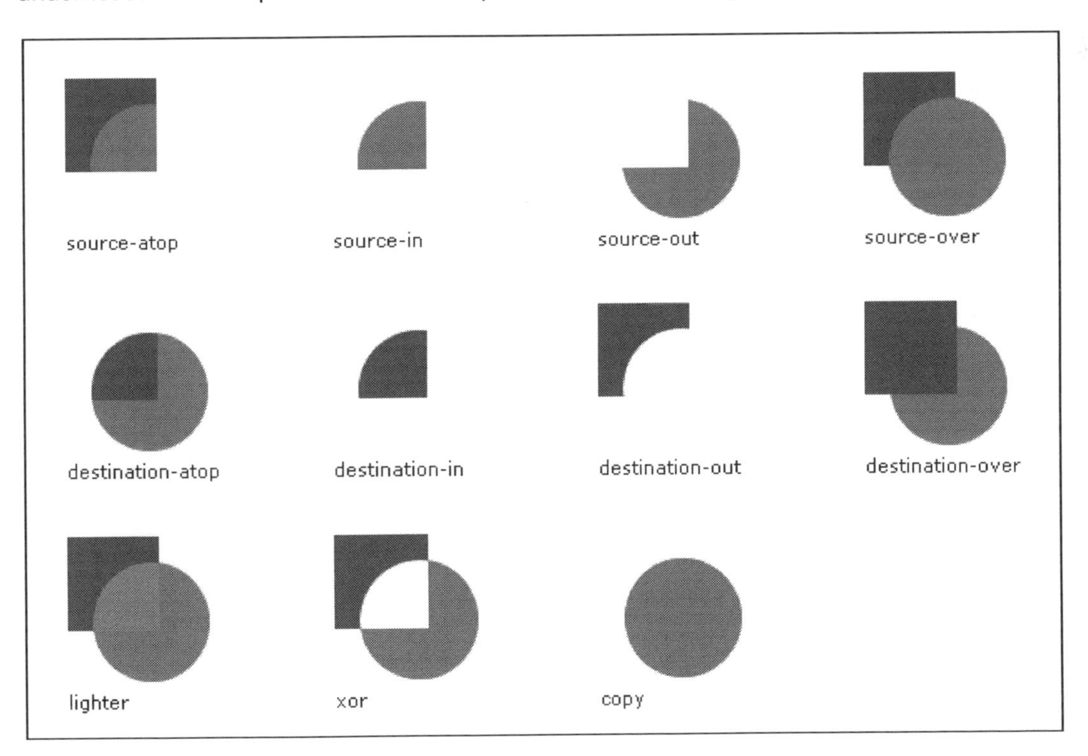

Getting ready...

The following is a description for each possible composite operation available with the HTML5 canvas API, where the red circle represents the source (S) and the blue square represents the destination (D). To further develop your understanding of composite operations, it helps to look at the corresponding operation while reading each description:

Operation	Description
`source-atop` (S atop D)	Display the source image wherever both images are opaque. Display the destination image wherever the destination image is opaque but the source image is transparent. Display transparency elsewhere.
`source-in` (S in D)	Display the source image wherever both the source image and destination image are opaque. Display transparency elsewhere.
`source-out` (S out D)	Display the source image wherever the source image is opaque and the destination image is transparent. Display transparency elsewhere.
`source-over` (S over D, default)	Display the source image wherever the source image is opaque. Display the destination image elsewhere.
`destination-atop` (S atop D)	Display the destination image wherever both images are opaque. Display the source image wherever the source image is opaque but the destination image is transparent. Display transparency elsewhere.
`destination-in` (S in D)	Display the destination image wherever both the destination image and source image are opaque. Display transparency elsewhere.
`destination -out` (S out D)	Display the destination image wherever the destination image is opaque and the source image is transparent. Display transparency elsewhere.
`destination -over` (S over D)	Display the destination image wherever the destination image is opaque. Display the destination image elsewhere.
`lighter` (S plus D)	Display the sum of the source image and destination image.
`xor` (S xor D)	Exclusive OR of the source image and destination image.
`copy` (D is ignored)	Display the source image instead of the destination image.

At the time of writing, dealing with composite operations is quite tricky because each of the five major browsers—Chrome, Firefox, Safari, Opera, and IE9—handle composite operations differently. Rather than showing you a chart of currently supported composite operations by browser at the time of writing, you should instead go online and search for something like "canvas composite operation support by browser" to see the current support for each browser if you intend on using them.

How to do it...

Follow these steps to create a live table of composite operations:

1. Define styles for the canvases and text displays:

```
/* select the div child element of the body */
body > div {
    width: 680px;
    height: 430px;
    border: 1px solid black;
    float: left;
    overflow: hidden;
}

canvas {
    float: left;
    margin-top: 30px;
}

div {
    font-size: 11px;
    font-family: verdana;
    height: 15px;
    float: left;
  width: 160px;
}

/* select the 1st, 5th, and 9th label div */
body > div > div:nth-of-type(4n+1) {
    margin-left: 40px;
}
```

2. Define the sizes and relative distances of each square and circle:

```
window.onload = function(){
    var squareWidth = 55;
    var circleRadius = 35;
    var rectCircleDistX = 50;
    var rectCircleDistY = 50;
```

3. Build an array of composite operations:

```
// define an array of composite operations
var operationArray = [];
operationArray.push("source-atop"); // 0
operationArray.push("source-in"); // 1
operationArray.push("source-out"); // 2
operationArray.push("source-over"); // 3
operationArray.push("destination-atop"); // 4
operationArray.push("destination-in"); // 5
operationArray.push("destination-out"); // 6
operationArray.push("destination-over"); // 7
operationArray.push("lighter"); // 8
operationArray.push("xor"); // 9
operationArray.push("copy"); // 10
```

4. Perform each operation and draw the result on the corresponding canvas:

```
    // draw each of the eleven operations
    for (var n = 0; n < operationArray.length; n++) {
        var thisOperation = operationArray[n];
        var canvas = document.getElementById(thisOperation);
        var context = canvas.getContext("2d");

        // draw rectangle
        context.beginPath();
        context.rect(40, 0, squareWidth, squareWidth);
        context.fillStyle = "blue";
        context.fill();

        // set the global composite operation
        context.globalCompositeOperation = thisOperation;

        // draw circle
        context.beginPath();
        context.arc(40 + rectCircleDistX, rectCircleDistY,
circleRadius, 0, 2 * Math.PI, false);
        context.fillStyle = "red";
        context.fill();
    }
};
```

5. Embed a canvas tag for each operation inside the body of the HTML document:

```
<body>
    <div>
        <canvas id="source-atop" width="160" height="90">
        </canvas>
        <canvas id="source-in" width="160" height="90">
        </canvas>
        <canvas id="source-out" width="160" height="90">
        </canvas>
        <canvas id="source-over" width="160" height="90">
        </canvas>
        <div>
            source-atop
        </div>
        <div>
            source-in
        </div>
        <div>
            source-out
        </div>
        <div>
            source-over
        </div>
        <canvas id="destination-atop" width="160" height="90">
        </canvas>
        <canvas id="destination-in" width="160" height="90">
        </canvas>
        <canvas id="destination-out" width="160" height="90">
        </canvas>
        <canvas id="destination-over" width="160" height="90">
        </canvas>
        <div>
            destination-atop
        </div>
        <div>
            destination-in
        </div>
        <div>
            destination-out
        </div>
        <div>
            destination-over
        </div>
```

```
                <canvas id="lighter" width="160" height="90">
                </canvas>
                <canvas id="xor" width="160" height="90">
                </canvas>
                <canvas id="copy" width="160" height="90">
                </canvas>
                <canvas width="160" height="90">
                </canvas>
                <div>
                    lighter
                </div>
                <div>
                    xor
                </div>
                <div>
                    copy
                </div>
            </div>
        </body>
```

How it works...

We can set a composite operation by using the `globalCompositeOperation` property of the canvas context:

```
context.globalCompositeOperation=[value];
```

The `globalCompositeOperaton` property accepts one of the eleven values, including `source-atop`, `source-in`, `source-out`, `source-over`, `destination-atop`, `destination-in`, `destination-out`, `destination-over`, `lighter`, `xor`, and `copy`. `Source` refers to everything drawn on the canvas after the operation, and `destination` refers to everything drawn on the canvas before the operation. Unless otherwise specified, the default composite operation is set to `source-over`, which basically means that each time something is drawn on the canvas, it's drawn on top of the stuff already there.

We can create an array for each composite operation and then loop through each one to draw the result onto the corresponding canvas. For each iteration, we can draw a square, set the composite operation, and then draw a circle.

Creating patterns with loops: drawing a gear

In this recipe, we'll create a mechanical gear by iteratively drawing a radial zigzag to form teeth and then drawing circles to form the body of the gear.

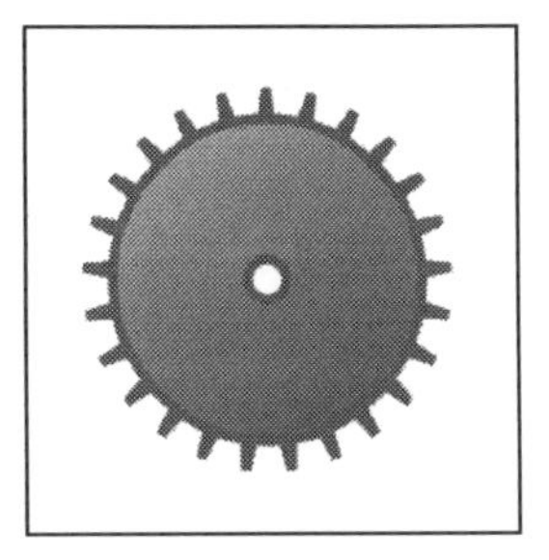

How to do it...

Follow these steps to draw a gear centered on the canvas:

1. Define a 2D canvas context and set the gear properties:

```
window.onload = function(){
    var canvas = document.getElementById("myCanvas");
    var context = canvas.getContext("2d");

    // gear position
    var centerX = canvas.width / 2;
    var centerY = canvas.height / 2;

  // radius of the teeth tips
    var outerRadius = 95;

  // radius of the teeth intersections
    var innerRadius = 50;

  // radius of the gear without the teeth
    var midRadius = innerRadius * 1.6;

  // radius of the hole
    var holeRadius = 10;

  // num points is the number of points that are required
  // to make the gear teeth.  The number of teeth on the gear
  // are equal to half of the number of points.  In this recipe,
  // we will use 50 points which corresponds to 25 gear teeth.
    var numPoints = 50;
```

2. Draw the gear teeth:

```
    // draw gear teeth
    context.beginPath();
  // we can set the lineJoinproperty to bevel so that the tips
  // of the gear teeth are flat and don't come to a sharp point
    context.lineJoin = "bevel";

  // loop through the number of points to create the gear shape
    for (var n = 0; n < numPoints; n++) {
        var radius = null;

    // draw tip of teeth on even iterations
        if (n % 2 == 0) {
            radius = outerRadius;
        }
    // draw teeth connection which lies somewhere between
    // the gear center and gear radius
        else {
            radius = innerRadius;
        }

        var theta = ((Math.PI * 2) / numPoints) * (n + 1);
        var x = (radius * Math.sin(theta)) + centerX;
        var y = (radius * Math.cos(theta)) + centerY;

    // if first iteration, use moveTo() to position
    // the drawing cursor
        if (n == 0) {
            context.moveTo(x, y);
        }
    // if any other iteration, use lineTo() to connect sub paths
        else {
            context.lineTo(x, y);
        }
    }

    context.closePath();

  // define the line width and stroke color
    context.lineWidth = 5;
    context.strokeStyle = "#004CB3";
    context.stroke();
```

3. Draw the gear body:

```
    // draw gear body
    context.beginPath();
    context.arc(centerX, centerY, midRadius, 0, 2 * Math.PI,
false);

  // create a linear gradient
    var grd = context.createLinearGradient(230, 0, 370, 200);
    grd.addColorStop(0, "#8ED6FF"); // light blue
    grd.addColorStop(1, "#004CB3"); // dark blue
    context.fillStyle = grd;
    context.fill();
    context.lineWidth = 5;
    context.strokeStyle = "#004CB3";
    context.stroke();
```

4. Draw the gear hole:

```
    // draw gear hole
    context.beginPath();
    context.arc(centerX, centerY, holeRadius, 0, 2 * Math.PI,
false);
    context.fillStyle = "white";
    context.fill();
    context.strokeStyle = "#004CB3";
    context.stroke();
};
```

5. Embed the canvas tag inside the body of the HTML document:

```
<canvas id="myCanvas" width="600" height="250" style="border:1px
solid black;">
</canvas>
```

How it works...

To draw a gear with the HTML5 canvas, we can start by drawing the teeth around the gear. One way to draw teeth around a gear is to draw a radial zigzag pattern with beveled line joins. One great example of a radial zigzag is a star, which has five points along an imaginary inner circle, and five more points along an imaginary outer circle. To create a star, we can set up a loop with 10 iterations, one iteration for each point. For even iterations, we can draw a point along the outer circle, and for odd iterations we can draw a point along the inner circle. Since our star would have 10 points, each point would be separated by (2π / 10) radians.

You might be asking yourself "What does a star have to do with gear teeth?". If we extend this logic to draw a zigzag shape of say 50 points instead of 10, we'll have effectively created a gear with 25 wedged teeth.

Once the gear teeth are taken care of, we can draw a circle and apply a linear gradient using the `createLinearGradient()` method, and then draw a smaller circle for the hole of the gear.

See also...

- *Animating mechanical gears* in *Chapter 5*

Randomizing shape properties: drawing a field of flowers

In this recipe, we'll embrace our inner hippie by creating a field of colorful flowers.

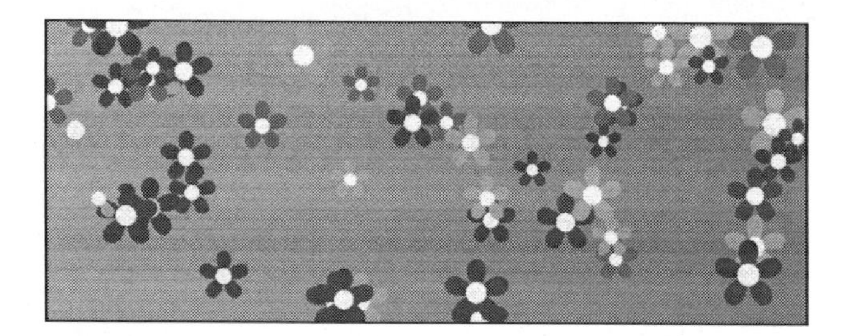

How to do it...

Follow these steps to draw randomized flowers all over the canvas:

1. Define the constructor of a `Flower` object:

```
// define Flower constructor
function Flower(context, centerX, centerY, radius, numPetals,
color){
    this.context = context;
    this.centerX = centerX;
    this.centerY = centerY;
    this.radius = radius;
    this.numPetals = numPetals;
    this.color = color;
}
```

2. Define a `draw` method of the `Flower` object that creates flower petals with a `for` loop and then draws a yellow center:

```
// Define Flower draw method
Flower.prototype.draw = function(){
    var context = this.context;
    context.beginPath();

    // draw petals
    for (var n = 0; n < this.numPetals; n++) {
        var theta1 = ((Math.PI * 2) / this.numPetals) * (n + 1);
        var theta2 = ((Math.PI * 2) / this.numPetals) * (n);

        var x1 = (this.radius * Math.sin(theta1)) + this.centerX;
        var y1 = (this.radius * Math.cos(theta1)) + this.centerY;
        var x2 = (this.radius * Math.sin(theta2)) + this.centerX;
        var y2 = (this.radius * Math.cos(theta2)) + this.centerY;

        context.moveTo(this.centerX, this.centerY);
        context.bezierCurveTo(x1, y1, x2, y2, this.centerX, this.
centerY);
    }

    context.closePath();
    context.fillStyle = this.color;
    context.fill();

    // draw yellow center
    context.beginPath();
    context.arc(this.centerX, this.centerY, this.radius / 5, 0, 2
* Math.PI, false);
    context.fillStyle = "yellow";
    context.fill();
};
```

3. Set the 2D canvas context:

```
window.onload = function(){
    var canvas = document.getElementById("myCanvas");
    var context = canvas.getContext("2d");
```

4. Create a green gradation for the background:

```
    // create a green gradation for background
    context.beginPath();
    context.rect(0, 0, canvas.width, canvas.height);
    var grd = context.createLinearGradient(0, 0, canvas.width,
canvas.height);
    grd.addColorStop(0, "#1EDE70"); // light green
    grd.addColorStop(1, "#00A747"); // dark green
    context.fillStyle = grd;
    context.fill();
```

5. Create an array of flower colors:

```
    // define an array of colors
    var colorArray = [];
    colorArray.push("red"); // 0
    colorArray.push("orange"); // 1
    colorArray.push("blue"); // 2
    colorArray.push("purple"); // 3
```

6. Create a loop that generates flowers with a random position, size, and color:

```
    // define number of flowers
    var numFlowers = 50;

    // draw randomly placed flowers
    for (var n = 0; n < numFlowers; n++) {
        var centerX = Math.random() * canvas.width;
        var centerY = Math.random() * canvas.height;
        var radius = (Math.random() * 25) + 25;
        var colorIndex = Math.round(Math.random() * (colorArray.
length - 1));

        var thisFlower = new Flower(context, centerX, centerY,
radius, 5, colorArray[colorIndex]);
        thisFlower.draw();
    }
};
```

7. Embed the canvas tag inside the body of the HTML document:

```
<canvas id="myCanvas" width="600" height="250" style="border:1px
solid black;">
</canvas>
```

How it works...

This recipe is all about randomizing object properties and drawing the results on the screen using HTML5 canvas. The idea is to create a bunch of flowers with varying positions, sizes, and colors.

To help aid us in creating a field of flowers, it's useful to create a `Flower` class that defines the properties of a flower and a method for drawing the flower. For this recipe, I've kept the number of petals constant, although you can certainly experiment with a varying number of petals for each flower on your own.

Drawing a flower is actually quite similar to our previous recipe, *Creating patterns with loops: drawing a gear*, only this time, we'll be drawing petals around a circle instead of zigzags. I've found that the easiest way to draw a petal with HTML5 canvas is to draw a Bezier curve whose starting point is connected to its ending point. The starting and ending points of the Bezier curve are at the center of the flower, and the control points are defined with each iteration in the `draw()` method of the `Flower` class.

Once our `Flower` class is set up and ready to go, we can create a loop that instantiates random `Flower` objects with each iteration and then render them with the `draw()` method.

If you try out this recipe for yourself, you'll see that the flowers are completely randomized each time you refresh the screen.

Creating custom shape functions: playing card suits

If a royal flush gets your adrenaline going, then this one's for you. In this recipe, we'll create drawing functions for the spade, heart, club, and diamond suits.

How to do it...

Follow these steps to draw a spade, heart, club, and diamond suit:

1. Define the drawSpade() function which draws a spade with four Bezier curves, two quadratic curves, and one straight line:

```
function drawSpade(context, x, y, width, height){
    context.save();
    var bottomWidth = width * 0.7;
    var topHeight = height * 0.7;
    var bottomHeight = height * 0.3;

    context.beginPath();
    context.moveTo(x, y);

    // top left of spade
    context.bezierCurveTo(
        x, y + topHeight / 2, // control point 1
        x - width / 2, y + topHeight / 2, // control point 2
        x - width / 2, y + topHeight // end point
    );

    // bottom left of spade
    context.bezierCurveTo(
        x - width / 2, y + topHeight * 1.3, // control point 1
        x, y + topHeight * 1.3, // control point 2
        x, y + topHeight // end point
    );

    // bottom right of spade
    context.bezierCurveTo(
        x, y + topHeight * 1.3, // control point 1
        x + width / 2, y + topHeight * 1.3, // control point 2
        x + width / 2, y + topHeight // end point
    );

    // top right of spade
    context.bezierCurveTo(
        x + width / 2, y + topHeight / 2, // control point 1
        x, y + topHeight / 2, // control point 2
        x, y // end point
    );

    context.closePath();
```

```
    context.fill();

    // bottom of spade
    context.beginPath();
    context.moveTo(x, y + topHeight);
    context.quadraticCurveTo(
        x, y + topHeight + bottomHeight, // control point
        x - bottomWidth / 2, y + topHeight + bottomHeight // end
point
    );
    context.lineTo(x + bottomWidth / 2, y + topHeight +
bottomHeight);
    context.quadraticCurveTo(
        x, y + topHeight + bottomHeight, // control point
        x, y + topHeight // end point
    );
    context.closePath();
    context.fillStyle = "black";
    context.fill();
    context.restore();
}
```

2. Define the drawHeart() function which draws a heart with four Bezier curves:

```
function drawHeart(context, x, y, width, height){
    context.save();
    context.beginPath();
    var topCurveHeight = height * 0.3;
    context.moveTo(x, y + topCurveHeight);
    // top left curve
    context.bezierCurveTo(
        x, y,
        x - width / 2, y,
        x - width / 2, y + topCurveHeight
    );

    // bottom left curve
    context.bezierCurveTo(
        x - width / 2, y + (height + topCurveHeight) / 2,
        x, y + (height + topCurveHeight) / 2,
        x, y + height
    );

    // bottom right curve
    context.bezierCurveTo(
```

```
        x, y + (height + topCurveHeight) / 2,
        x + width / 2, y + (height + topCurveHeight) / 2,
        x + width / 2, y + topCurveHeight
    );

    // top right curve
    context.bezierCurveTo(
        x + width / 2, y,
        x, y,
        x, y + topCurveHeight
    );

    context.closePath();
    context.fillStyle = "red";
    context.fill();
    context.restore();
}
```

3. Define the drawClub() function which draws a club with four circles, two quadratic curves, and one straight line:

```
function drawClub(context, x, y, width, height){
    context.save();
    var circleRadius = width * 0.3;
    var bottomWidth = width * 0.5;
    var bottomHeight = height * 0.35;
    context.fillStyle = "black";

    // top circle
    context.beginPath();
    context.arc(
        x, y + circleRadius + (height * 0.05),
        circleRadius, 0, 2 * Math.PI, false
    );
    context.fill();

    // bottom right circle
    context.beginPath();
    context.arc(
        x + circleRadius, y + (height * 0.6),
        circleRadius, 0, 2 * Math.PI, false
    );
    context.fill();

    // bottom left circle
```

```
    context.beginPath();
    context.arc(
        x - circleRadius, y + (height * 0.6),
        circleRadius, 0, 2 * Math.PI, false
    );
    context.fill();

    // center filler circle
    context.beginPath();
    context.arc(
        x, y + (height * 0.5),
        circleRadius / 2, 0, 2 * Math.PI, false
    );
    context.fill();

    // bottom of club
    context.moveTo(x, y + (height * 0.6));
    context.quadraticCurveTo(
        x, y + height,
        x - bottomWidth / 2, y + height
    );
    context.lineTo(x + bottomWidth / 2, y + height);
    context.quadraticCurveTo(
        x, y + height,
        x, y + (height * 0.6)
    );
    context.closePath();
    context.fill();
    context.restore();
}
```

4. Define the drawDiamond() function which draws a diamond with four straight lines:

```
function drawDiamond(context, x, y, width, height){
    context.save();
    context.beginPath();
    context.moveTo(x, y);

    // top left edge
    context.lineTo(x - width / 2, y + height / 2);

    // bottom left edge
    context.lineTo(x, y + height);

    // bottom right edge
```

```
        context.lineTo(x + width / 2, y + height / 2);

        // closing the path automatically creates
        // the top right edge
        context.closePath();

        context.fillStyle = "red";
        context.fill();
        context.restore();
    }
```

5. When the page loads, define the canvas context and then use the four drawing functions to render a spade, a heart, a club, and a diamond:

```
window.onload = function(){
    var canvas = document.getElementById("myCanvas");
    var context = canvas.getContext("2d");

    drawSpade(context, canvas.width * 0.2, 70, 75, 100);
    drawHeart(context, canvas.width * 0.4, 70, 75, 100);
    drawClub(context, canvas.width * 0.6, 70, 75, 100);
    drawDiamond(context, canvas.width * 0.8, 70, 75, 100);
};
```

6. Embed the canvas tag inside the body of the HTML document:

```
<canvas id="myCanvas" width="600" height="250" style="border:1px
solid black;">
</canvas>
```

How it works...

This recipe demonstrates how any shape can be drawn by combining the four major types of sub paths provided by the HTML5 canvas: straight lines, arcs, Quadratic curves, and Bezier curves.

To draw a spade, we can connect four Bezier curves to form the top portion, and we can use two Quadratic curves and a straight line to form the bottom portion. To draw a heart, we can connect four Bezier curves in much the same way that we created the spade, except that the point of the shape is on the bottom instead of the top. To create a club, we can draw three circles using arcs for the top portion, and similar to the spade, we can use two Quadratic curves and a straight line to form the bottom portion. Finally, to draw a diamond, we can simply connect four straight lines.

Putting it all together: drawing a jet

In this recipe, we'll push the limits of the HTML5 canvas drawing API by drawing a vector-style jet using lines, curves, shapes, colors, linear gradients, and radial gradients.

How to do it...

Follow these steps to draw a vector-style jet:

1. Define a 2D canvas context and set the line join style:

```
window.onload = function(){
    var canvas = document.getElementById("myCanvas");
    var context = canvas.getContext("2d");
  var grd;

    context.lineJoin = "round";
```

2. Draw the right tail wing:

```
    // outline right tail wing
    context.beginPath();
    context.moveTo(248, 60); //13
    context.lineTo(262, 45); // 12
    context.lineTo(285, 56); //11
    context.lineTo(284, 59); // 10
    context.lineTo(276, 91); // 9
    context.closePath();
    context.fillStyle = "#495AFE";
    context.fill();
    context.lineWidth = 4;
    context.stroke();

    // right tail wing detail
    context.beginPath();
```

```
context.moveTo(281, 54); // 10
context.lineTo(273, 84); // 9
context.closePath();
context.lineWidth = 2;
context.stroke();
```

3. Draw the right wing:

```
// outline right wing
context.beginPath();
context.moveTo(425, 159);
context.lineTo(449, 91); // 4
context.lineTo(447, 83); // 5
context.lineTo(408, 67); // 6
context.lineTo(343, 132); // 7
context.fillStyle = "#495AFE";
context.fill();
context.lineWidth = 4;
context.stroke();

// right wing detail
context.beginPath();
context.moveTo(420, 158);
context.lineTo(447, 83); // 4
context.lineWidth = 2;
context.stroke();

context.beginPath();
context.moveTo(439, 102);
context.lineTo(395, 81);
context.lineWidth = 2;
context.stroke();
```

4. Draw the body and top of the tail:

```
// outline body
context.beginPath();
context.moveTo(541, 300); // 1
context.quadraticCurveTo(529, 252, 490, 228); // 2
context.quadraticCurveTo(487, 160, 303, 123); // 3

// outline tail
context.lineTo(213, 20); // 14
context.lineTo(207, 22); // 15
context.bezierCurveTo(208, 164, 255, 207, 412, 271); // 27
context.lineTo(427, 271); // 28
```

```
context.quadraticCurveTo(470, 296, 541, 300); // 1
context.closePath();
grd = context.createLinearGradient(304, 246, 345, 155);
grd.addColorStop(0, "#000E91"); // dark blue
grd.addColorStop(1, "#495AFE"); // light blue
context.fillStyle = grd;
context.fill();
context.lineWidth = 4;
context.stroke();

// tail detail
context.beginPath();
context.moveTo(297, 124);
context.lineTo(207, 22);
context.lineWidth = 2;
context.stroke();
```

5. Draw the left tail wing:

```
// outline left tail wing
context.beginPath();
context.moveTo(303, 121); // 8
context.lineTo(297, 125); // 8
context.lineTo(255, 104);
context.lineWidth = 2;
context.stroke();

context.beginPath();
context.moveTo(212, 80);
context.lineTo(140, 85); // 18
context.lineTo(138, 91); // 19
context.lineTo(156, 105); // 20
context.lineTo(254, 104);
context.lineTo(254, 100);
context.lineWidth = 4;
context.fillStyle = "#495AFE";
context.fill();
context.stroke();

// left tail wing detail
context.beginPath();
context.moveTo(140, 86); // 18
context.lineTo(156, 100); // 20
context.lineTo(254, 100);
context.lineTo(209, 77);
context.lineWidth = 2;
context.stroke();
```

6. Draw the left wing:

```
// outline left wing
context.beginPath();
context.moveTo(262, 166); // 22
context.lineTo(98, 208); // 23
context.lineTo(96, 215); // 24
context.lineTo(136, 245); // 25
context.lineTo(339, 218);
context.lineTo(339, 215);
context.closePath();
context.fillStyle = "#495AFE";
context.fill();
context.lineWidth = 4;
context.stroke();

// left wing detail
context.beginPath();
context.moveTo(98, 210);
context.lineTo(136, 240); // 25
context.lineTo(339, 213);
context.lineWidth = 2;
context.stroke();

context.beginPath();
context.moveTo(165, 235);
context.lineTo(123, 203);
context.lineWidth = 2;
context.stroke();
```

7. Draw the side detail:

```
// side detail
context.beginPath();
context.moveTo(427, 271);
context.lineTo(423, 221);
context.quadraticCurveTo(372, 175, 310, 155);
context.lineWidth = 4;
context.stroke();
```

8. Draw the nose detail:

```
// nose detail
context.beginPath();
context.moveTo(475, 288);
context.quadraticCurveTo(476, 256, 509, 243);
context.quadraticCurveTo(533, 268, 541, 300); // 1
```

```
context.quadraticCurveTo(501, 300, 475, 288);
grd = context.createLinearGradient(491, 301, 530, 263);
grd.addColorStop(0, "#9D0000"); // dark red
grd.addColorStop(1, "#FF0000"); // light red
context.fillStyle = grd;
context.fill();
context.lineWidth = 4;
context.stroke();

context.beginPath();
context.moveTo(480, 293);
context.quadraticCurveTo(480, 256, 513, 246);
context.lineWidth = 2;
context.stroke();
```

9. Draw the cockpit:

```
// cockpit detail
context.beginPath();
context.moveTo(442, 169);
context.quadraticCurveTo(419, 176, 415, 200);
context.quadraticCurveTo(483, 250, 490, 228);
context.quadraticCurveTo(480, 186, 439, 170);
context.lineWidth = 4;
context.stroke();
grd = context.createRadialGradient(473, 200, 20, 473, 200, 70);
grd.addColorStop(0, "#E1E7FF"); // dark gray
grd.addColorStop(1, "#737784"); // light gray
context.fillStyle = grd;
context.fill();

context.beginPath();
context.moveTo(448, 173);
context.quadraticCurveTo(425, 176, 420, 204);
context.lineWidth = 2;
context.stroke();

context.beginPath();
context.moveTo(470, 186);
context.quadraticCurveTo(445, 190, 440, 220);
context.lineWidth = 2;
context.stroke();
```

10. Draw the intake:

```
        // intake outline
        context.beginPath();
        context.moveTo(420, 265);
        context.lineTo(416, 223);
        context.bezierCurveTo(384, 224, 399, 270, 420, 265);
        context.closePath();
        context.fillStyle = "#001975";
        context.fill();
        context.lineWidth = 4;
        context.stroke();

        context.beginPath();
        context.moveTo(420, 265);
        context.lineTo(402, 253);
        context.lineWidth = 2;
        context.stroke();

        context.beginPath();
        context.moveTo(404, 203);
        context.bezierCurveTo(364, 204, 379, 265, 394, 263);
        context.lineWidth = 2;
        context.stroke();
    };
```

11. Embed the canvas tag inside the body of the HTML document:

```
<canvas id="myCanvas" width="650" height="350" style="border:1px
solid black;">
</canvas>
```

How it works...

This recipe combines the use of lines, Quadratic curves, Bezier curves, paths, shapes, solid fills, linear gradients, and radial gradients. Although it's true that the HTML5 canvas is quite rudimentary, it does provide everything that we need to make great drawings, including a vector-style jet.

To draw a jet with the HTML5 canvas, we can start by drawing a jet in Adobe Photoshop or some other image editor with a drawing area size equal to the size of our canvas, which in this case is 650 x 350 pixels. Next, we can use our cursor to find the major points that form the jet shape by hovering over the end points of each line in our drawing and recording the x, y coordinates. With these coordinates in hand, we can draw the major outline of the jet with a line width of 4, and we can go back and fill in the finer details of the jet using a line width of 2.

It's good practice to draw the portions of the drawing farthest away from the viewer first because each shape that you draw on the canvas will overlap the previous shapes. If you take a look at the preceding code, you'll notice that the right wing was drawn first, followed by the body of the jet, followed by the left wing. This is because the right wing is farthest from the viewer while the left wing is closest to the viewer.

Once the line drawing is complete, we can fill in the jet with solid colors, add a linear gradient to the body, and add a radial gradient to the cockpit to give the drawing some depth. Finally, we can add a bold red gradation to the nose of the plane, preparing it for take-off and inspiring our imagination.

3
Working with Images and Videos

In this chapter, we will cover:

- Drawing an image
- Cropping an image
- Copying and pasting sections of the canvas
- Working with video
- Getting image data
- Introduction to pixel manipulation: inverting image colors
- Inverting video colors
- Converting image colors to grayscale
- Converting a canvas drawing into a data URL
- Saving a canvas drawing as an image
- Loading the canvas with a data URL
- Creating a pixelated image focus

Introduction

This chapter focuses on yet another very exciting topic of the HTML5 canvas, images and videos. Along with providing basic functionality for positioning, sizing, and cropping images and videos, the HTML5 canvas API also allows us to access and modify the color and transparency of each pixel for both mediums. Let's get started!

Drawing an image

Let's jump right in by drawing a simple image. In this recipe, we'll learn how to load an image and draw it somewhere on the canvas.

Follow these steps to draw an image in the center of the canvas:

How to do it...

1. Define the canvas context:

```
window.onload = function(){
    var canvas = document.getElementById("myCanvas");
    var context = canvas.getContext("2d");
```

2. Create an `image` object, set the `onload` property to a function that draws the image, and then set the source of the image:

```
    var imageObj = new Image();
    imageObj.onload = function(){
        var destX = canvas.width / 2 - this.width / 2;
        var destY = canvas.height / 2 - this.height / 2;

        context.drawImage(this, destX, destY);
    };
    imageObj.src = "jet_300x214.jpg";
};
```

3. Embed the canvas tag inside the body of the HTML document:

```
<canvas id="myCanvas" width="600" height="250" style="border:1px
solid black;">
</canvas>
```

How it works...

To draw an image, we first need to create an `image` object using new `Image()`. Notice that we've set the `onload` property of the `image` object *before* defining the source of the image.

It's good practice to define what we want to do with the image when it loads *before* setting its source. Theoretically, if we were to define the source of the image before we define the `onload` property; the image could possibly load before the definition is complete (although, it's very unlikely).

The key method in this recipe is the `drawImage()` method:

```
context.drawImage(imageObj,destX,destY);
```

Where `imageObj` is the `image` object, and `destX` and `destY` is where we want to position the image.

There's more...

In addition to defining an image position with `destX` and `destY`, we can also add two additional parameters, `destWidth` and `destHeight` to define the size of our image:

```
context.drawImage(imageObj,destX,destY,destWidth,destHeight);
```

For the most part, it's a good idea to stay away from resizing an image with the `drawImage()` method, simply because the quality of the scaled image will be noticeably reduced, similar to the result when we resize an image with the width and height properties of an HTML image element. If image quality is something you're concerned about (why on earth wouldn't you be?), it's usually best to work with thumbnail images alongside bigger images if you're creating an application that needs scaled images. If, on the other hand, your application dynamically shrinks and expands images, using the `drawImage()` method with `destWidth` and `destHeight` to scale images is a perfectly acceptable approach.

Cropping an image

In this recipe, we'll crop out a section of an image and then draw the result onto the canvas.

Follow these steps to crop out a section of an image and draw the result onto the canvas.

How to do it...

1. Define the canvas context:

```
window.onload = function(){
    var canvas = document.getElementById("myCanvas");
    var context = canvas.getContext("2d");
```

2. Create an image object, set the `onload` property to a function that crops the image, and then set the source of the image:

```
    var imageObj = new Image();
    imageObj.onload = function(){
    // source rectangular area
        var sourceX = 550;
        var sourceY = 300;
        var sourceWidth = 300;
        var sourceHeight = 214;

    // destination image size and position
        var destWidth = sourceWidth;
        var destHeight = sourceHeight;
        var destX = canvas.width / 2 - destWidth / 2;
        var destY = canvas.height / 2 - destHeight / 2;

        context.drawImage(this, sourceX, sourceY, sourceWidth,
sourceHeight, destX, destY, destWidth, destHeight);
    };
    imageObj.src = "jet_1000x714.jpg";
};
```

3. Embed the canvas tag inside the body of the HTML document:

```
<canvas id="myCanvas" width="600" height="250" style="border:1px
solid black;">
</canvas>
```

How it works...

In the last recipe, we discussed two different ways that we can use the `drawImage()` method to draw images on the canvas. In the first case, we can pass an `image` object and a position to simply draw an image at the given position. In the second case, we can pass an `image` object, a position, and a size to draw an image at the given position with the given size. Additionally, we can also add six more parameters to the `drawImage()` method if we wanted to crop an image:

```
Context.drawImage(imageObj,sourceX,sourceY,sourceWidth, sourceHight,
sourceHeight,sourceHeight, destX, destY, destWidth, destHeight);
```

Take a look at the following diagram:

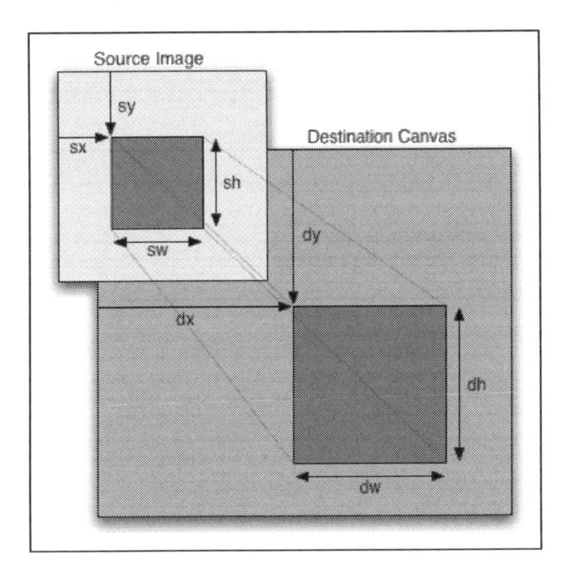

As you can see, `sourceX` and `sourceY` refer to the top-left corner of the cropped region in the source image. `sourceWidth` and `sourceHeight` refer to the width and height of the cropped image from the source. `destX` and `destY` refer to the position of the cropped image on the canvas, and `destWidth` and `destHeight` refer to the width and height of the resulting cropped image.

If you don't intend to scale a cropped image, then `destWidth` equals `sourceWidth` and `destHeight` equals `sourceHeight`.

Copying and pasting sections of the canvas

In this recipe, we'll cover yet another interesting usage of the `drawImage()` method—copying sections of the canvas. First, we'll draw a spade in the center of the canvas, then we'll copy the right side of the spade and then paste it to the left, and then we'll copy the left side of the spade and then paste it to the right.

Follow these steps to draw a spade in the center of the canvas and then copy-and-paste sections of the shape back onto the canvas:

How to do it...

1. Define the canvas context:

```
window.onload = function(){
    // drawing canvas and context
    var canvas = document.getElementById("myCanvas");
    var context = canvas.getContext("2d");
```

2. Draw a spade in the center of the canvas using the `drawSpade()` function that we created in *Chapter 2, Shape Drawing and Composites*:

```
    // draw spade
    var spadeX = canvas.width / 2;
    var spadeY = 20;
    var spadeWidth = 140;
    var spadeHeight = 200;

    // draw spade in center of canvas
    drawSpade(context, spadeX, spadeY, spadeWidth, spadeHeight);
```

3. Copy the right half of the spade and then paste it on the canvas to the left of the spade using the `drawImage()` method:

```
    context.drawImage(
    canvas,
    spadeX,         // source x
    spadeY,         // source y
    spadeWidth / 2,     // source width
```

```
        spadeHeight,        // source height
        spadeX - spadeWidth,  // dest x
        spadeY,          // dest y
        spadeWidth / 2,      // dest width
        spadeHeight         // dest height
    );
```

4. Copy the left half of the spade and then paste it on the canvas to the right of the spade using the `drawImage()` method:

```
        context.drawImage(
        canvas,
        spadeX - spadeWidth / 2,  // source x
        spadeY,            // source y
        spadeWidth / 2,        // source width
        spadeHeight,         // source height
        spadeX + spadeWidth / 2,   // dest x
        spadeY,            // dest y
        spadeWidth / 2,        // dest width
        spadeHeight          // dest height
    );
};
```

5. Embed the canvas inside the body of the HTML document:

```
<canvas id="myCanvas" width="600" height="250" style="border:1px
solid black;">
</canvas>
```

How it works...

To copy a section of the canvas, we can pass the `canvas` object to the `drawImage()` method instead of an `image` object:

```
Context.drawImage(canvas,sourceX,sourceY,sourceWidth, sourceHight, sou
rceHeight,sourceHeight, destX, destY, destWidth, destHeight);
```

As we'll see in the next recipe, not only can we copy sections of an image or a canvas with `drawImage()`, we can also copy sections of HTML5 video.

Working with video

Although the HTML5 canvas API doesn't provide a direct method for drawing videos on the canvas like it does for images, we can certainly work with videos by capturing frames from a hidden video tag and then copying them onto the canvas with a loop.

Getting ready...

Before we get started, let's talk about the supported HTML5 video formats for each browser. At the time of writing, the video format war continues to rage on, in which all of the major browsers—Chrome, Firefox, Opera, Safari, and IE—continue to drop and add support for different video formats. To make things worse, each time a major browser adds or drops support for a particular video format, developers have to once again re-formulate the minimal set of video formats that's required for their applications to work across all browsers.

At the time of writing, the three major video formats are Ogg Theora, H.264, and WebM. For the video recipes in this chapter, we'll be using a combination of Ogg Theora and H.264. When working with video, it's strongly advised that you do a search online to see what the current status is for video support as it is a subject to change at any moment.

There's more! Once you've decided which video formats to support, you'll probably need a video format converter to convert the video file that you have on hand to other video formats. One great option for converting video formats is the Miro Video Converter, which supports video format conversions for just about any video format including Ogg Theora, H.264, or WebM formats.

Miro Video Converter is probably the most common video converter available at the time of writing, although you can certainly use any other video format converter of your liking. You can download Miro Video Converter from: `http://www.mirovideoconverter.com/`.

Follow these steps to draw a video onto the canvas:

How to do it...

1. Create a cross-browser method that requests an animation frame:

```
window.requestAnimFrame = (function(callback){
    return window.requestAnimationFrame ||
    window.webkitRequestAnimationFrame ||
    window.mozRequestAnimationFrame ||
    window.oRequestAnimationFrame ||
    window.msRequestAnimationFrame ||
    function(callback){
        window.setTimeout(callback, 1000 / 60);
    };
})();
```

2. Define the `drawFrame()` function which copies the current video frame, pastes it onto the canvas using the `drawImage()` method, and then requests a new animation frame to draw the next frame:

```
function drawFrame(context, video){
    context.drawImage(video, 0, 0);
    requestAnimFrame(function(){
        drawFrame(context, video);
    });
}
```

3. Define the canvas context, get the video tag, and draw the first video frame:

```
window.onload = function(){
    var canvas = document.getElementById("myCanvas");
    var context = canvas.getContext("2d");
    var video = document.getElementById("myVideo");
    drawFrame(context, video);
};
```

4. Embed the canvas and the video tag inside the body of the HTML document:

```
<video id="myVideo" autoplay="true" loop="true"
style="display:none;">
    <source src="BigBuckBunny_640x360.ogv" type="video/ogg"/
><source src="BigBuckBunny_640x360.mp4" type="video/mp4"/>
</video>
<canvas id="myCanvas" width="600" height="360" style="border:1px
solid black;">
</canvas>
```

How it works...

To draw a video on an HTML5 canvas, we first need to embed a hidden video tag in the HTML document. In this recipe, and in future video recipes, I've used the Ogg Theora and H.264 (mp4) video formats.

Next, when the page loads, we can use our cross-browser `requestAnimFrame()` method to capture the video frames as fast as the browser will allow and then draw them onto the canvas.

Getting image data

Now that we know how to draw images and videos, let's try accessing the image data to see what kind of properties we can play with.

WARNING: This recipe must run on a web server due to security constraints with the `getImageData()` method.

Getting ready...

Before we get started working with image data, it's important that we cover canvas security and the RGBA color space.

So why is canvas security important with respect to accessing image data? Simply put, in order to access image data, we need to use the `getImateData()` method of the canvas context which will throw a `SECURITY_ERR` exception if we try accessing image data from an image residing on a non-web server file system, or if we try accessing image data from an image on a different domain. In other words, if you're going to try out these demos for yourself, they won't work if your files reside on your local file system. You'll need to run the rest of the recipes in this chapter on a web server.

Next, since pixel manipulation is all about altering the RGB values of pixels, we should probably cover the RGB color model and the RGBA color space while we're at it. RGB represents the red, green, and blue components of a pixel's color. Each component is an integer between 0 and 255, where 0 represents no color and 255 represents full color. RGB values are often times represented as follows:

```
rgb(red,green,blue)
```

Here are some common color values represented with the RGB color model:

```
rgb(0,0,0) = black
rgb(255,255,255) = white
rgb(255,0,0) = red
rgb(0,255,0) = green
rgb(0,0,255) = blue
rgb(255,255,0) = yellow
rgb(255,0,255) = magenta
rgb(0,255,255) = cyan
```

In addition to RGB, pixels can also have an alpha channel which refers to its opacity. An alpha channel of 0 is a fully transparent pixel, and an alpha channel of 255 is a fully opaque pixel. RGBA color space simply refers to the RGB color model (RGB) plus the alpha channel (A).

Be careful not to confuse the alpha channel range of HTML5 canvas pixels, which are integers 0 to 255, and the alpha channel range of CSS colors, which are decimals 0.0 to 1.0.

Follow these steps to write out the image data properties of an image:

How to do it...

1. Define a canvas context:

```
window.onload = function(){
    var canvas = document.getElementById("myCanvas");
    var context = canvas.getContext("2d");
```

2. Create an `image` object, set the `onload` property to a function which draws the image:

```
    var imageObj = new Image();
    imageObj.onload = function(){
        var sourceWidth = this.width;
        var sourceHeight = this.height;
        var destX = canvas.width / 2 - sourceWidth / 2;
        var destY = canvas.height / 2 - sourceHeight / 2;
        var sourceX = destX;
```

```
            var sourceY = destY;

        // draw image on canvas
            context.drawImage(this, destX, destY);
```

3. Get the image data, write out its properties, and then set the source of the `image` object outside of the `onload` definition:

```
        // get image data from the rectangular area
        // of the canvas containing the image
            var imageData = context.getImageData(sourceX, sourceY,
sourceWidth, sourceHeight);
            var data = imageData.data;

        // write out the image data properties
            var str = "width=" + imageData.width + ", height=" +
imageData.height + ", data length=" + data.length;
            context.font = "12pt Calibri";
            context.fillText(str, 4, 14);
        };
        imageObj.src = "jet_300x214.jpg";
};
```

4. Embed the canvas tag into the body of the HTML document:

```
<canvas id="myCanvas" width="600" height="250" style="border:1px
solid black;">
</canvas>
```

How it works...

The idea behind this recipe is to draw an image, get its image data, and then write out the image data properties to the screen. As you can see from the preceding code, we can get the image data using the `getImageData()` method of the canvas context:

```
context.getImageData(sourceX,sourceY,sourceWidth,sourceHeight);
```

Notice that the `getImageData()` method only works with the canvas context and not the `image` object itself. As a result, in order to get image data, we must first draw an image onto the canvas and then use `getImageData()` method of the canvas context.

The `ImageData` object contains three properties: `width`, `height`, and `data`. As you can see from the screenshot in the beginning of this recipe, our `ImageData` object contains a `width` property of 300, a `height` property of 214, and a `data` property which is an array of pixel information, which in this case has a length of 256,800 elements. The key to the `ImageData` object, in all honesty, is the `data` property. The `data` property contains the RGBA information for each pixel in our image. Since our image is made up of 300 * 214 = 64,200 pixels, the length of this array is 4 * 64,200 = 256,800 elements.

Introduction to pixel manipulation: inverting image colors

Now that we know how to access image data, including the RGBA for every pixel in an image or video, our next step is to explore the possibilities of pixel manipulation. In this recipe, we'll invert the colors of an image by inverting the color of each pixel.

WARNING: This recipe must be run on a web server due to security constraints with the `getImageData()` method.

Follow these steps to invert the colors of an image:

How to do it...

1. Define the canvas context:

```
window.onload = function(){
    var canvas = document.getElementById("myCanvas");
    var context = canvas.getContext("2d");
```

2. Create an `image` object and set the `onload` property to a function that draws the image and gets the image data:

```
    var imageObj = new Image();
    imageObj.onload = function(){
        var sourceWidth = this.width;
        var sourceHeight = this.height;
        var sourceX = canvas.width / 2 - sourceWidth / 2;
        var sourceY = canvas.height / 2 - sourceHeight / 2;
        var destX = sourceX;
        var destY = sourceY;
```

```
            context.drawImage(this, destX, destY);

            var imageData = context.getImageData(sourceX, sourceY,
    sourceWidth, sourceHeight);
            var data = imageData.data;
```

3. Loop through all of the pixels in the image and invert the colors:

```
            for (var i = 0; i < data.length; i += 4) {
                data[i] = 255 - data[i]; // red
                data[i + 1] = 255 - data[i + 1]; // green
                data[i + 2] = 255 - data[i + 2]; // blue
                // i+3 is alpha (the fourth element)
            }
```

4. Overwrite the original image with the manipulated image, and then set the source of the image outside of the `onload` definition:

```
            // overwrite original image with
            // new image data
            context.putImageData(imageData, destX, destY);
        };
        imageObj.src = "jet_300x214.jpg";
    };
```

5. Embed the canvas tag into the body of the HTML document:

```
<canvas id="myCanvas" width="600" height="250" style="border:1px
solid black;">
</canvas>
```

How it works...

To invert the color of an image using HTML5 canvas, we can simply loop through all of the pixels in an image and then invert each pixel using a color inverting algorithm. Don't worry it's easier than it sounds. To invert a pixel's color, we can invert each of its RGB components by subtracting each value from 255 as follows:

```
data[i  ] = 255 - data[i  ]; // red
data[i+1] = 255 - data[i+1]; // green
data[i+2] = 255 - data[i+2]; // blue
```

Once the pixels have been updated, we can redraw the image using the `putImageData()` method of the canvas context:

```
context.putImageData(imageData, destX, destY);
```

This method basically allows us to draw an image using image data instead of a source image with the `drawImage()` method.

Inverting video colors

The purpose of this recipe is to demonstrate how to perform pixel manipulations on videos in much the same way as we did with images. In this recipe, we'll invert the colors of a short video clip.

WARNING: This recipe must be run on a web server due to security constraints with the `getImageData()` method.

Follow these steps to invert the colors of a video:

How to do it...

1. Create a cross-browser method that requests an animation frame:

```
window.requestAnimFrame = (function(callback){
    return window.requestAnimationFrame ||
    window.webkitRequestAnimationFrame ||
    window.mozRequestAnimationFrame ||
    window.oRequestAnimationFrame ||
    window.msRequestAnimationFrame ||
    function(callback){
        window.setTimeout(callback, 1000 / 60);
    };
})();
```

2. Define the `drawFrame()` function that captures the current video frame, inverts the colors, draws the frame on the canvas, and then requests a new animation frame:

```
function drawFrame(canvas, context, video){
    context.drawImage(video, 0, 0);

    var imageData = context.getImageData(0, 0, canvas.width, 
canvas.height);
    var data = imageData.data;

    for (var i = 0; i < data.length; i += 4) {
        data[i] = 255 - data[i]; // red
        data[i + 1] = 255 - data[i + 1]; // green
        data[i + 2] = 255 - data[i + 2]; // blue
        // i+3 is alpha (the fourth element)
    }

    // overwrite original image
    context.putImageData(imageData, 0, 0);

    requestAnimFrame(function(){
        drawFrame(canvas, context, video);
    });
}
```

3. Define the canvas context, get the video tag, and draw the first animation frame:

```
window.onload = function(){
    var canvas = document.getElementById("myCanvas");
    var context = canvas.getContext("2d");
    var video = document.getElementById("myVideo");
    drawFrame(canvas, context, video);
};
```

4. Embed the video and canvas element into the body of the HTML document:

```
<video id="myVideo" autoplay="true" loop="true" 
style="display:none;">
    <source src="BigBuckBunny_640x360.ogv" type="video/ogg"/
><source src="BigBuckBunny_640x360.mp4" type="video/mp4"/>
</video>
<canvas id="myCanvas" width="640" height="360" style="border:1px 
solid black;">
</canvas>
```

How it works...

Similarly to the previous recipe, we can perform pixel manipulations on video in much the same way that we did with images because the `getImageData()` method gets the image data from the canvas context regardless of how the context was rendered. In this recipe, we can simply invert the color of each pixel on the canvas for each video frame provided by the `requestAnimFrame()` method.

Converting image colors to grayscale

In this recipe, we'll explore another common pixel manipulation algorithm, converting colors to grayscale.

[WARNING: This recipe must be ran on a web server due to security constraints with the `getImageData()` method.]

Follow these steps to convert the colors of an image to grayscale:

How to do it...

1. Define the canvas context:

```
window.onload = function(){
    var canvas = document.getElementById("myCanvas");
    var context = canvas.getContext("2d");
```

2. Create an `image` object and set the `onload` property to a function that draws the image and gets the image data:

```
    var imageObj = new Image();
    imageObj.onload = function(){
        var sourceWidth = this.width;
```

```
            var sourceHeight = this.height;
            var destX = canvas.width / 2 - sourceWidth / 2;
            var destY = canvas.height / 2 - sourceHeight / 2;
            var sourceX = destX;
            var sourceY = destY;

            context.drawImage(this, destX, destY);

            var imageData = context.getImageData(sourceX, sourceY,
sourceWidth, sourceHeight);
            var data = imageData.data;
```

3. Loop through the pixels in the image and convert the colors to grayscale using the equation for brightness:

```
            for (var i = 0; i < data.length; i += 4) {
                var brightness = 0.34 * data[i] + 0.5 * data[i + 1] +
0.16 * data[i + 2];

                data[i] = brightness; // red
                data[i + 1] = brightness; // green
                data[i + 2] = brightness; // blue
                // i+3 is alpha (the fourth element)
            }
```

4. Overwrite the original image with the manipulated image and then set the image source after the `onload` definition:

```
            // overwrite original image
            context.putImageData(imageData, destX, destY);
        };
        imageObj.src = "jet_300x214.jpg";
};
```

5. Embed the canvas element inside the body of the HTML document:

```
<canvas id="myCanvas" width="600" height="250" style="border:1px
solid black;">
</canvas>
```

How it works...

To convert an RGB color into a gradation of gray, we need to obtain the brightness of the color. We can use the equation of brightness to obtain the grayscale value of a colored pixel. This equation is based on the fact that humans are most sensitive to green light, followed by red light, and are least sensitive to blue light:

```
Brightness = 0.34 * R + 0.5 * G + 0.16 * B
```

To account for physiological effects, notice that we've added more weight to the green value (most sensitive) followed by the red value (less sensitive) followed by the blue value (least sensitive).

With this equation in hand, we can simply loop through all of the pixels in our image, calculate the perceived brightness, assign this value to each of the RGB values, and then re-draw the image onto the canvas.

Converting a canvas drawing into a data URL

In addition to image data, we can also extract an image data URL which is basically just a very long text string containing encoded information about the canvas image. Data URLs are extremely handy if we want to save the canvas drawing in local storage or in an offline database. In this recipe, we'll draw a cloud shape, get its data URL, and then insert it into the HTML page so that we can see what it looks like.

Follow these steps to convert a canvas drawing into a data URL:

How to do it...

1. Define the canvas context and draw a cloud shape:

```
window.onload = function(){
    var canvas = document.getElementById("myCanvas");
    var context = canvas.getContext("2d");

    var startX = 200;
    var startY = 100;

    // draw cloud shape
    context.beginPath();
    context.moveTo(startX, startY);
    context.bezierCurveTo(startX - 40, startY + 20, startX - 40,
startY + 70, startX + 60, startY + 70);
    context.bezierCurveTo(startX + 80, startY + 100, startX + 150,
startY + 100, startX + 170, startY + 70);
    context.bezierCurveTo(startX + 250, startY + 70, startX + 250,
startY + 40, startX + 220, startY + 20);
    context.bezierCurveTo(startX + 260, startY - 40, startX + 200,
startY - 50, startX + 170, startY - 30);
    context.bezierCurveTo(startX + 150, startY - 75, startX + 80,
startY - 60, startX + 80, startY - 30);
    context.bezierCurveTo(startX + 30, startY - 75, startX - 20,
startY - 60, startX, startY);
```

```
        context.closePath();

        context.lineWidth = 5;
        context.fillStyle = "#8ED6FF";
        context.fill();
        context.strokeStyle = "#0000ff";
        context.stroke();
```

2. Get the data URL of the canvas using the `toDataURL()` method of the `canvas` object:

```
        // save canvas image as data url (png format by default)
        var dataURL = canvas.toDataURL();
```

3. Insert the (long) data URL into a `<p>` tag so that we can see it:

```
        // insert url into the HTML document so we can see it
        document.getElementById("dataURL").innerHTML = "<b>dataURL:</
b> " + dataURL;
};
```

4. Embed the canvas tag inside the body of the HTML document and create a `<p>` tag which will be used to store the data URL:

```
<canvas id="myCanvas" width="600" height="250" style="border:1px
solid black;">
</canvas>
<p id="dataURL" style="width:600px;word-wrap: break-word;">
</p>
```

How it works...

The key to this recipe is the `toDataURL()` method which converts a canvas drawing into a data URL:

```
var dataURL = canvas.toDataURL();
```

When running this demo, you'll see a very long data URL that looks something like this:


```
data:image/png;base64,iVBORw0KGgoAAAANSUhEUgAAAlg
AAAD6CAYAAAB9LTkQAAAgAElEQVR4Xu3dXbAUxd3H8f+5i09
VrEjuDlRFBSvoo1ETD/HmEcQIXskRc6FViaA+N7woRlNJUDQm4
kueeiS+INz4wEGfilwocLxSUASvDMf4XokpQbFKuAtYSdWT3PXz
/885C3t2Z3dndntme3q+W7Uehn7k/3sj96enpGhAcCCCCAAAI
IIICAV4ERr6VRGAIIIIAAAggggIAQsBgECCCCAAAIIIICAZwECl
mdQikMAAQQQQAABBAhYjAEEEEEAAAQQQQMCzAAHLMyjFIYAAAgg
ggAACBCzGAAIIIIAAAggg4FmAgOUZl0OIQQAABBBBAAAECFmMAA
QQQQAABBBDwLEDA8gxKcQgggAACCCCAAAGLMYAAAggggAACCHgWI
```

```
GB5BqU4BBBAAAEEEECAgMUYQAABBBBAAAEEPAsQsDyDUhwCCCCAA
AIIIEDAYgwggAACCCCAAAKeBQhYnkEpDgEEEEAAAQQQIGAxBhBAA
AEEEEAAAc8CBCzPoBSHAAIIIIAAAggQsBgDCCCAAAIIIICAZwECl
mdQikMAAQQQQAABBAhYjAEEEEAAAQQQQMCzAAHLMyjFIYAAAgggg
AACBCzGAAIIIIAAAggg4FmAgOUZlOIQQAABBBBAAAECFmMAAQQQQ
AABBBDwLEDA8gxKcQgggAACCCCAAAGLMYAAAggggAACCHgWIGB5
BqU4BBBAAAEEEECAgMUYQAABBBBAAAEEPAsQsDyDUhwCCCCAAAI
IIEDAYgwggAACCCCAAAKeBQhYnkEpDgEEEEAAAQQQIGAxBhBAAA
EEEEAAAc8CBCzPoBSHAAIIIIAAAggQsBgDCCCAAAIIIICAZwECl
mdQikMAAQQQQAABBAhYjAEEEEAAAQQQQMCzAAHLMyj
```


What you're looking at here is just a small snippet of the entire data URL. The important part to pay attention to in the URL is the very beginning, which starts with `data:image/png;base64`. This means that the data URL is a PNG image which is represented by a base 64 encoding.

Unlike image data, which is a native array of pixel data, an image data URL is special because it's a string that can be stored with local storage, or it can be passed to a web server to be saved in an offline database. In other words, image data is useful for inspecting and manipulating each individual pixel that makes up an image, while image data URLs are intended to be used for storing the canvas drawing and to be passed between the client and server.

Saving a canvas drawing as an image

In addition to saving the canvas drawing in local storage or in an offline database, we can also use an image data URL to save the canvas drawing as an image so that a user can then save it to their local computer. In this recipe, we'll get the image data URL of the canvas drawing and then set it to the source of an `image` object so that a user can right click and download the image as a PNG.

Follow these steps to save a canvas drawing as an image:

How to do it...

1. Define the canvas context and draw a cloud shape:

```
window.onload = function(){
    var canvas = document.getElementById("myCanvas");
    var context = canvas.getContext("2d");

    // draw cloud
    context.beginPath(); // begin custom shape
    context.moveTo(170, 80);
    context.bezierCurveTo(130, 100, 130, 150, 230, 150);
```

```
        context.bezierCurveTo(250, 180, 320, 180, 340, 150);
        context.bezierCurveTo(420, 150, 420, 120, 390, 100);
        context.bezierCurveTo(430, 40, 370, 30, 340, 50);
        context.bezierCurveTo(320, 5, 250, 20, 250, 50);
        context.bezierCurveTo(200, 5, 150, 20, 170, 80);
        context.closePath(); // complete custom shape
        context.lineWidth = 5;
        context.fillStyle = "#8ED6FF";
        context.fill();
        context.strokeStyle = "#0000ff";
        context.stroke();
```

2. Get the data URL:

```
        // save canvas image as data url (png format by default)
        var dataURL = canvas.toDataURL();
```

3. Set the source of an image tag to the data URL so that a user can download it:

```
        // set canvasImg image src to dataURL
        // so it can be saved as an image
        document.getElementById("canvasImg").src = dataURL;
    };
```

4. Embed the canvas tag in the body of the HTML document and add an image tag which will contain the canvas drawing:

```
<canvas id="myCanvas" width="578" height="200">
</canvas>
<p>
    Image:
</p>
<img id="canvasImg" alt="Right click to save me!">
```

How it works...

After drawing something on the canvas, we can create an image that the user can save by getting the image data URL using the `toDataURL()` method, and then setting the source of an `image` object to the data URL. Once the image has loaded (which is nearly instantaneous because the image is being loaded directly and doesn't have to make a request to a web server), the user can right click on the image to save it to their local computer.

Loading the canvas with a data URL

To load the canvas with a data URL, we can extend the previous recipe by creating an `image` object with the data URL and then drawing it on the canvas using our good friend `drawImage()`. In this recipe, we'll make a simple Ajax call to get the data URL from a text file and then use the URL to draw the image on the canvas. In the real world of course, you'll probably be fetching the image data URL from local storage or by calling a data service.

Follow these steps to load a canvas drawing with a data URL:

How to do it...

1. Define the `loadCanvas()` function which takes a data URL as input, defines a canvas context, creates a new image using the data URL, and then draws the image onto the canvas once it has loaded:

```
function loadCanvas(dataURL){
    var canvas = document.getElementById("myCanvas");
    var context = canvas.getContext("2d");

    // load image from data url
    var imageObj = new Image();
    imageObj.onload = function(){
        context.drawImage(this, 0, 0);
    };

    imageObj.src = dataURL;
}
```

2. Make an AJAX call to get a data URL stored on your server, and then call `loadCanvas()` with the response text when the response is received:

```
window.onload = function(){
    // make ajax call to get image data url
    var request = new XMLHttpRequest();
    request.open("GET", "dataURL.txt", true);
    request.onreadystatechange = function(){
        if (request.readyState == 4) {
            if (request.status == 200) { // successful response
                loadCanvas(request.responseText);
            }
        }
    };
    request.send(null);
};
```

3. Embed the canvas tag inside the body of the HTML document:

```
<canvas id="myCanvas" width="600" height="250" style="border:1px
solid black;">
</canvas>
```

How it works...

To get the image data URL from a web server, we can set up an AJAX call (Asynchronous JavaScript and XML) to make a request to a web server and get the data URL as a response. When we get a status code of 200, which means that the request and response was successful, we can get the image data URL from `request.responseText`, and then pass it to the `loadCanvas()` function. This function will then create a new `image` object, set its source to the data URL, and then draw the image onto the canvas once it has loaded.

Creating a pixelated image focus

Looking for a fancy way to focus an image? How about a pixelated image focus? In this recipe, we'll explore the art of image pixelation by looping through an algorithm that pixelates an image less and less until it's completely focused.

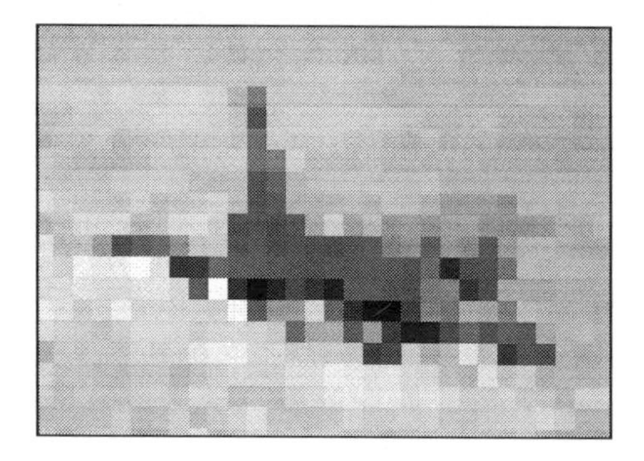

WARNING: This recipe must be run on a web server due to security constraints with the `getImageData()` method.

Follow these steps to create a pixilation function that slowly focuses an image:

How to do it...

1. Define the `focusImage()` function which de-pixelates an image based on a pixilation value:

```
function focusImage(canvas, context, imageObj, pixelation){
    var sourceWidth = imageObj.width;
    var sourceHeight = imageObj.height;
    var sourceX = canvas.width / 2 - sourceWidth / 2;
    var sourceY = canvas.height / 2 - sourceHeight / 2;
    var destX = sourceX;
    var destY = sourceY;

    var imageData = context.getImageData(sourceX, sourceY,
sourceWidth, sourceHeight);
    var data = imageData.data;

    for (var y = 0; y < sourceHeight; y += pixelation) {
        for (var x = 0; x < sourceWidth; x += pixelation) {
            // get the color components of the sample pixel
            var red = data[((sourceWidth * y) + x) * 4];
            var green = data[((sourceWidth * y) + x) * 4 + 1];
            var blue = data[((sourceWidth * y) + x) * 4 + 2];

            // overwrite pixels in a square below and to
            // the right of the sample pixel, whos width and
            // height are equal to the pixelation amount
            for (var n = 0; n < pixelation; n++) {
                for (var m = 0; m < pixelation; m++) {
                    if (x + m < sourceWidth) {
                        data[((sourceWidth * (y + n)) + (x + m)) *
4] = red;
                        data[((sourceWidth * (y + n)) + (x + m)) *
4 + 1] = green;
                        data[((sourceWidth * (y + n)) + (x + m)) *
4 + 2] = blue;
                    }
                }
            }
        }
    }

    // overwrite original image
    context.putImageData(imageData, destX, destY);
}
```

2. Define the canvas context, fps value that determines how fast or slow the image focuses, the corresponding time interval, and the initial pixilation amount:

```
window.onload = function(){
    var canvas = document.getElementById("myCanvas");
    var context = canvas.getContext("2d");
    var fps = 20; // frames / second
    var timeInterval = 1000 / fps; // milliseconds

    // define initial pixelation.  The higher the value,
    // the more pixelated the image is.  The image is
    // perfectly focused when pixelation = 1;
    var pixelation = 40;
```

3. Create a new `image` object, set the `onload` property to a function that creates a timed loop that calls the `focusImage()` function and decrements the pixilation value for each call until the image is focused, and then set the image source outside of the `onload` definition:

```
    var imageObj = new Image();
    imageObj.onload = function(){
        var sourceWidth = imageObj.width;
        var sourceHeight = imageObj.height;
        var destX = canvas.width / 2 - sourceWidth / 2;
        var destY = canvas.height / 2 - sourceHeight / 2;

        var intervalId = setInterval(function(){
            context.drawImage(imageObj, destX, destY);

            if (pixelation < 1) {
                clearInterval(intervalId);
            }
            else {
                focusImage(canvas, context, imageObj, pixelation--
);
            }
        }, timeInterval);
    };
    imageObj.src = "jet_300x214.jpg";
};
```

4. Embed the canvas tag into the body of the HTML document:

```
<canvas id="myCanvas" width="600" height="250" style="border:1px
solid black;">
</canvas>
```

How it works...

Before jumping into the pixelation algorithm, let's define pixelation. Pixelation of an image occurs when the human eye can detect the individual pixels that make up the image. Old school video game graphics and small images that have been enlarged are good examples of pixilation. In layman terms, if we define pixilation as a condition in which the pixels that make up the image are visible, this simply means that the pixels themselves are fairly large. In fact, the larger the pixels are, the more pixelated the image becomes. We can use this observation to create a pixilation algorithm.

To create an algorithm that pixelates an image, we can take color samples of the image and then draw oversized pixels in its place. As pixels need to be square, we can construct pixel sizes of 1 x 1 (standard pixel size), 2 x 2, 3 x 3, 4 x 4, and so on. The larger the pixels are, the more pixelated the image will look.

Until now, our recipes have simply looped through all of the pixels in the `data` property and converted them with a simple algorithm, without paying much attention to which pixels are being updated. In this recipe, however, we'll need to inspect sample pixels by looking at specific areas in the image based on x,y coordinates. We can use the following equations to pick out the RGBA components of a pixel based on the x, y coordinates:

```
var red = data[((sourceWidth * y) + x) * 4];
var green = data[((sourceWidth * y) + x) * 4 + 1];
var blue = data[((sourceWidth * y) + x) * 4 + 2];
```

With these equations in hand, we can use `setInterval()` to render a series of pixelated images over time, in which each successive pixelated image is less pixelated than the previous image, until the pixilation value equals 0 and the image is restored to its original state.

4
Mastering Transformations

In this chapter, we will cover:

- Translating the canvas context
- Rotating the canvas context
- Scaling the canvas context
- Creating a mirror transform
- Creating custom transforms
- Shearing the canvas context
- Handling multiple transforms with the state stack
- Transforming a circle into an oval
- Rotating an image
- Drawing a simple logo and randomizing its position, rotation, and scale

Introduction

This chapter will reveal the power of canvas transformations, which can drastically simplify complex drawings and provide new functionality that we wouldn't have had otherwise. Until now, we've been positioning elements on the screen directly with x and y coordinates. This can quickly become a problem if you've worked out the coordinates for each point of a complex drawing, and then later decide that the entire drawing needs to be repositioned, rotated, or scaled. Canvas transforms solve this problem by enabling the developer to translate, rotate, and scale entire sections of the canvas without having to rework the coordinates of each point that make up a drawing. In addition, canvas transforms also enable the developer to rotate and scale images and text, which isn't possible without transforms. Let's get started!

Translating the canvas context

In this recipe, we'll learn how to perform the most basic and commonly used transformation available with the HTML5 canvas API—translation. If you're unfamiliar with transformation terminologies, "translation" is just a fancy way of saying "move". In this case, we'll be moving the context to a new location on the canvas.

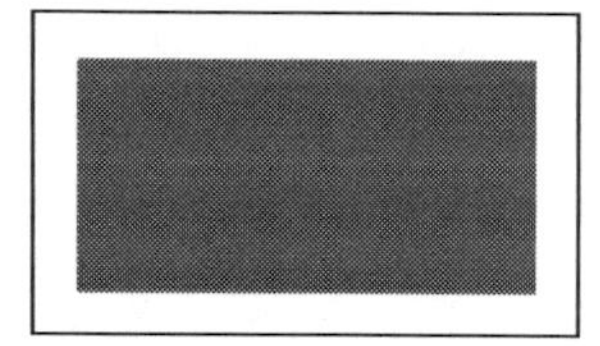

How to do it...

Follow these steps to draw a translated rectangle moved to the center of the canvas:

1. Define the canvas context and the dimensions for the rectangle:

```
window.onload = function(){
    var canvas = document.getElementById("myCanvas");
    var context = canvas.getContext("2d");

    var rectWidth = 150;
    var rectHeight = 75;
```

2. Translate the context to the center of the canvas:

```
    // translate context to center of canvas
    context.translate(canvas.width / 2, canvas.height / 2);
```

3. Draw a rectangle whose center lies on the top-left corner of the translated canvas context:

```
    context.fillStyle = "blue";
    context.fillRect(-rectWidth / 2, -rectHeight / 2, rectWidth,
rectHeight);
};
```

4. Embed the canvas tag inside the body of the HTML document:

```
<canvas id="myCanvas" width="600" height="250" style="border:1px
solid black;">
</canvas>
```

How it works...

Here's how it works!

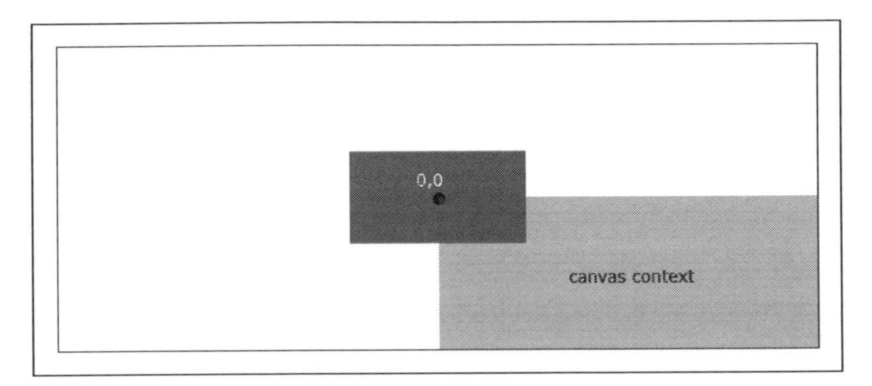

The idea behind HTML5 canvas transformations is to transform the canvas context in some way and then draw onto the canvas. In this recipe, we've translated the canvas context such that the top-left corner of the context has moved to the center of the canvas:

```
context.translate(tx,ty);
```

The `tx` parameter corresponds to the horizontal translation, and the `ty` parameter corresponds to the vertical translation. Once the context has been transformed, we can draw a rectangle centered on the top-left corner of the canvas context. The end result is a translated rectangle that's been moved to the center of the canvas.

Rotating the canvas context

The next type of transformation available with the HTML5 canvas API, and quite arguably the handiest, is the rotation transform. In this recipe, we'll first position the canvas context with a translation transform, and then we'll rotate the context with `rotate()` method.

How to do it...

Follow these steps to draw a rotated rectangle:

1. Define the canvas context and the dimensions for the rectangle:

```
window.onload = function(){
    var canvas = document.getElementById("myCanvas");
    var context = canvas.getContext("2d");

    var rectWidth = 150;
    var rectHeight = 75;
```

2. Translate the canvas context and then rotate it by 45 degrees:

```
    // translate context to center of canvas
    context.translate(canvas.width / 2, canvas.height / 2);

    // rotate context 45 degrees clockwise
    context.rotate(Math.PI / 4);
```

3. Draw the rectangle:

```
    context.fillStyle = "blue";
    context.fillRect(-rectWidth / 2, -rectHeight / 2, rectWidth,
rectHeight);
};
```

4. Embed the canvas tag inside the body of the HTML document:

```
<canvas id="myCanvas" width="600" height="250" style="border:1px
solid black;">
</canvas>
```

How it works...

Here's how it works!

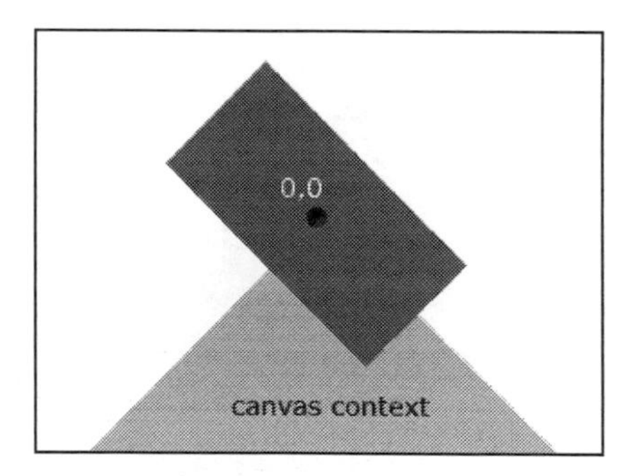

To position and rotate the rectangle, we can translate the canvas context to the center of the canvas as we did in the previous recipe, and then we can rotate the canvas context using the rotation transform, which rotates the context about the top-left corner of the context:

```
canvas.rotate(theta);
```

The parameter `theta` is in radians, and the transform rotates the context clockwise. Once the context has been translated and rotated, we can then draw the rectangle centered on the top-left corner of the context. The end result is a rotated rectangle centered on the canvas.

Notice that we've achieved this result by chaining two different transforms, a translation and a rotation. Each of the three transformations provided by the HTML5 canvas API apply a transformation matrix to the current state. For example, if we applied three translations one after another that moved the canvas context 10 pixels to the right, the net result would be a translation 30 pixels to the right.

If we had wanted to rotate the rectangle about a different point, say the bottom-right corner of the rectangle, we could simply draw the bottom-right corner of the rectangle at the origin of the canvas context.

Translations and rotations are the most common transformation chains used when creating complex HTML5 canvas drawings. As we'll see in the next chapter, rotations are exceptionally useful when animating shapes that spin about an axis.

See also...

- *Swinging a pendulum* in *Chapter 5*
- *Animating mechanical gears* in *Chapter 5*
- *Animating a clock* in *Chapter 5*

Scaling the canvas context

In addition to translations and rotations, the HTML5 canvas API also provides us with a means for scaling the canvas context. In this recipe, we'll scale down the height of the canvas context using the `scale()` method.

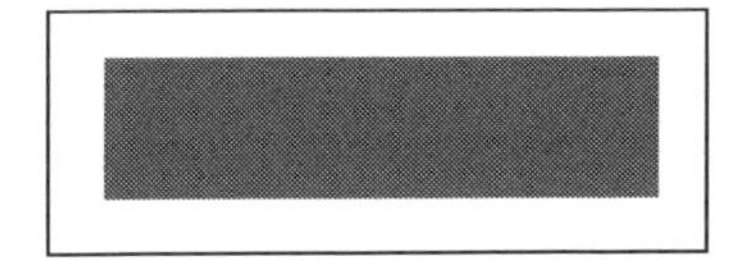

How to do it...

Follow these steps to draw a scaled rectangle:

1. Define the canvas context and the dimensions for the rectangle:

```
window.onload = function(){
    var canvas = document.getElementById("myCanvas");
    var context = canvas.getContext("2d");

    var rectWidth = 150;
    var rectHeight = 75;
```

2. Translate the canvas context and then scale the canvas context height by 50%:

```
    // translate context to center of canvas
    context.translate(canvas.width / 2, canvas.height / 2);

    // scale down canvas height by half
    context.scale(1, 0.5);
```

3. Draw a rectangle whose center lies on the top-left corner of the canvas context:

```
    context.fillStyle = "blue";
    context.fillRect(-rectWidth / 2, -rectHeight / 2, rectWidth, 
rectHeight);
};
```

4. Embed the canvas tag inside the body of the HTML document:

```
<canvas id="myCanvas" width="600" height="250" style="border:1px 
solid black;">
</canvas>
```

How it works...

To scale the canvas context, we can simply use the scale transform:

```
context.scale(sx,sy);
```

In the context's default state, the `sx` and `sy` parameters are normalized to `1` and `1`. As you might expect, the `sx` parameter corresponds to the horizontal scale, and the `sy` parameter corresponds to the vertical scale.

In this recipe, we've shrunk the vertical context by 50% by setting the `sy` parameter to a value of `0.5`. If we assign `sy` to a value greater than `1`, on the other hand, the context will stretch vertically. As we will see in the next recipe, if we assign negative values to either the `sx` or `sy` values, we will end up inverting the canvas context either horizontally or vertically, creating a mirror transform.

See also...

- *Oscillating a bubble* in *Chapter 5*

Creating a mirror transform

Another interesting use of the scale transformation is its ability to mirror the canvas context vertically or horizontally. In this recipe, we'll mirror the canvas context horizontally, and then write out some backwards text.

How to do it...

Follow these steps to write text backwards:

1. Define the canvas context:

```
window.onload = function(){
    var canvas = document.getElementById("myCanvas");
    var context = canvas.getContext("2d");
```

2. Translate the canvas context and then flip the context horizontally using a negative `x` value:

```
    // translate context to center of canvas
    context.translate(canvas.width / 2, canvas.height / 2);

    // flip context horizontally
    context.scale(-1, 1);
```

3. Write "Hello World!":

```
    context.font = "30pt Calibri";
    context.textAlign = "center";
    context.fillStyle = "blue";
    context.fillText("Hello World!", 0, 0);
};
```

4. Embed the canvas tag into the body of the HTML document:

```
<canvas id="myCanvas" width="600" height="250" style="border:1px
solid black;">
</canvas>
```

How it works...

To create a mirror transform using the HTML5 canvas API, we can assign a negative value to `sx` or `sy` when using the `scale` method of the canvas context:

```
context.scale(-sx,-sy);
```

In this recipe, we've translated the canvas context to the center of the canvas, and then inverted the context horizontally by applying a `-sx` value with the `scale()` transform.

Creating a custom transform

If you're looking to perform a custom transformation other than a translation, scale, or rotation, the HTML5 canvas API also provides a method which allows us to define a custom transformation matrix that can be applied to the current context. In this recipe, we'll manually create a translational transform to demonstrate how the `transform()` method works.

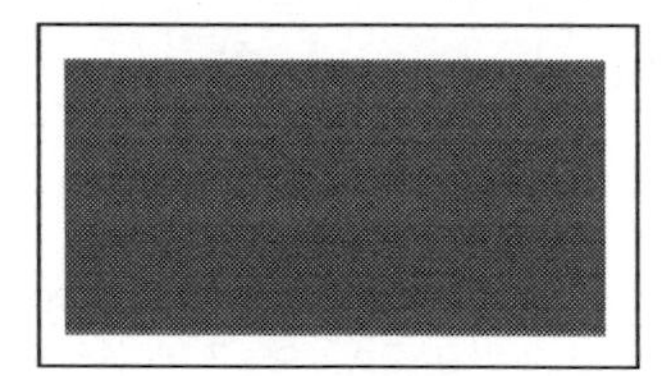

How to do it...

Follow these steps to perform a custom transform:

1. Define the canvas context and the dimensions for our rectangle:

```
window.onload = function(){
    var canvas = document.getElementById("myCanvas");
    var context = canvas.getContext("2d");

    var rectWidth = 150;
    var rectHeight = 75;
```

2. Apply a custom transform by manually translating the canvas context:

```
    // translation matrix:
    //  1  0  tx
    //  0  1  ty
    //  0  0  1
    var tx = canvas.width / 2;
    var ty = canvas.height / 2;

    // apply custom transform
    context.transform(1, 0, 0, 1, tx, ty);
```

3. Draw the rectangle:

```
        context.fillStyle = "blue";
        context.fillRect(-rectWidth / 2, -rectHeight / 2, rectWidth,
    rectHeight);
    };
```

4. Embed the canvas element into the body of the HTML document:

```
<canvas id="myCanvas" width="600" height="250" style="border:1px
solid black;">
</canvas>
```

How it works...

In this recipe, we've created a custom translation transform by applying a custom translation transformation matrix to the context state. A transformation matrix is simply a 2-dimensional matrix that can be used to transform the current matrix into a new one. Custom transformations can be applied to the context state using the `transform()` method of the canvas context:

```
context.transform(a,b,c,d,e,f);
```

Where the parameters `a`, `b`, `c`, `d`, `e`, and `f` correspond to the following components of a transformation matrix:

$$\begin{bmatrix} x' \\ y' \\ 1 \end{bmatrix} = \begin{bmatrix} a & c & e \\ b & d & f \\ 0 & 0 & 1 \end{bmatrix} \begin{bmatrix} x \\ y \\ 1 \end{bmatrix}$$

Here, *x'* and *y'* are the new matrix *x* and *y* components after applying the transformation. The transformation matrix for a translation transform looks as follows:

$$\begin{bmatrix} x' \\ y' \\ 1 \end{bmatrix} = \begin{bmatrix} 1 & 0 & t_x \\ 0 & 1 & t_y \\ 0 & 0 & 1 \end{bmatrix} \begin{bmatrix} x \\ y \\ 1 \end{bmatrix}$$

Where *tx* is the horizontal translation, and *ty* is the vertical translation.

There's more...

In addition to the `transform()` method, which *applies* a transformation matrix to the current context state, we can also *set* the transformation matrix using the `setTransform()` method of the canvas context:

```
context.setTransform(a,b,c,d,e,f);
```

This method can be useful if you want to directly set the transformation matrix of the context with a formulated transformation matrix, instead of obtaining the same result through a series of transformations.

Shearing the canvas context

In this recipe, we'll use what we've learned from the `transform()` method of the canvas context to create a custom shear transformation to skew the canvas context horizontally.

How to do it...

Follow these steps to draw a sheared rectangle:

1. Define the canvas context and the dimensions for the rectangle:

```
window.onload = function(){
    var canvas = document.getElementById("myCanvas");
    var context = canvas.getContext("2d");

    var rectWidth = 150;
    var rectHeight = 75;
```

2. Translate the canvas context and then apply a custom shear transform to the context:

```
    // shear matrix:
    //  1  sx  0
    //  sy  1  0
    //  0  0  1

    var sx = 0.75; // 0.75 horizontal shear
    var sy = 0; // no vertical shear
```

```
        // translate context to center of canvas
        context.translate(canvas.width / 2, canvas.height / 2);

        // apply custom transform
        context.transform(1, sy, sx, 1, 0, 0);
```

3. Draw the rectangle:

```
        context.fillStyle = "blue";
        context.fillRect(-rectWidth / 2, -rectHeight / 2, rectWidth,
rectHeight);
};
```

4. Embed the canvas element inside the body of the HTML document:

```
<canvas id="myCanvas" width="600" height="250" style="border:1px
solid black;">
</canvas>
```

How it works...

To shear the canvas context, we can apply the following transformation matrix:

$$\begin{bmatrix} x' \\ y' \\ 1 \end{bmatrix} = \begin{bmatrix} 1 & S_x & 0 \\ S_y & 1 & 0 \\ 0 & 0 & 1 \end{bmatrix} \begin{bmatrix} x \\ y \\ 1 \end{bmatrix}$$

We can use the `transform()` method with the following parameters:

```
context.transform(1,sy,sx,1,0,0);
```

The more we increase the value of `sx`, the greater the context is sheared horizontally. The more we increase the value of `sy`, the greater the context is sheared vertically.

Handling multiple transforms with the state stack

Now that we have a good handle on transformations with the HTML5 canvas API, we're now in a position to further explore the canvas state stack and see what it can do for us with respect to transformations. In *Chapter 2, Shape Drawing and Composites*, we covered the state stack, a very powerful yet sometimes overlooked property of the canvas API. Although the canvas state stack can help with managing styling, it's most common usage is to save and restore transformation states. In this recipe, we'll perform multiple transformations while saving the canvas state between each transformation, and then draw a sequence of rectangles after restoring each state to see the effects.

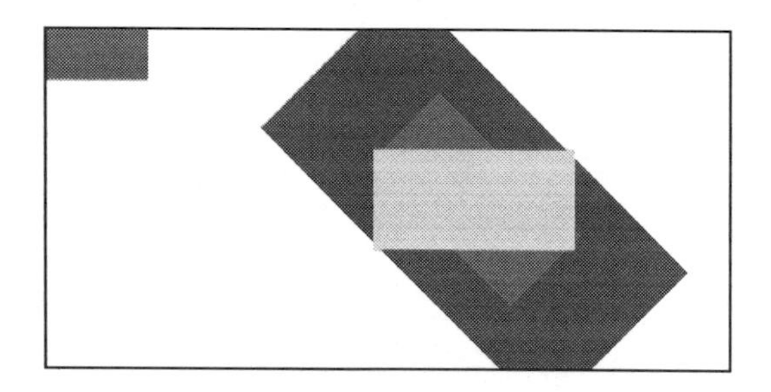

How to do it...

Follow these steps to construct a state stack with four different states and then draw a rectangle after popping each state:

1. Define the canvas context and the dimensions for our rectangle:

```
window.onload = function(){
    var canvas = document.getElementById("myCanvas");
    var context = canvas.getContext("2d");

    var rectWidth = 150;
    var rectHeight = 75;
```

2. Push the current transformation state, the default state, onto the state stack, and translate the context:

```
    context.save(); // save state 1
    context.translate(canvas.width / 2, canvas.height / 2);
```

3. Push the current transformation state, the translated state, onto the stack, and rotate the context:

```
    context.save(); // save state 2
    context.rotate(Math.PI / 4);
```

4. Push the current transformation state, the translated and rotated state, onto the stack, and scale the context:

```
    context.save(); // save state 3
    context.scale(2, 2);
```

5. Draw a blue rectangle:

```
  // draw the rectangle
    context.fillStyle = "blue";
    context.fillRect(-rectWidth / 2, -rectHeight / 2, rectWidth,
rectHeight);
```

6. Restore the previous state from the state stack by popping off the current state, and then draw a red rectangle:

```
    context.restore(); // restore state 3
    context.fillStyle = "red";
    context.fillRect(-rectWidth / 2, -rectHeight / 2, rectWidth,
rectHeight);
```

7. Restore the previous state from the state stack by popping off the current state, and then draw a yellow rectangle:

```
    context.restore(); // restore state 2
    context.fillStyle = "yellow";
    context.fillRect(-rectWidth / 2, -rectHeight / 2, rectWidth,
rectHeight);
```

8. Restore the previous state from the state stack by popping off the current state, and then draw a green rectangle:

```
    context.restore(); // restore state 1
    context.fillStyle = "green";
    context.fillRect(-rectWidth / 2, -rectHeight / 2, rectWidth,
rectHeight);
};
```

9. Embed the canvas tag into the body of the HTML document:

```
<canvas id="myCanvas" width="600" height="250" style="border:1px
solid black;">
</canvas>
```

How it works...

This recipe performs a series of three transformations, a translation, a rotation, and a scale transform, while pushing each transformation state onto the state stack with the `save()` operation. When the blue rectangle is drawn, it's centered, rotated, and scaled. At this point, the state stack has four states (from bottom to top):

1. Default state
2. Translated state
3. Translated and rotated state
4. Current state (translated, rotated, and scaled state)

After the blue rectangle is drawn, we use the `restore()` method to pop off the top state in the state stack, and restore the canvas context to the third state, in which the canvas context is translated and rotated. The red rectangle is drawn, and you can see that it's been translated and rotated, but not scaled. Next, we use the `restore()` method once again to pop off the top state in the state stack, and restore the second state, in which the canvas context is merely translated. We then draw a yellow rectangle, which is indeed just translated. Finally, we call the `restore()` method one last time to pop off the top state in the state stack, and return us to the default state. When we draw the green rectangle, it appears at the origin, because no transformation has been applied.

Using the state stack, we can jump between transformation states so that we don't have to constantly reset the state back to its default state and then translate each element separately. In addition, we can also use save-restore combinations to encapsulate transformations for a small piece of code without affecting shapes drawn afterwards.

Transforming a circle into an oval

One of the most common applications of the scale transform is to stretch a circle horizontally or vertically to create an oval. In this recipe, we'll create an oval by translating the canvas context, stretching it horizontally, and then drawing a circle.

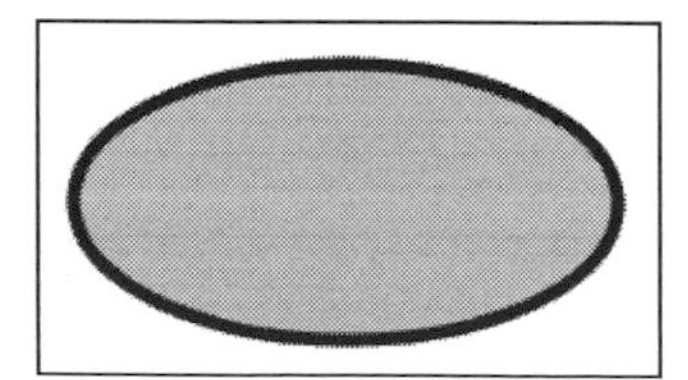

How to do it...

Follow these steps to draw an oval:

1. Define a canvas context:

```
window.onload = function(){
    var canvas = document.getElementById("myCanvas");
    var context = canvas.getContext("2d");
```

2. Push the current transformation state, which is the default state, onto the state stack:

```
    context.save(); // save state
```

3. Define the dimensions of the circle:

```
    var centerX = 0;
    var centerY = 0;
    var radius = 50;
```

4. Translate the canvas context to the center of the canvas, and then scale the context width to stretch it outwards:

```
    context.translate(canvas.width / 2, canvas.height / 2);
    context.scale(2, 1);
```

5. Draw the circle:

```
    context.beginPath();
    context.arc(centerX, centerY, radius, 0, 2 * Math.PI, false);
```

6. Restore the previous transformation state, which was the default state, and also pop off the current transformation state from the state stack:

```
    context.restore(); // restore original state
```

7. Apply styling to the oval:

```
    context.fillStyle = "#8ED6FF";
    context.fill();
    context.lineWidth = 5;
    context.strokeStyle = "black";
    context.stroke();
};
```

8. Embed the canvas tag into the body of the HTML document:

```
<canvas id="myCanvas" width="600" height="250" style="border:1px
solid black;">
</canvas>
```

How it works...

To draw an oval using the HTML5 canvas API, we can simply translate the context to its desired position with the `translate()` method, stretch the context either vertically or horizontally with the `scale()` method, and then draw the circle. In this recipe, we've stretched the canvas context horizontally to create an oval that's twice as wide as it is tall.

As we want to apply a stroke style to the oval, we can use a save-restore combination to encapsulate the transformations used to create the oval so that they don't affect the styling of the oval afterwards.

If you try this recipe out for yourself, and you remove the `save()` and `restore()` methods, you'll find that the thickness of the line at the top and bottom of the oval is 5 pixels, and the thickness of the line on the sides of the oval is 10 pixels, because the stroke style has also been stretched horizontally along with the circle.

See also...

- *Oscillating a bubble* in *Chapter 5*

Rotating an image

In this recipe, we'll rotate an image by translating and rotating the canvas context, and then drawing an image on the transformed context.

How to do it...

Follow these steps to rotate an image:

1. Define a canvas context:

```
window.onload = function(){
    var canvas = document.getElementById("myCanvas");
    var context = canvas.getContext("2d");
```

2. Create a new `image` object and set its `onload` property:

```
    var imageObj = new Image();
    imageObj.onload = function(){
```

3. When the image loads, translate the context to the center of the canvas, rotate the context by 45 degrees counter-clockwise, and then draw the image:

```
        // translate context to center of canvas
        context.translate(canvas.width / 2, canvas.height / 2);

        // rotate context by 45 degrees counter clockwise
        context.rotate(-1 * Math.PI / 4);
        context.drawImage(this, -1 * imageObj.width / 2, -1 *
imageObj.height / 2);
    };
```

4. Set the source of the image:

```
    imageObj.src = "jet_300x214.jpg";
};
```

5. Embed the canvas tag inside the body of the HTML document:

```
<canvas id="myCanvas" width="600" height="250" style="border:1px
solid black;">
</canvas>
```

How it works...

To rotate an image, we can simply position the canvas context with the `translate()` method, rotate the context with the `rotate()` method, and then draw the image with the `drawImage()` method.

There's more...

It's also worth noting that in addition to rotating an image, another common transform used with images is the mirror transform. To mirror an image, we could have translated the context to the desired position, inverted the context horizontally with `scale(-1,1)` or inverted the context vertically with `scale(1,-1)`, and then drawn the image using `drawImage()`.

See also...

- *Creating a mirror transform* recipe

Drawing a simple logo and randomizing its position, rotation, and scale

The purpose of this recipe is to demonstrate the practical use of transformations by transforming a complex shape. In this case, our complex shape will be a logo, which is just some text with a couple of wavy lines below it. Transformations are exceedingly useful when we want to translate, rotate, or scale complex shapes. It's very common for developers to create functions that draw something complicated at the origin, and then use transforms to move it somewhere on the screen. In this recipe, we'll draw five randomly positioned, rotated, and scaled logos on the screen.

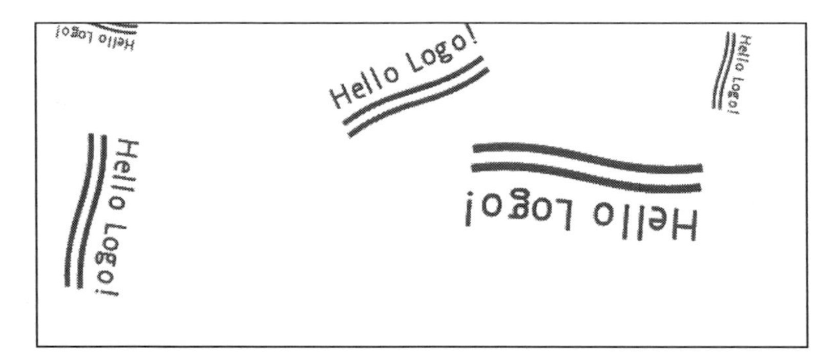

How to do it...

Follow these steps to draw five randomly positioned, rotated, and scaled logos:

1. Define the `drawLogo()` function which draws a simple logo by writing out text and drawing two waves below it:

```
function drawLogo(context){
    // draw Hello Logo! text
    context.beginPath();
    context.font = "10pt Calibri";
    context.textAlign = "center";
    context.textBaseline = "middle";
    context.fillStyle = "blue";
    context.fillText("Hello Logo!", 0, 0);
    context.closePath();

  // define style for both waves
    context.lineWidth = 2;
    context.strokeStyle = "blue";

    // draw top wave
```

```
        context.beginPath();
        context.moveTo(-30, 10);
        context.bezierCurveTo(-5, 5, 5, 15, 30, 10);
        context.stroke();

        // draw bottom wave
        context.beginPath();
        context.moveTo(-30, 15);
        context.bezierCurveTo(-5, 10, 5, 20, 30, 15);
        context.stroke();
    }
```

2. Define the `getRandomX()` function that returns a random `X` value between 0 and the canvas width:

```
function getRandomX(canvas){
    return Math.round(Math.random() * canvas.width);
}
```

3. Define the `getRandomY()` function that returns a random `Y` value between 0 and the canvas height:

```
function getRandomY(canvas){
    return Math.round(Math.random() * canvas.height);
}
```

4. Define the `getRandomSize()` function that returns a random size between 0 and 5:

```
function getRandomSize(){
    return Math.round(Math.random() * 5);
}
```

5. Define the `getRandomAngle()` function that returns a random angle between 0 and 2π:

```
function getRandomAngle(){
    return Math.random() * Math.PI * 2;
}
```

6. Define the canvas context:

```
window.onload = function(){
    var canvas = document.getElementById("myCanvas");
    var context = canvas.getContext("2d");
```

7. Create a loop that draws five randomly positioned, rotated, and scaled logos:

```
    // draw 5 randomly transformed logos
    for (var n = 0; n < 5; n++) {
        context.save();
```

```
            // translate to random position
            context.translate(getRandomX(canvas), getRandomY(canvas));

            // rotate by random angle
            context.rotate(getRandomAngle());

            // scale by random size
            var randSize = getRandomSize();
            context.scale(randSize, randSize);

            // draw logo
            drawLogo(context);
            context.restore();
        }
    };
```

8. Embed the canvas tag inside the body of the HTML document:

```
<canvas id="myCanvas" width="600" height="250" style="border:1px
solid black;">
</canvas>
```

How it works...

Firstly, to draw our simple logo, we can create a function called `drawLogo()` that writes out the text **Hello Logo!** at the origin and then draws two wavy lines using the `bezierCurveTo()` method for each wave.

Next, to draw five randomly positioned, rotated, and scaled logos, we can create a few utility functions that return random values for the position, rotation, and scale, and then create a `for` loop that uses a save-restore combination for each iteration to induce state scope, perform the three transformations, and then draw the logo with the `drawLogo()` method. If you try out this recipe for yourself, you'll see that each of the five logos are positioned, rotated, and scaled differently each time you refresh the screen.

5

Bringing the Canvas to Life with Animation

In this chapter, we will cover:

- Creating an Animation class
- Creating a linear motion
- Creating an acceleration
- Creating an oscillation
- Oscillating a bubble
- Swinging a pendulum
- Animating mechanical gears
- Animating a clock
- Simulating particle physics
- Creating microscopic life forms
- Stressing the canvas and displaying the FPS

Introduction

In the first half of this book, we covered the fundamental capabilities of the HTML5 canvas, including path drawing, shape drawing, working with images and video, and transformations. This chapter focuses on animation, which is not a part of the HTML5 canvas API. Although the API doesn't provide us with animation functionality, we can certainly create an Animation class that can be used to support animation projects. We'll cover the essential types of motion including linear motion, accelerations, and oscillations, and we'll use what we've learned to create some really awesome demos. Let's get started!

Creating an Animation class

As the HTML5 canvas API doesn't provide methods for animation, we'll have to create our own Animation class for handling an animation stage. This recipe will cover the basics of animation and provide an Animation class for all of our future animation projects.

Getting ready...

As browsers and computer hardware are not created equally, it's important to understand that the optimal **FPS** (**Frames Per Second**) value for each animation varies depending on the browser, the computer's hardware, and the animation's algorithm. Therefore, it would be quite difficult for a developer to figure out what the best FPS value is for each user. Fortunately, browsers are now implementing a `requestAnimationFrame` method of the `window` object which can automatically determine the best FPS for animations (thank goodness). As we'll see later in this chapter, a typical FPS value for a smooth animation is somewhere between 40 and 60 frames per second.

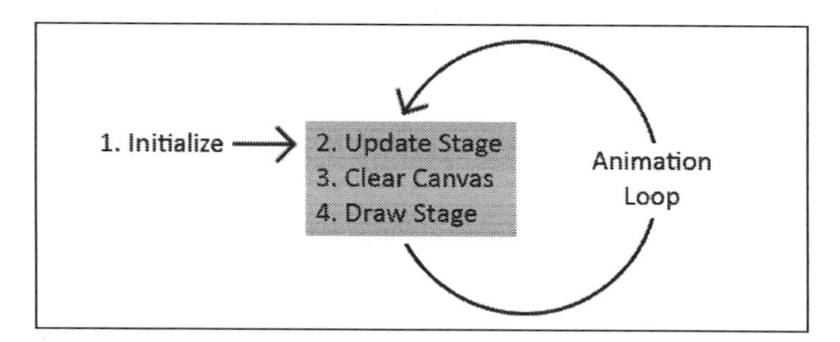

Take a look at the preceding diagram. To create an animation, we first need to initialize the objects on our stage. We can refer to the canvas as a "stage" because the objects in the canvas that will be moving can be seen as "actors" on the stage. Moreover, the stage analogy provides us with a sense that stuff is *happening* in the canvas, instead of just sitting there. Once our objects are initialized, we can start an animation loop that updates the stage, clears the canvas, redraws the stage, and then request a new animation frame.

As this behavior can define any type of animation, it makes a lot of sense for us to create an Animation class that handles these steps for us under the covers.

How to do it...

Follow these steps to create an Animation class which will support the animation recipes in this chapter:

1. Define the `Animation` constructor and create a cross-browser `requestAnimationFrame` method:

```
var Animation = function(canvasId){
    this.canvas = document.getElementById(canvasId);
    this.context = this.canvas.getContext("2d");
    this.t = 0;
    this.timeInterval = 0;
    this.startTime = 0;
    this.lastTime = 0;
    this.frame = 0;
    this.animating = false;

    // provided by Paul Irish
    window.requestAnimFrame = (function(callback){
        return window.requestAnimationFrame ||
        window.webkitRequestAnimationFrame ||
        window.mozRequestAnimationFrame ||
        window.oRequestAnimationFrame ||
        window.msRequestAnimationFrame ||
        function(callback){
            window.setTimeout(callback, 1000 / 60);
        };
    })();
};
```

2. Define the `getContext()` method:

```
Animation.prototype.getContext = function(){
    return this.context;
};
```

3. Define the `getCanvas()` method:

```
Animation.prototype.getCanvas = function(){
    return this.canvas;
};
```

4. Define the `clear()` method which clears the canvas:

```
Animation.prototype.clear = function(){
    this.context.clearRect(0, 0, this.canvas.width, this.canvas.
height);
};
```

5. Define the `setStage()` method that sets the `stage()` function. This function will execute for each animation frame:

```
Animation.prototype.setStage = function(func){
    this.stage = func;
};
```

6. Define the `isAnimating()` method:

```
Animation.prototype.isAnimating = function(){
    return this.animating;
};
```

7. Define the `getFrame()` method that returns the frame number:

```
Animation.prototype.getFrame = function(){
    return this.frame;
};
```

8. Define the `start()` method that starts the animation:

```
Animation.prototype.start = function(){
    this.animating = true;
    var date = new Date();
    this.startTime = date.getTime();
    this.lastTime = this.startTime;

    if (this.stage !== undefined) {
        this.stage();
    }

    this.animationLoop();
};
```

9. Define the `stop()` method that stops the animation:

```
Animation.prototype.stop = function(){
    this.animating = false;
};
```

10. Define the `getTimeInterval()` method that returns the time in milliseconds between the last frame and the current frame:

```
Animation.prototype.getTimeInterval = function(){
    return this.timeInterval;
};
```

11. Define the `getTime()` method that returns the time in milliseconds that the animation has been running:

```
Animation.prototype.getTime = function(){
    return this.t;
};
```

12. Define the `getFps()` method that returns the current FPS of the animation:

```
Animation.prototype.getFps = function(){
    return this.timeInterval > 0 ? 1000 / this.timeInterval : 0;
};
```

13. Define the `animationLoop()` method that handles the animation loop:

```
Animation.prototype.animationLoop = function(){
    var that = this;

    this.frame++;
    var date = new Date();
    var thisTime = date.getTime();
    this.timeInterval = thisTime - this.lastTime;
    this.t += this.timeInterval;
    this.lastTime = thisTime;

    if (this.stage !== undefined) {
        this.stage();
    }

    if (this.animating) {
        requestAnimFrame(function(){
            that.animationLoop();
        });
    }
};
```

How it works...

The idea of the `Animation` class is to simplify our animation projects by encapsulating and hiding all of the logic that animations require, such as providing the time interval between frames, handling the animation loop, and clearing the canvas.

The key to the `Animation` class is inside the `Animation` constructor, where we set the `requestAnimFrame` method of the `window` object. This method acts as a cross-browser implementation of the `requestAnimationFrame`, which allows the user's browser to decide what the optimal FPS of the animation should be. The FPS is completely dynamic and will change throughout the animation.

Our `Animation` class also provides some handy methods such as `getTimeInterval()`, which returns the number of milliseconds since the last animation frame, the `getTime()` method which returns the number of milliseconds the animation has ran since it was started, a `start()` method which starts the animation, a `stop()` method which stops the animation, and a `clear()` method which clears the canvas.

Now that we have a working `Animation` class ready for prime time, the rest of the animations in this chapter, and your future animation projects as well, will be a piece of cake.

Creating a linear motion

In this recipe, we'll try out our `Animation` class by creating a simple linear motion animation by moving a box from the left of the canvas to the right of the canvas:

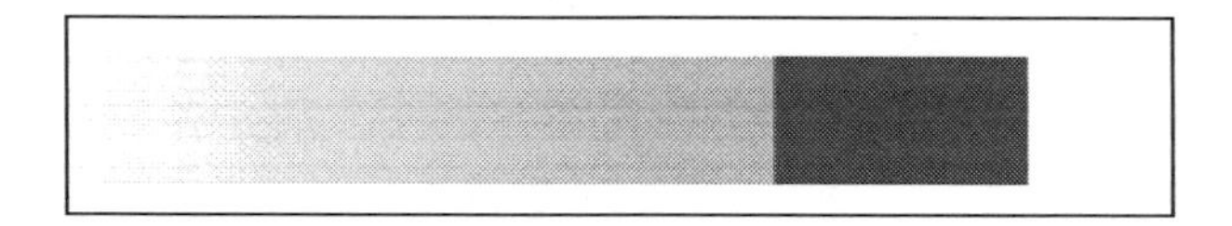

How to do it...

Follow these steps to move a box from one side of the canvas to the other:

1. Link to the `Animation` class:

```
<head>
    <script src="animation.js">
    </script>
```

2. Instantiate an `Animation` object and get the canvas context:

```
    <script>
        window.onload = function(){
            var anim = new Animation("myCanvas");
            var canvas = anim.getCanvas();
            var context = anim.getContext();
```

3. Define the box's linear speed and create a `box` object that contains the box's position and size:

```
            var linearSpeed = 100; // pixels / second
            var box = {
                x: 0,
                y: canvas.height / 2 - 25,
                width: 100,
                height: 50
            };
```

4. Set the `stage()` function, which updates the box's position, clears the canvas, and draws the box:

```
        anim.setStage(function(){
            // update
            var linearDistEachFrame = linearSpeed * this.
getTimeInterval() / 1000;

            if (box.x < canvas.width - box.width) {
                box.x += linearDistEachFrame;
            }
            else {
                anim.stop();
            }

            // clear
            this.clear();

            // draw
            context.beginPath();
            context.fillStyle = "blue";
            context.fillRect(box.x, box.y, box.width, box.height);
        });
```

5. Start the animation:

```
        anim.start();
    };
    </script>
</head>
```

6. Embed the canvas inside the body of the HTML document:

```
<body>
    <canvas id="myCanvas" width="600" height="250"
style="border:1px solid black;">
    </canvas>
</body>
```

How it works...

To create a simple linear motion, first we need to instantiate a new `Animation` object, and then get the canvas and context. Next, we can define the speed of the box, which for this recipe we've set to 100 pixels / second, and we can create a `box` object that contains the box's position and size.

Now that our box has been initialized, we can define the `stage()` function which will be executed within the animation loop. For each animation loop, we can update the position of the box by first calculating the distance that the box moved between the last frame and the current frame, and then update the box's x position by adding the distance that it travelled. Once the box reaches the edge of the canvas, we can stop the animation by calling `stop()`.

Finally, once the `stage()` function has been defined, we can start the animation with the `start()` method.

See also...

- *Drawing a rectangle* in *Chapter 2*

Creating acceleration

Now that we have a handle on the basics of animation, let's try something a little bit more complex by accelerating a box downwards due to the force of gravity.

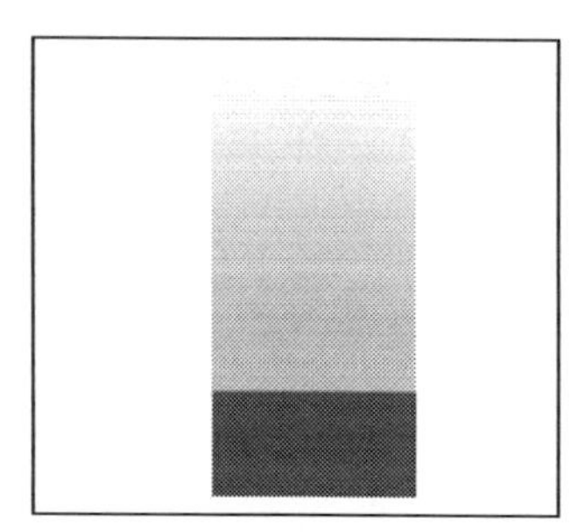

How to do it...

Follow these steps to draw a box at the top of the canvas which falls downward due to the force of gravity:

1. Link to the `Animation` class:

```
<head>
    <script src="animation.js">
    </script>
```

2. Instantiate an `Animation` object and get the canvas context:

```
<script>
    window.onload = function(){
        var anim = new Animation("myCanvas");
        var canvas = anim.getCanvas();
        var context = anim.getContext();
```

3. Define gravity and create a `box` object that contains the box's position, x and y velocity, and size:

```
        var gravity = 2; // pixels / second^2
        var box = {
            x: canvas.width / 2 - 50,
            y: 0,
            vx: 0,
            vy: 0,
            width: 100,
            height: 50
        };
```

4. Set the `stage()` function which updates the box, clears the canvas, and draws the box:

```
        anim.setStage(function(){
            // update
    if (this.getTime() > 1000) {
                var speedIncrementEachFrame = gravity * anim.
getTimeInterval() / 1000; // pixels / second
                box.vy += speedIncrementEachFrame;
                box.y += box.vy * this.getTimeInterval();

                if (box.y > canvas.height - box.height) {
                    box.y = canvas.height - box.height;
                    this.stop();
                }
    }

            // clear
            this.clear();

            // draw
            context.beginPath();
            context.fillStyle = "blue";
            context.fillRect(box.x, box.y, box.width, box.
height);
        });
```

5. Start the animation:

```
                anim.start();
            };
        </script>
    </head>
```

6. Embed the canvas inside the body of the HTML document:

```
<body>
    <canvas id="myCanvas" width="600" height="250"
style="border:1px solid black;">
    </canvas>
</body>
```

How it works...

To create an acceleration, we can increment the velocity of the box, update the position of the box with the new velocity, clear the canvas, and then draw the box.

We can calculate the new y velocity of the box for each frame by adding the change in velocity due to gravity, which is set to 2 pixels / second^2:

```
var speedIncrementEachFrame = gravity * anim.getTimeInterval() / 1000;
// pixels / second
box.vy += speedIncrementEachFrame;
```

Next, we can calculate the new y position of the box by adding the distance that it travelled since the last frame:

```
box.y += box.vy * this.getTimeInterval();
```

In other words, the change in y position is equal to the box's velocity multiplied by the change in time (the time interval).

Finally, we can add a condition that checks to see if the box has reached the bottom of the canvas, and if it has, we can then stop the animation with the `stop()` method.

Accelerations are particularly useful when applying forces to an object or particle. Some examples of applied forces include gravity, air resistance, damping, floor friction, and electromagnetic forces. For really intensive animations that require a lot of physics, you might consider looking for an open source vector library to help handle velocities and accelerations in both the x and y direction.

See also...

- *Drawing a rectangle* in *Chapter 2*

Creating oscillation

In this recipe, we'll explore the third major type of motion—oscillation. Some good examples of oscillations are a bouncing weight attached to a spring, an oscillating bubble, or a pendulum that swings back and forth.

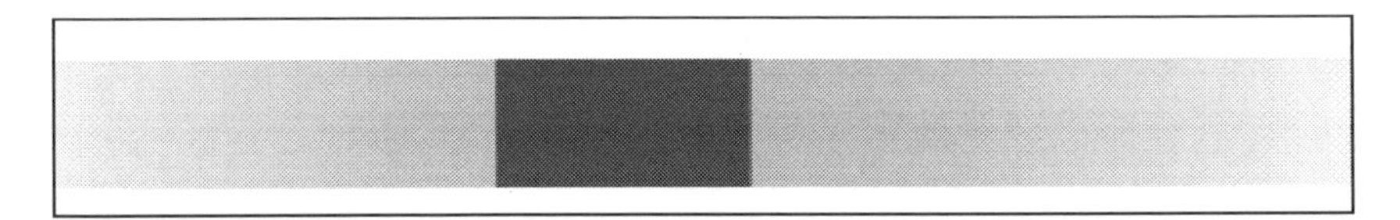

How to do it...

Follow these steps to oscillate a box back and forth:

1. Link to the `Animation` class:

```
<head>
    <script src="animation.js">
    </script>
```

2. Instantiate an `Animation` object and get the canvas context:

```
    <script>
        window.onload = function(){
            var anim = new Animation("myCanvas");
            var canvas = anim.getCanvas();
            var context = anim.getContext();
```

3. Create a `box` object that contains the box's position and size:

```
            var box = {
                x: 250,
                y: canvas.height / 2 - 25,
                width: 100,
                height: 50
            };
```

4. Define the parameters required for the harmonic oscillation equation:

```
            var centerX = canvas.width / 2 - box.width / 2;
            var amplitude = 150; // pixels
            var period = 2000; // ms
```

5. Set the `stage()` function which updates the box's position based on the harmonic oscillation equation, clears the canvas, and then draws the box:

```
            anim.setStage(function(){
        // update
        box.x = amplitude * Math.sin(anim.getTime() * 2 * Math.PI
/ period) + centerX;

        // clear
        this.clear();

        // draw
                context.beginPath();
                context.rect(box.x, box.y, box.width, box.height);
                context.fillStyle = "blue";
                context.fill();
            });
```

6. Start the animation:

```
            anim.start();
        };
    </script>
</head>
```

7. Embed the canvas inside the body of the HTML document:

```
<body>
    <canvas id="myCanvas" width="600" height="250"
style="border:1px solid black;">
    </canvas>
</body>
```

How it works...

Once the page loads, we can instantiate a new `Animation` object and then get the canvas and context.

Next, we can create a `box` object which defines the box's position and size, and then define the variables required for the equation of harmonic oscillation:

```
x(t) = A * sin (t * 2π / T + Φ) + x0
```

For this recipe, we've set the amplitude `A` to `150`, the period `T` to `2` seconds, and the offset `x0` and the phase difference `Φ` to `0`.

For each animation frame, we can leverage the equation for harmonic oscillation to update the box's position, clear the canvas, and then draw the box using the `rect()` method.

Finally, we can start the animation using the `start()` method.

See also...

- *Drawing a rectangle* in *Chapter 2*

Oscillating a bubble

In this recipe, we'll create a life-like oscillating bubble using the principles of harmonic oscillation and canvas transformations.

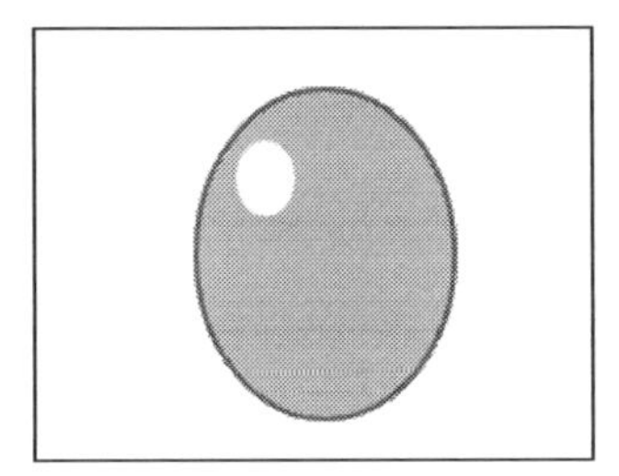

How to do it...

Follow these steps to create a life-like oscillating bubble floating in the air:

1. Link to the `Animation` class:

```
<head>
    <script src="animation.js">
    </script>
```

2. Instantiate an `Animation` object and get the canvas context:

```
    <script>
        window.onload = function(){
            // instantiate new animation object
            var anim = new Animation("myCanvas");
            var context = anim.getContext();
            var canvas = anim.getCanvas();
```

3. Set the `stage()` function which updates the width and height scale of the bubble, clears the canvas, scales the canvas context, and then draws the bubble:

```
            anim.setStage(function(){
                // update
                var widthScale = Math.sin(this.getTime() / 200) *
0.1 + 0.9;
```

```
                    var heightScale = -1 * Math.sin(this.getTime() /
200) * 0.1 + 0.9;

                    // clear
                    this.clear();

                    //draw
                    context.beginPath();
                    context.save();
                    context.translate(canvas.width / 2, canvas.height
/ 2);
                    context.scale(widthScale, heightScale);
                    context.arc(0, 0, 65, 0, 2 * Math.PI, false);
                    context.restore();
                    context.fillStyle = "#8ED6FF";
                    context.fill();
                    context.lineWidth = 2;
                    context.strokeStyle = "#555";
                    context.stroke();

                    context.beginPath();
                    context.save();
                    context.translate(canvas.width / 2, canvas.height
/ 2);
                    context.scale(widthScale, heightScale);
                    context.arc(-30, -30, 15, 0, 2 * Math.PI, false);
                    context.restore();
                    context.fillStyle = "white";
                    context.fill();
                });
```

4. Start the animation:

```
                anim.start();
            };
        </script>
</head>
```

5. Embed the canvas tag inside the body of the HTML document:

```
<body>
    <canvas id="myCanvas" width="600" height="250"
style="border:1px solid black;">
    </canvas>
</body>
```

How it works...

Before we talk about oscillating a bubble, it's a good idea to first cover how we can use canvas transformations to stretch the bubble in both the x and y direction. To draw a bubble that has been stretched horizontally, we can translate the context to the center of the canvas, scale the context horizontally, and then draw a bubble. To draw a bubble that has been stretched vertically, we can translate it to the center of the canvas, scale the context vertically, and then draw the bubble.

In order to oscillate the bubble, we need to alternate which direction the canvas is scaled in such a way that the horizontal scale and the vertical scale always equals a constant, which in our case is 1.8, so that the volume of the bubble remains constant. Once this relationship is in place, we can use the equation of harmonic oscillation to oscillate both the x and y scale of the bubble.

When the page first loads, we can instantiate a new `Animation` object and get the canvas and context. Next, we can set the `stage()` function which is responsible for updating the bubble, clearing the canvas, and then drawing the bubble for each animation frame. To update the bubble for each frame, we can calculate the horizontal and vertical scale of the bubble by using the equation of harmonic oscillation. Next, we can clear the canvas, and then draw the bubble using the `arc()` method.

Finally, once the `stage()` function has been set, we can start the animation with the `start()` method.

See also...

- *Drawing a circle* in *Chapter 2*
- *Scaling the canvas context* in *Chapter 4*
- *Transforming a circle into an oval* in *Chapter 4*

Swinging a pendulum

Unlike the bubble recipe, whose width and height oscillate as a function of time, in this recipe we'll create a pendulum whose *angle* oscillates as a function of time.

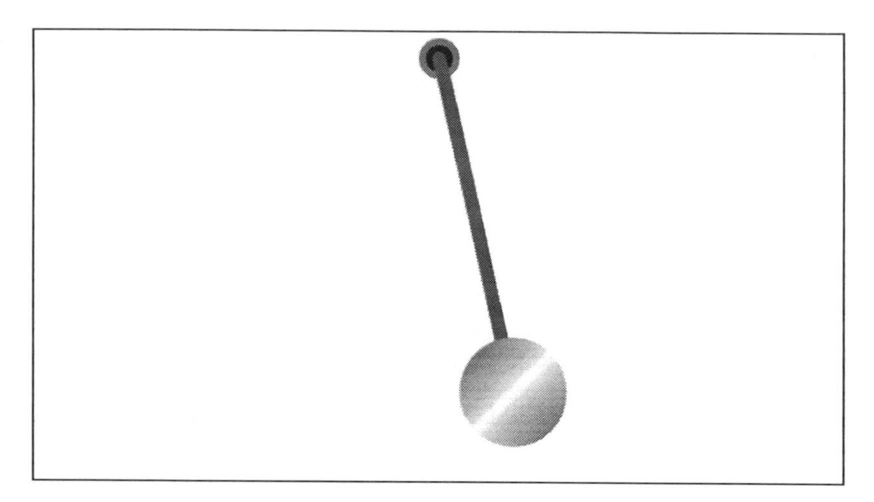

How to do it...

Follow these steps to swing a pendulum back and forth:

1. Link to the `Animation` class:

```
<head>
    <script src="animation.js">
    </script>
```

2. Instantiate a new `Animation` object and get the canvas context:

```
    <script>
        window.onload = function(){
            var anim = new Animation("myCanvas");
            var canvas = anim.getCanvas();
            var context = anim.getContext();
```

3. Define the properties of the pendulum:

```
            var amplitude = Math.PI / 4; // 45 degrees
            var period = 4000; // ms
            var theta = 0;
            var pendulumLength = 250;
            var pendulumWidth = 10;
            var rotationPointX = canvas.width / 2;
            var rotationPointY = 20;
```

4. Set the `stage()` function which updates the angle of the pendulum, clears the canvas, and then draws the pendulum:

```
            anim.setStage(function(){
                // update
                theta = (amplitude * Math.sin((2 * Math.PI * this.
getTime()) / period)) + Math.PI / 2;

                // clear
                this.clear();

                // draw top circle
                context.beginPath();
                context.arc(rotationPointX, rotationPointY, 15, 0,
2 * Math.PI, false);
                context.fillStyle = "#888";
                context.fill();

                // draw top inner circle
                context.beginPath();
                context.arc(rotationPointX, rotationPointY, 10, 0,
2 * Math.PI, false);
                context.fillStyle = "black";
                context.fill();

                // draw shaft
                context.beginPath();
                var endPointX = rotationPointX + (pendulumLength *
Math.cos(theta));
                var endPointY = rotationPointY + (pendulumLength *
Math.sin(theta));
                context.beginPath();
                context.moveTo(rotationPointX, rotationPointY);
                context.lineTo(endPointX, endPointY);
                context.lineWidth = pendulumWidth;
                context.lineCap = "round";
                context.strokeStyle = "#555";
                context.stroke();

                // draw bottom circle
                context.beginPath();
                context.arc(endPointX, endPointY, 40, 0, 2 * Math.
PI, false);
                var grd = context.createLinearGradient(endPointX -
50, endPointY - 50, endPointX + 50, endPointY + 50);
```

```
                    grd.addColorStop(0, "#444");
                    grd.addColorStop(0.5, "white");
                    grd.addColorStop(1, "#444");
                    context.fillStyle = grd;
                    context.fill();
                });
```

5. Start the animation:

```
                anim.start();
            };
        </script>
    </head>
```

6. Embed the canvas inside the body of the HTML document:

```
<body>
    <canvas id="myCanvas" width="600" height="330"
style="border:1px solid black;">
    </canvas>
</body>
```

How it works...

When the page loads, we can instantiate a new `Animation` object and then get the canvas and context. Next, we can define the properties of our pendulum, including the angular amplitude, the period, the initial angle theta, the pendulum length, width, and the center of rotation.

Once our pendulum has been initialized, we can set the `stage()` function which will update the pendulum angle with the equation of harmonic oscillation, clear the canvas, and then immediately redraw the pendulum.

We can create a pendulum by drawing a couple of circles at the rotation point, drawing a thick line from the rotation point to the weight of the pendulum to form the shaft, and then drawing a big circle at the end of the line that has a nice diagonal gray gradient to create the illusion of a polished surface.

Once the `stage()` function has been set, we can start the animation with the `start()` method.

See also...

- *Drawing a line* in *Chapter 1*
- *Drawing a circle* in *Chapter 2*
- *Working with custom shapes and fill styles* in *Chapter 2*

Animating mechanical gears

For the mechanics and engineers out there, this one's for you. In this recipe, we'll create a system of interconnected rotating gears.

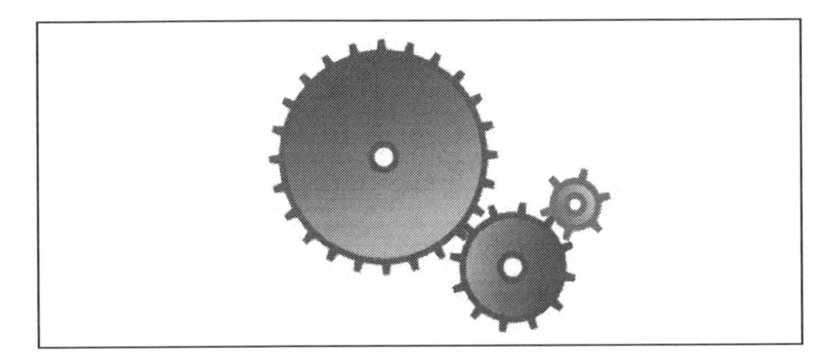

How to do it...

Follow these steps to animate a system of interconnected gears:

1. Link to the `Animation` class:

```
<head>
    <script src="animation.js">
    </script>
```

2. Define the constructor for the `Gear` class:

```
    <script>
        function Gear(config){
            this.x = config.x;
            this.y = config.y;
            this.outerRadius = config.outerRadius;
            this.innerRadius = config.innerRadius;
            this.holeRadius = config.holeRadius;
            this.numTeeth = config.numTeeth;
            this.theta = config.theta;
            this.thetaSpeed = config.thetaSpeed;
            this.lightColor = config.lightColor;
            this.darkColor = config.darkColor;
            this.clockwise = config.clockwise;
            this.midRadius = config.outerRadius - 10;
        }
```

3. Define the `draw` method of the `Gear` class which draws a `gear` object:

```
Gear.prototype.draw = function(context){
    context.save();
    context.translate(this.x, this.y);
    context.rotate(this.theta);

    // draw gear teeth
    context.beginPath();
    // we can set the lineJoin property to bevel so that
the tips
    // of the gear teeth are flat and don't come to a
sharp point
    context.lineJoin = "bevel";

    // loop through the number of points to create the
gear shape
    var numPoints = this.numTeeth * 2;
    for (var n = 0; n < numPoints; n++) {
        var radius = null;

        // draw tip of teeth on even iterations
        if (n % 2 == 0) {
            radius = this.outerRadius;
        }
        // draw teeth connection which lies somewhere
between
        // the gear center and gear radius
        else {
            radius = this.innerRadius;
        }

        var theta = ((Math.PI * 2) / numPoints) * (n + 1);
        var x = (radius * Math.sin(theta));
        var y = (radius * Math.cos(theta));

        // if first iteration, use moveTo() to position
        // the drawing cursor
        if (n == 0) {
            context.moveTo(x, y);
        }
        // if any other iteration, use lineTo() to connect
sub paths
        else {
            context.lineTo(x, y);
```

```
                }
            }

            context.closePath();

            // define the line width and stroke color
            context.lineWidth = 5;
            context.strokeStyle = this.darkColor;
            context.stroke();

            // draw gear body
            context.beginPath();
            context.arc(0, 0, this.midRadius, 0, 2 * Math.PI,
false);

            // create a linear gradient
            var grd = context.createLinearGradient(-1 * this.
outerRadius / 2, -1 * this.outerRadius / 2, this.outerRadius / 2,
this.outerRadius / 2);
            grd.addColorStop(0, this.lightColor);
            grd.addColorStop(1, this.darkColor);
            context.fillStyle = grd;
            context.fill();
            context.lineWidth = 5;
            context.strokeStyle = this.darkColor;
            context.stroke();

            // draw gear hole
            context.beginPath();
            context.arc(0, 0, this.holeRadius, 0, 2 * Math.PI,
false);
            context.fillStyle = "white";
            context.fill();
            context.strokeStyle = this.darkColor;
            context.stroke();
            context.restore();
        };
```

4. Instantiate an `Animation` object and get the canvas context:

```
        window.onload = function(){
            var anim = new Animation("myCanvas");
            var canvas = anim.getCanvas();
            var context = anim.getContext();
```

5. Build an array of `gear` objects:

```
var gears = [];

// add blue gear
gears.push(new Gear({
    x: 270,
    y: 105,
    outerRadius: 90,
    innerRadius: 50,
    holeRadius: 10,
    numTeeth: 24,
    theta: 0,
    thetaSpeed: 1 / 1000,
    lightColor: "#B1CCFF",
    darkColor: "#3959CC",
    clockwise: false
}));

// add red gear
gears.push(new Gear({
    x: 372,
    y: 190,
    outerRadius: 50,
    innerRadius: 15,
    holeRadius: 10,
    numTeeth: 12,
    theta: 0.14,
    thetaSpeed: 2 / 1000,
    lightColor: "#FF9E9D",
    darkColor: "#AD0825",
    clockwise: true
}));

// add orange gear
gears.push(new Gear({
    x: 422,
    y: 142,
    outerRadius: 28,
    innerRadius: 5,
    holeRadius: 7,
    numTeeth: 6,
    theta: 0.35,
    thetaSpeed: 4 / 1000,
    lightColor: "#FFDD87",
    darkColor: "#D25D00",
    clockwise: false
}));
```

6. Set the `stage()` function which updates the rotation of each gear, clears the canvas, and then draws the gears:

```
            anim.setStage(function(){
                // update
                for (var i = 0; i < gears.length; i++) {
                    var gear = gears[i];
                    var thetaIncrement = gear.thetaSpeed * this.
getTimeInterval();
                    gear.theta += gear.clockwise ? thetaIncrement
: -1 * thetaIncrement;
                }

                // clear
                this.clear();

                // draw
                for (var i = 0; i < gears.length; i++) {
                    gears[i].draw(context);
                }
            });
```

7. Start the animation:

```
            anim.start();
        };
    </script>
</head>
```

8. Embed the canvas inside the body of the HTML document:

```
<body>
    <canvas id="myCanvas" width="600" height="250"
style="border:1px solid black;">
    </canvas>
</body>
```

How it works...

To create a system of rotating gears, we can reuse the gear drawing procedure from *Chapter 2* and create a `Gear` class that has some additional properties such as number of teeth, color, theta, and theta speed. `theta` defines the angular position of the gear and `thetaSpeed` defines the angular speed of the gear. We can also add a `clockwise` property to the `Gear` class that defines the direction of the gear rotation.

Once the page loads, we can instantiate a new `Animation` object and get the canvas and context. Next, we can initialize some gears by instantiating `Gear` objects and pushing them onto the gears array. Now that our stage is initialized, we can set the `stage()` function which will update the angle of each gear, clear the canvas, and then draw each of the gears using the `draw()` method of the `Gear` class.

Now that the `stage()` function has been set, we can start the animation with the `start()` method.

See also...

- *Drawing a circle* in *Chapter 2*
- *Creating patterns with loops: drawing a gear* in *Chapter 2*

Animating a clock

For those of you who slip into a trance when you're developing cool projects, where time seems to melt away, this one's for you. In this recipe, we'll create a nifty animated clock to remind us of the real-world time outside of cyber space.

How to do it...

Follow these steps to animate the hour, minute, and second hands on a clock:

1. Link to the `Animation` class:

```
<head>
    <script src="animation.js">
    </script>
```

2. Instantiate an `Animation` object, get the canvas context, and define the clock radius:

```
<script>
    window.onload = function(){
        var anim = new Animation("myCanvas");
        var canvas = anim.getCanvas();
        var context = anim.getContext();
        var clockRadius = 75;
```

3. Set the `stage()` function which gets the current time, calculates the angle for the hour hand, minute hand, and second hand, clears the canvas, and then draws the clock:

```
        anim.setStage(function(){

            // update
            var date = new Date();
            var hours = date.getHours();
            var minutes = date.getMinutes();
            var seconds = date.getSeconds();

            hours = hours > 12 ? hours - 12 : hours;

            var hour = hours + minutes / 60;
            var minute = minutes + seconds / 60;

    // clear
    this.clear();

    // draw
            var context = anim.getContext();
            context.save();
            context.translate(canvas.width / 2, canvas.height
/ 2);

            // draw clock body
            context.beginPath();
            context.arc(0, 0, clockRadius, 0, Math.PI * 2,
true);

            var grd = context.createLinearGradient(-
clockRadius, -clockRadius, clockRadius, clockRadius);
            grd.addColorStop(0, "#F8FCFF"); // light blue
            grd.addColorStop(1, "#A1CCEE"); // dark blue
            context.fillStyle = grd;
```

```
context.fill();

// draw numbers
context.font = "16pt Calibri";
context.fillStyle = "#024F8C";
context.textAlign = "center";
context.textBaseline = "middle";
for (var n = 1; n <= 12; n++) {
    var theta = (n - 3) * (Math.PI * 2) / 12;
    var x = clockRadius * 0.8 * Math.cos(theta);
    var y = clockRadius * 0.8 * Math.sin(theta);
    context.fillText(n, x, y);
}

context.save();

// apply drop shadow
context.shadowColor = "#bbbbbb";
context.shadowBlur = 5;
context.shadowOffsetX = 1;
context.shadowOffsetY = 1;

// draw clock rim
context.lineWidth = 3;
context.strokeStyle = "#005EA8";
context.stroke();

context.restore();

// draw hour hand
context.save();
var theta = (hour - 3) * 2 * Math.PI / 12;
context.rotate(theta);
context.beginPath();
context.moveTo(-10, -4);
context.lineTo(-10, 4);
context.lineTo(clockRadius * 0.6, 1);
context.lineTo(clockRadius * 0.6, -1);
context.fill();
context.restore();

// minute hand
context.save();
var theta = (minute - 15) * 2 * Math.PI / 60;
```

```
            context.rotate(theta);
            context.beginPath();
            context.moveTo(-10, -3);
            context.lineTo(-10, 3);
            context.lineTo(clockRadius * 0.9, 1);
            context.lineTo(clockRadius * 0.9, -1);
            context.fill();
            context.restore();

            // second hand
            context.save();
            var theta = (seconds - 15) * 2 * Math.PI / 60;
            context.rotate(theta);
            context.beginPath();
            context.moveTo(-10, -2);
            context.lineTo(-10, 2);
            context.lineTo(clockRadius * 0.8, 1);
            context.lineTo(clockRadius * 0.8, -1);
            context.fillStyle = "red";
            context.fill();
            context.restore();

            context.restore();
        });
```

4. Start the animation:

```
            anim.start();
        };
    </script>
</head>
```

5. Embed the canvas inside the body of the HTML document:

```
<body>
    <canvas id="myCanvas" width="600" height="250"
style="border:1px solid black;">
    </canvas>
</body>
```

How it works...

When the page loads, we can instantiate a new `Animation` object and then get the canvas and context. Next, we can start defining the `stage()` function which is responsible for updating the clock, clearing the canvas, and then drawing the clock for each animation loop.

In the update portion of the code, we can instantiate a new `Date()` object and then get the hours, minutes, and seconds. Next, we can adjust the hour and minute to represent a 12-hour time (AM and PM).

After clearing the canvas, we can begin drawing the clock:

- Translate the canvas context to the center of the canvas with the `translate()` method
- Draw the body with the `arc()` method
- Create a loop that draws the numbers of the clock around the edge with the `fillText()` method
- Apply a drop shadow with the `shadowOffsetX` and `shadowOffsetY` properties
- Draw the clock rim by stroking the circle with `stroke()`
- Draw each of the clock hands by rotating the canvas context and then drawing a thin trapezoid whose thickest end resides at the center.

Finally, once the `stage()` function has been set, we can start the animation with the `start()` method.

See also...

- *Working with text* in *Chapter 1*
- *Drawing a circle* in *Chapter 2*
- *Working with custom shapes and fill styles* in *Chapter 2*

Simulating particle physics

Now that we've covered the basics of classical physics, let's put it all together. In this recipe, we'll simulate particle physics by modeling gravity, boundary conditions, collision damping, and floor friction.

How to do it...

Follow these steps to launch a particle inside the canvas and observe it's projectile path as it bounces on the walls, gradually falls down to the floor due to gravity, and then slows to a stop due to floor friction:

1. Link to the `Animation` class:

```
<head>
    <script src="animation.js">
    </script>
```

2. Define the `applyPhysics()` function which takes a particle as input and updates its position and velocity based on physics variables such as gravity, collision damping, and floor friction:

```
        function applyPhysics(anim, particle){
            // physics globals
            var gravity = 1500; // pixels / second^2
            var collisionDamper = 0.8; // 80% velocity lost when
collision occurs
            var floorFriction = 100; // pixels / second^2
            var timeInterval = anim.getTimeInterval();
            var canvas = anim.getCanvas();

            // gravity
            particle.vy += gravity * timeInterval / 1000;

            // position
            particle.y += particle.vy * timeInterval / 1000;
            particle.x += particle.vx * timeInterval / 1000;

            // floor condition
            if (particle.y > (canvas.height - particle.radius)) {
                particle.y = canvas.height - particle.radius;
                particle.vy *= -1;
                particle.vy *= collisionDamper;
            }

            // floor friction
            if (particle.y == canvas.height - particle.radius) {
                if (particle.vx > 0.1) {
                    particle.vx -= floorFriction * timeInterval /
1000;
                }
                else if (particle.vx < -0.1) {
```

```
                    particle.vx += floorFriction * timeInterval /
1000;
                }
                else {
                    particle.vx = 0;
                }
            }

            // ceiling  condition
            if (particle.y < (particle.radius)) {
                particle.y = particle.radius;
                particle.vy *= -1;
                particle.vy *= collisionDamper;
            }

            // right wall condition
            if (particle.x > (canvas.width - particle.radius)) {
                particle.x = canvas.width - particle.radius;
                particle.vx *= -1;
                particle.vx *= collisionDamper;
            }

            // left wall condition
            if (particle.x < (particle.radius)) {
                particle.x = particle.radius;
                particle.vx *= -1;
                particle.vx *= collisionDamper;
            }
        }
```

3. Instantiate a new `Animation` object and get the canvas context:

```
window.onload = function(){
    var anim = new Animation("myCanvas");
    var canvas = anim.getCanvas();
    var context = anim.getContext();
```

4. Initialize a `particle` object with a position, x and y velocity, and radius:

```
    var particle = {
        x: 10,
        y: canvas.height - 10,
        vx: 600, // px / second
        vy: -900, // px / second
        radius: 10
    };
```

5. Set the `stage()` function which updates the particle by passing it to the `applyPhysics()` function, clears the canvas, and then draws the particle:

```
            anim.setStage(function(){
                // update
                applyPhysics(this, particle);

                // clear
                this.clear();

                // draw
                context.beginPath();
                context.arc(particle.x, particle.y, particle.
radius, 0, 2 * Math.PI, false);
                context.fillStyle = "blue";
                context.fill();
            });
```

6. Start the animation:

```
            anim.start();
        };
    </script>
</head>
```

7. Embed the canvas tag inside the body of the HTML document:

```
<body>
    <canvas id="myCanvas" width="600" height="250"
style="border:1px solid black;">
    </canvas>
</body>
```

How it works...

To simulate particle physics, we need to handle the particle's x and y position and the particle's velocity in both the x and y direction for each frame. The key to understanding particle physics simulations is to remember that the movement of the particle in the system is based on the sum of all the forces acting on the particle. In our case, gravity will be pulling the particle downwards, collisions against the walls, ceiling, and floor will reduce the particle's velocity according to the collision damper constant, and floor friction will reduce the particle's horizontal speed when it rolls on the floor.

To start off, when the page loads we can instantiate a new `Animation` object and then get the canvas and context. Next, we can initialize a particle with a position, initial velocity, and size. Now that we've initialized the actors on the stage (the particle), we can set the `stage()` function which will update the particle, clear the canvas, and then draw the particle for each animation frame.

The update logic happens inside the `applyPhysics()` function, which is passed a reference to the `Animation` object, and also the `particle` object. The `applyPhysics()` function walks through a list of conditions that updates the particle's position and velocity.

After the `applyPhysics()` function has been called and the particle has been updated, we can clear the canvas and then draw the particle by drawing a simple circle whose radius is equal to the radius of the particle.

Finally, once the `stage()` function has been set, we can start the animation with the `start()` method.

There's more...

If you really wanted to get fancy, you could even add additional forces such as air resistance. As a general rule of thumb, the more forces that you add to a particle simulation, the more life-like it becomes. You can play around with different initial positions and velocities to see different projectile paths.

See also...

- *Drawing a circle* in *Chapter 2*

Creating microscopic life forms

Have you ever seen microscopic life forms in a microscope and observed how they wiggle around? This recipe is inspired by the alien-like world of micro-organisms. In this recipe, we'll create 100 random microbes and let them loose in the canvas.

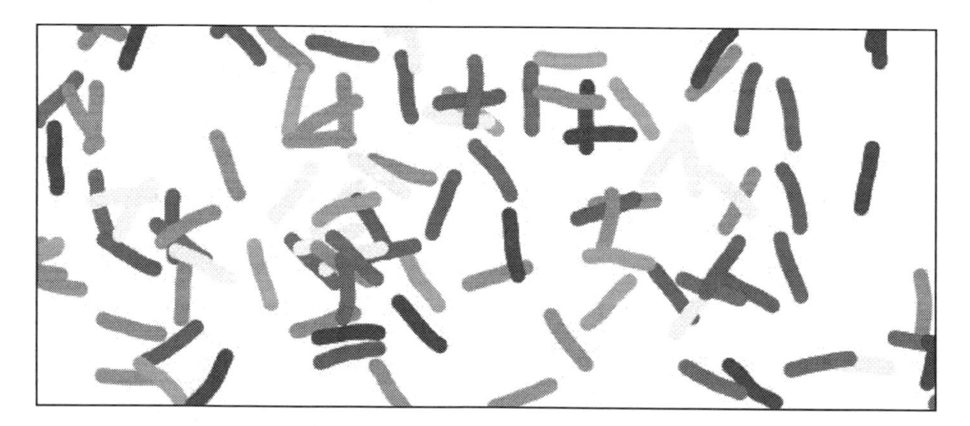

How to do it...

Follow these steps to create wiggling microbes moving inside the canvas:

1. Link to the `Animation` class:

```
<head>
    <script src="animation.js">
    </script>
```

2. Define the `getRandColor()` function that returns a random color:

```
    <script>
        function getRandColor(){
            var colors = ["red", "orange", "yellow", "green",
"blue", "violet"];
            return colors[Math.floor(Math.random() * colors.
length)];
        }
```

3. Define the `getRandTheta()` function that returns a random theta:

```
        function getRandTheta(){
            return Math.random() * 2 * Math.PI;
        }
```

4. Define the `updateMicrobes()` function that updates `microbe` objects by adding a new head segment with a randomly generated angle to each microbe, and then removing the tail segment:

```
        function updateMicrobes(anim, microbes){
            var canvas = anim.getCanvas();
            var angleVariance = 0.2;

            for (var i = 0; i < microbes.length; i++) {
                var microbe = microbes[i];
                var angles = microbe.angles;

        /*
         * good numNewSegmentsPerFrame values:
         * 60fps -> 1
         * 10fps -> 10
         *
         * for a linear relationship, we can use the equation:
         * n = mf + b, where n = numNewSegmentsPerFrame and f =
FPS
         * solving for m and b, we have:
         * n = (-0.18)f + 11.8
         */
```

```
                    var numNewSegmentsPerFrame = Math.round(-0.18 *
anim.getFps() + 11.8);

                    for (var n = 0; n < numNewSegmentsPerFrame; n++) {
                        // create first angle if no angles
                        if (angles.length == 0) {
                            microbe.headX = canvas.width / 2;
                            microbe.headY = canvas.height / 2;
                            angles.push(getRandTheta());
                        }

                        var headX = microbe.headX;
                        var headY = microbe.headY;
                        var headAngle = angles[angles.length - 1];

                        // create new head angle
                        var dist = anim.getTimeInterval() / (10 *
numNewSegmentsPerFrame);
                        // increase new head angle by an amount equal
to
                        // -0.1 to 0.1
                        var newHeadAngle = headAngle + ((angleVariance
/ 2) - Math.random() * angleVariance);
                        var newHeadX = headX + dist * Math.
cos(newHeadAngle);
                        var newHeadY = headY + dist * Math.
sin(newHeadAngle);

                        // change direction if collision occurs
                        if (newHeadX >= canvas.width || newHeadX <= 0
|| newHeadY >= canvas.height || newHeadY <= 0) {
                            newHeadAngle += Math.PI / 2;
                            newHeadX = headX + dist * Math.
cos(newHeadAngle);
                            newHeadY = headY + dist * Math.
sin(newHeadAngle);
                        }

                        microbe.headX = newHeadX;
                        microbe.headY = newHeadY;
                        angles.push(newHeadAngle);

                        // remove tail angle
                        if (angles.length > 20) {
                            angles.shift();
                        }
                    }
                }
            }
```

5. Define the `drawMicrobes()` function that draws all of the microbes:

```
function drawMicrobes(anim, microbes){
    var segmentLength = 2; // px
    var context = anim.getContext();

    for (var i = 0; i < microbes.length; i++) {
        var microbe = microbes[i];

        var angles = microbe.angles;
        context.beginPath();
        context.moveTo(microbe.headX, microbe.headY);

        var x = microbe.headX;
        var y = microbe.headY;

        // start with the head and end with the tail
        for (var n = angles.length - 1; n >= 0; n--) {
            var angle = angles[n];

            x -= segmentLength * Math.cos(angle);
            y -= segmentLength * Math.sin(angle);
            context.lineTo(x, y);
        }

        context.lineWidth = 10;
        context.lineCap = "round";
        context.lineJoin = "round";
        context.strokeStyle = microbe.color;
        context.stroke();
    }
}
```

6. Instantiate an `Animation` object and get the canvas context:

```
window.onload = function(){
    var anim = new Animation("myCanvas");
    var canvas = anim.getCanvas();
    var context = anim.getContext();
```

7. Initialize 100 microbes:

```
    // init microbes
    var microbes = [];
    for (var n = 0; n < 100; n++) {
        // each microbe will be an array of angles
        microbes[n] = {
            headX: 0,
            headY: 0,
            angles: [],
            color: getRandColor()
        };
    }
```

8. Set the `stage()` function that updates the microbes by calling the `updateMicrobes()` function, clears the canvas, and then draws the microbes by calling the `drawMicrobes()` function:

```
                anim.setStage(function(){
                    // update
                    updateMicrobes(this, microbes);

                    // clear
                    this.clear();

                    // draw
                    drawMicrobes(this, microbes);
                });
```

9. Start the animation:

```
                anim.start();
            };
        </script>
    </head>
```

10. Embed the canvas inside the body of the HTML document:

```
    <body>
        <canvas id="myCanvas" width="600" height="250"
    style="border:1px solid black;">
        </canvas>
    </body>
```

How it works...

To create a micro-organism, we can draw a series of connected segments to create a short snake-like creature. We can represent a micro-organism as an object containing a head position and an array of angles. These angles represent the angle between segments.

This recipe initializes 100 randomized micro-organisms and positions them in the center of the canvas. Our `stage()` function contains the `updateMicrobes()` and `drawMicrobes()` function.

The `updateMicrobes()` function loops through all of the microbe objects, adds a new head segment, and removes the tail segment for each microbe. In this way, the segments of each microbe will wiggle as they move across the canvas. When the head of a microbe hits the edge of the canvas, its angle will be increased by 90 degrees so that it bounces back into the canvas area.

The `drawMicrobes()` function loops through all of the `microbe` objects, positions the drawing cursor at the head for each microbe, and then draws 20 line segments according to the angle of each segment.

See also...

- *Drawing a spiral* in *Chapter 1*
- *Creating a drawing application* in *Chapter 6*

Stressing the canvas and displaying the FPS

After seeing the last recipe, you might be thinking "Is there a limit to how many microbes we can animate?" The straightforward answer to this question is yes. As the 2D context of the HTML5 canvas is not hardware-accelerated, and as our animations are driven purely by JavaScript, there is definitely a point where the browser will start to choke if it's working overtime. To illustrate this, we can draw the FPS of our animation and observe the relationship between the number of microbes on the screen and the FPS value.

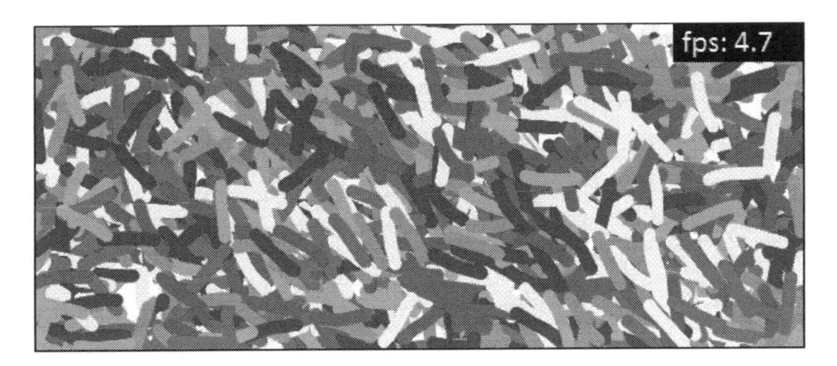

How to do it...

Follow these steps to stress the canvas and display the FPS:

1. Link to the `Animation` class:

```
<head>
    <script src="animation.js">
    </script>
```

2. Define the `drawFps()` function that draws the FPS value in the top-right corner of the canvas:

```
        function drawFps(anim, fps){
            var canvas = anim.getCanvas();
            var context = anim.getContext();

            context.fillStyle = "black";
            context.fillRect(canvas.width - 100, 0, 100, 30);

            context.font = "18pt Calibri";
            context.fillStyle = "white";
            context.fillText("fps: " + fps.toFixed(1), canvas.
width - 93, 22);
        }
```

3. Define the `getRandColor()` function that returns a random color:

```
    <script>
        function getRandColor(){
            var colors = ["red", "orange", "yellow", "green",
"blue", "violet"];
            return colors[Math.floor(Math.random() * colors.
length)];
        }
```

4. Define the `getRandTheta()` function that returns a random theta:

```
        function getRandTheta(){
            return Math.random() * 2 * Math.PI;
        }
```

5. Define the `updateMicrobes()` function that updates `microbe` objects by adding a new head segment with a randomly generated angle to each microbe and then removing the tail segment:

```
        function updateMicrobes(anim, microbes){
            var canvas = anim.getCanvas();
            var angleVariance = 0.2;

            for (var i = 0; i < microbes.length; i++) {
                var microbe = microbes[i];
                var angles = microbe.angles;

                /*
               * good numNewSegmentsPerFrame values:
               * 60fps -> 1
               * 10fps -> 10
```

```
                 *
                 * for a linear relationship, we can use the
equation:
                 * n = mf + b, where n = numNewSegmentsPerFrame and f
= FPS
                 * solving for m and b, we have:
                 * n = (-0.18)f + 11.8
                 */

                  var numNewSegmentsPerFrame = Math.round(-0.18 *
anim.getFps() + 11.8);

                  for (var n = 0; n < numNewSegmentsPerFrame; n++) {
                      // create first angle if no angles
                      if (angles.length == 0) {
                          microbe.headX = canvas.width / 2;
                          microbe.headY = canvas.height / 2;
                          angles.push(getRandTheta());
                      }

                      var headX = microbe.headX;
                      var headY = microbe.headY;
                      var headAngle = angles[angles.length - 1];

                      // create new head angle
                      var dist = anim.getTimeInterval() / (10 *
numNewSegmentsPerFrame);
                      // increase new head angle by an amount equal
to
                      // -0.1 to 0.1
                      var newHeadAngle = headAngle + ((angleVariance
/ 2) - Math.random() * angleVariance);
                      var newHeadX = headX + dist * Math.
cos(newHeadAngle);
                      var newHeadY = headY + dist * Math.
sin(newHeadAngle);

                      // change direction if collision occurs
                      if (newHeadX >= canvas.width || newHeadX <= 0
|| newHeadY >= canvas.height || newHeadY <= 0) {
                          newHeadAngle += Math.PI / 2;
                          newHeadX = headX + dist * Math.
cos(newHeadAngle);
                          newHeadY = headY + dist * Math.
sin(newHeadAngle);
```

```
                    }

                    microbe.headX = newHeadX;
                    microbe.headY = newHeadY;
                    angles.push(newHeadAngle);

                    // remove tail angle
                    if (angles.length > 20) {
                        angles.shift();
                    }
                }
            }
        }
```

6. Define the `drawMicrobes()` function that draws all of the microbes:

```
        function drawMicrobes(anim, microbes){
            var segmentLength = 2; // px
            var context = anim.getContext();

            for (var i = 0; i < microbes.length; i++) {
                var microbe = microbes[i];

                var angles = microbe.angles;
                context.beginPath();
                context.moveTo(microbe.headX, microbe.headY);

                var x = microbe.headX;
                var y = microbe.headY;

                // start with the head and end with the tail
                for (var n = angles.length - 1; n >= 0; n--) {
                    var angle = angles[n];

                    x -= segmentLength * Math.cos(angle);
                    y -= segmentLength * Math.sin(angle);
                    context.lineTo(x, y);
                }

                context.lineWidth = 10;
                context.lineCap = "round";
                context.lineJoin = "round";
                context.strokeStyle = microbe.color;
                context.stroke();
            }
        }
```

7. Instantiate an `Animation` object and get the canvas context:

```
window.onload = function(){
    var anim = new Animation("myCanvas");
    var canvas = anim.getCanvas();
    var context = anim.getContext();
```

8. Initialize 1,500 microbes:

```
    // init microbes
    var microbes = [];
    for (var n = 0; n < 1500; n++) {
        // each microbe will be an array of angles
        microbes[n] = {
            headX: 0,
            headY: 0,
            angles: [],
            color: getRandColor()
        };
    }
```

9. Set the `stage()` function which updates the microbes, updates the FPS value every 10 frames, clears the canvas, and then draws the microbes and the FPS value:

```
    var fps = 0;

    anim.setStage(function(){
        // update
        updateMicrobes(this, microbes);

        if (anim.getFrame() % 10 == 0) {
            fps = anim.getFps();
        }

        // clear
        this.clear();

        // draw
        drawMicrobes(this, microbes);
        drawFps(this, fps);
    });
```

10. Start the animation:

```
            anim.start();
        };
    </script>
</head>
```

11. Embed the canvas inside the body of the HTML document:

```
<body>
    <canvas id="myCanvas" width="600" height="250"
style="border:1px solid black;">
    </canvas>
</body>
```

How it works...

To draw the FPS of the animation, we can create the `drawFps()` function that takes in an FPS value as input, draws a black box in the upper-right corner of the canvas, and then writes out the FPS value. To avoid updating the FPS too frequently, we can store a copy of the FPS value in the variable `FPS`, and update it every 10 frames. In this way, the FPS will update, at the most, six times per second.

To stress the canvas, we can simply initialize more microbes. In this recipe, we've initialized 1,500 microbes. If you try out the code for yourself, you can play with different numbers to see how the FPS is affected.

There's more...

As mentioned earlier, a typical animation should run at about 40 to 60 FPS. If the FPS drops below 30, you'll start to notice a slight lag in the animation. When testing in Google Chrome on a 32-bit Windows 7 machine with a 2.2 GHz AMD processor and 2 GB of RAM (yes I know, I need to upgrade), I was seeing about 5 FPS when animating 1,500 microbes. It doesn't look bad, but it's not great. When animating 2,000 microbes or more, the animation starts to look unacceptably choppy.

Almost all of the animations that we've created with the 2D context perform great on desktops and laptops. However, if you find yourself in a situation where your animations are computationally expensive enough that they aren't performing well in the 2D context, you might consider using WebGL instead (we'll cover WebGL in *Chapter 9, Introduction to WebGL*). Unlike the 2D context, WebGL leverages hardware acceleration. At the time of writing, the 2D context in all of the major browsers does not utilize hardware acceleration. Using WebGL does come at a cost, however, because it's much more difficult to develop and maintain WebGL animations than it is to create 2D context animations.

See also...

- *Working with text* in *Chapter 1*
- *Drawing a spiral* in *Chapter 1*
- *Creating a drawing application* in *Chapter 6*

6
Interacting with the Canvas: Attaching Event Listeners to Shapes and Regions

In this chapter, we will cover:

- Creating an Events class
- Working with canvas mouse coordinates
- Attaching mouse event listeners to regions
- Attaching touch event listeners to regions on a mobile device
- Attaching event listeners to images
- Dragging-and-dropping shapes
- Dragging-and-dropping images
- Creating an image magnifier
- Creating a drawing application

Introduction

So far, we've learned how to draw on the canvas, work with images and video, and create fluid animations. This chapter focuses on canvas interactivity. Until now, all of our canvas projects have been very unresponsive and disengaged from the user. Although the HTML5 canvas API doesn't provide us with a means for attaching event listeners to shapes and regions, we can certainly achieve this functionality by extending the API. According to the HTML5 specification, once a shape is drawn, we have no access to it as an object like we do with DOM elements in an HTML document. Until the HTML5 canvas specification includes methods for attaching event listeners to shapes and regions, (hopefully it will some day), we'll need to construct our own Events class which will enable us to do so. Our class will enable us to attach event listeners to regions which wrap one or more shapes, similar to attaching event listeners to DOM elements.

This is quite a powerful notion because it enables us to draw shapes in the canvas that users can interact with. Our Events class will support **mousedown**, **mouseup**, **mouseover**, **mouseout**, **mousemove**, **touchstart**, **touchend**, and **touchmove** events.

> Although most of the recipes in this chapter utilize mouse events, they can also be modified to support mobile touch events by replacing `mousedown` with `touchstart`, `mouseup` with `touchend`, and `mousemove` with `touchmove`.

Let's get started!

Creating an Events class

Similar to *Chapter 5, Bringing the Canvas to Life with Animation*, where we created a custom class to handle animations, in this chapter we'll create a custom class to handle canvas events.

As canvas shapes are not accessible as objects (bummer!), there's nothing for us to attach event listeners to like we would with a div element as follows:

```
document.getElementById("foo").addEventListener("mouseup", function()
{
  // do stuff
}, false);
```

So what can we do? If we follow the pattern of the canvas API, in which the beginning of a shape is defined with `beginPath()`, and the end of the shape is defined by `closePath()`, we can extend this idea one step further by introducing the concept of regions, which encapsulate multiple shapes. Furthermore, it would be really nice if we could add event listeners to a region in a similar manner that we add event listeners to DOM elements as follows:

```
this.addRegionEventListener("mouseup", function() {
 // do stuff
});
```

The goal of the Events class is to do just that by extending the canvas API to support canvas events by introducing regions which can be attached with desktop event listeners such as `mousedown`, `mouseup`, `mouseover`, `mouseout`, and `mousemove`, and also mobile event listeners such as `touchstart`, `touchend`, and `touchmove`.

Rather than typing out the Events class by hand, you may consider downloading the class from the online resources for this book at `www.html5canvastutorials.com/cookbook`.

How to do it...

Follow these steps to create an Events class which will enable us to attach event listeners to shapes and regions on the canvas:

1. Define the `Events` constructor:

```
var Events = function(canvasId){
    this.canvas = document.getElementById(canvasId);
    this.context = this.canvas.getContext("2d");
    this.stage = undefined;
    this.listening = false;

    // desktop flags
    this.mousePos = null;
    this.mouseDown = false;
    this.mouseUp = false;
    this.mouseOver = false;
    this.mouseMove = false;

    // mobile flags
    this.touchPos = null;
    this.touchStart = false;
    this.touchMove = false;
    this.touchEnd = false;

    // Region Events
    this.currentRegion = null;
```

```
    this.regionIndex = 0;
    this.lastRegionIndex = -1;
    this.mouseOverRegionIndex = -1;
};
```

2. Define the `getContext()` method which returns the canvas context:

```
Events.prototype.getContext = function(){
    return this.context;
};
```

3. Define the `getCanvas()` method which returns the canvas DOM element:

```
Events.prototype.getCanvas = function(){
    return this.canvas;
};
```

4. Define the `clear()` method which clears the canvas:

```
Events.prototype.clear = function(){
    this.context.clearRect(0, 0, this.canvas.width, this.canvas.
height);
};
```

5. Define the `getCanvasPos()` method which returns the canvas position:

```
Events.prototype.getCanvasPos = function(){
    var obj = this.getCanvas();
    var top = 0;
    var left = 0;
    while (obj.tagName != "BODY") {
        top += obj.offsetTop;
        left += obj.offsetLeft;
        obj = obj.offsetParent;
    }
    return {
        top: top,
        left: left
    };
};
```

6. Define the `setStage()` method which sets the `stage()` function:

```
Events.prototype.setStage = function(func){
    this.stage = func;
    this.listen();
};
```

7. Define the `reset()` method which sets the mouse position and the touch position, resets the region index, calls the `stage()` function, and then resets the event flags:

```
Events.prototype.reset = function(evt){
    if (!evt) {
        evt = window.event;
    }

    this.setMousePosition(evt);
    this.setTouchPosition(evt);
    this.regionIndex = 0;

    if (this.stage !== undefined) {
        this.stage();
    }

    // desktop flags
    this.mouseOver = false;
    this.mouseMove = false;
    this.mouseDown = false;
    this.mouseUp = false;

    // mobile touch flags
    this.touchStart = false;
    this.touchMove = false;
    this.touchEnd = false;
};
```

8. Define the `listen()` method which adds event listeners to the canvas element:

```
Events.prototype.listen = function(){
    var that = this;

    if (this.stage !== undefined) {
        this.stage();
    }

    // desktop events
    this.canvas.addEventListener("mousedown", function(evt){
        that.mouseDown = true;
        that.reset(evt);
    }, false);

    this.canvas.addEventListener("mousemove", function(evt){
        that.reset(evt);
```

```
        }, false);

        this.canvas.addEventListener("mouseup", function(evt){
            that.mouseUp = true;
            that.reset(evt);
        }, false);

        this.canvas.addEventListener("mouseover", function(evt){
            that.reset(evt);
        }, false);

        this.canvas.addEventListener("mouseout", function(evt){
            that.mousePos = null;
        }, false);

        // mobile events
        this.canvas.addEventListener("touchstart", function(evt){
            evt.preventDefault();
            that.touchStart = true;
            that.reset(evt);
        }, false);

        this.canvas.addEventListener("touchmove", function(evt){
            evt.preventDefault();
            that.reset(evt);
        }, false);

        this.canvas.addEventListener("touchend", function(evt){
            evt.preventDefault();
            that.touchEnd = true;
            that.reset(evt);
        }, false);
    };
```

9. Define the `getMousePos()` method which returns the mouse position for desktop applications:

```
Events.prototype.getMousePos = function(evt){
    return this.mousePos;
};
```

10. Define the `getTouchPos()` method which returns the touch position for mobile applications:

```
Events.prototype.getTouchPos = function(evt){
    return this.touchPos;
};
```

11. Define the `setMousePos()` method which sets the mouse position:

```
Events.prototype.setMousePosition = function(evt){
    var mouseX = evt.clientX - this.getCanvasPos().left + window.
pageXOffset;
    var mouseY = evt.clientY - this.getCanvasPos().top + window.
pageYOffset;
    this.mousePos = {
        x: mouseX,
        y: mouseY
    };
};
```

12. Define the `setTouchPos()` method which sets the touch position:

```
Events.prototype.setTouchPosition = function(evt){
    if (evt.touches !== undefined && evt.touches.length == 1) { //
Only deal with one finger
        var touch = evt.touches[0]; // Get the information for
finger #1
        var touchX = touch.pageX - this.getCanvasPos().left +
window.pageXOffset;
        var touchY = touch.pageY - this.getCanvasPos().top +
window.pageYOffset;

        this.touchPos = {
            x: touchX,
            y: touchY
        };
    }
};
```

13. Define the `beginRegion()` method which is used to define a new region:

```
Events.prototype.beginRegion = function(){
    this.currentRegion = {};
    this.regionIndex++;
};
```

14. Define the `addRegionEventListener()` method which is used to add an event listener to a region:

```
Events.prototype.addRegionEventListener = function(type, func){
    var event = (type.indexOf('touch') == -1) ? 'on' + type :
type;
    this.currentRegion[event] = func;
};
```

15. Define the `closeRegion()` method which is used to close a region and determine if an event has occurred with respect to the current region:

```
Events.prototype.closeRegion = function(){
    var pos = this.touchPos || this.mousePos;

    if (pos !== null && this.context.isPointInPath(pos.x, pos.y))
{
        if (this.lastRegionIndex != this.regionIndex) {
            this.lastRegionIndex = this.regionIndex;
        }

        // handle onmousedown
        if (this.mouseDown && this.currentRegion.onmousedown !==
undefined) {
            this.currentRegion.onmousedown();
            this.mouseDown = false;
        }

        // handle onmouseup
        else if (this.mouseUp && this.currentRegion.onmouseup !==
undefined) {
            this.currentRegion.onmouseup();
            this.mouseUp = false;
        }

        // handle onmouseover
        else if (!this.mouseOver && this.regionIndex != this.
mouseOverRegionIndex && this.currentRegion.onmouseover !==
undefined) {
            this.currentRegion.onmouseover();
            this.mouseOver = true;
            this.mouseOverRegionIndex = this.regionIndex;
        }

        // handle onmousemove
        else if (!this.mouseMove && this.currentRegion.onmousemove
!== undefined) {
            this.currentRegion.onmousemove();
            this.mouseMove = true;
        }

        // handle touchstart
        if (this.touchStart && this.currentRegion.touchstart !==
undefined) {
            this.currentRegion.touchstart();
```

```
                this.touchStart = false;
            }

            // handle touchend
            if (this.touchEnd && this.currentRegion.touchend !==
undefined) {
                this.currentRegion.touchend();
                this.touchEnd = false;
            }

            // handle touchmove
            if (!this.touchMove && this.currentRegion.touchmove !==
undefined) {
                this.currentRegion.touchmove();
                this.touchMove = true;
            }

        }
        else if (this.regionIndex == this.lastRegionIndex) {
            this.lastRegionIndex = -1;
            this.mouseOverRegionIndex = -1;

            // handle mouseout condition
            if (this.currentRegion.onmouseout !== undefined) {
                this.currentRegion.onmouseout();
            }
        }
    };
```

How it works...

Even though the HTML5 canvas API doesn't provide a way for us to easily handle event listeners, it does provide one key method that will make it possible:

```
context.isPointInPath(x,y);
```

The `isPointInPath()` method returns true if the given coordinates reside within *any* path drawn on the canvas. As the canvas is a bitmap, the concept of layers and shapes has no meaning here, so we'll have to figure out a way to leverage the `isPointInPath()` method for determining whether or not a given coordinate, in particular the mouse coordinates, resides within a specific region of the canvas. Once we can detect whether or not the mouse cursor is on top of a particular region, we can add additional logic to handle `mouseover`, `mousemove`, `mouseout`, `mousedown`, `mouseup`, `touchstart`, `touchend`, and `touchmove` events.

Before getting in any deeper, let's make up an example and formulate a procedure for simulating region events, and then use what we've learned to lay out the methods we'll need to create the `Events` class. Let's say that we want to draw a triangle, a rectangle, and a circle on the canvas, and then we want to alert some text when the user places their cursor over the circle. We could first draw the triangle, and then see whether the mouse coordinates reside within the current path using `isPointInPath()`. If the method returns false, we know that the mouse cursor is somewhere outside of the triangle. Next, we could draw the rectangle, and again check whether the mouse coordinates reside within any path, which at this point includes the triangle and the rectangle. If `isPointInPath()` still returns false, we now know that the mouse cursor is somewhere outside of the triangle and the rectangle. Finally, we can draw the circle, and once again check whether the mouse coordinates reside within any path on the canvas, which now includes the triangle, rectangle, and circle. If the method returns true, then the mouse is indeed over the circle. If it returns false, then the mouse cursor is somewhere outside the triangle, rectangle, and circle.

Of course, this only works if we assume that the cursor is already positioned somewhere on the canvas before the elements are actually drawn. The only way that we can detect whether the mouse cursor is on top of an element after the cursor has moved is to redraw our elements each time an event is triggered, and then check whether the mouse coordinates exist within a shape after drawing each element. We can accomplish this by defining the `stage()` function with the `setStage()` method of the `Events` class.

Next, we need a way to define the beginning and the end of a region. We can create a `beginRegion()` method which defines a new `Region` object. The `Region` object can have eight properties: `mouseover`, `mouseout`, `mousemove`, `mousedown`, `mouseup`, `touchstart`, `touchend`, and `touchmove`, all of which are user-defined functions. Next, we can create a method called `addRegionEventListener()` which can be used to attach region events which require an event type and the function to be called when the event occurs. Since we have a method that begins a new region, we also need to create a `closeRegion()` method. This method contains most of the logic required to determine if one of the eight events has occurred. Finally, we can create a `listen()` method which adds event listeners to the canvas element in order to appropriately handle the region events.

The Events class described in this recipe works by defining regions with the `beginRegion()` and `closeRegion()` methods, and then redrawing the regions each time an event is triggered in order to detect which which region the event belongs to. The advantage of this approach is that it's easy to implement and that we only need one canvas element.

Although, this approach works beautifully for canvas applications that have a reasonable number of regions with attached event listeners, it may not be the best approach for applications using a large number of regions. Applications that require thousands of regions, each with their own event listeners, may run into performance issues due to the number of shapes being redrawn each time the mouse moves.

For such applications, a more complex approach can be used by assigning each region its own canvas and then stacking the canvases on top of each other so that the regions don't have to be redrawn each time an event is triggered. One great example of this approach is the KineticJS library (`http://www.kineticjs.com`).

Working with canvas mouse coordinates

To get our feet wet with the `Events` class, we'll keep it simple by getting the mouse coordinates of the cursor using the `getMousePos()` method from the `Events` class and then displaying it in the top-left corner of the canvas. The `getMousePos()` method returns the mouse coordinates relative to the canvas, which takes into account the offset position of the canvas relative to the page, and also the scroll position of the page.

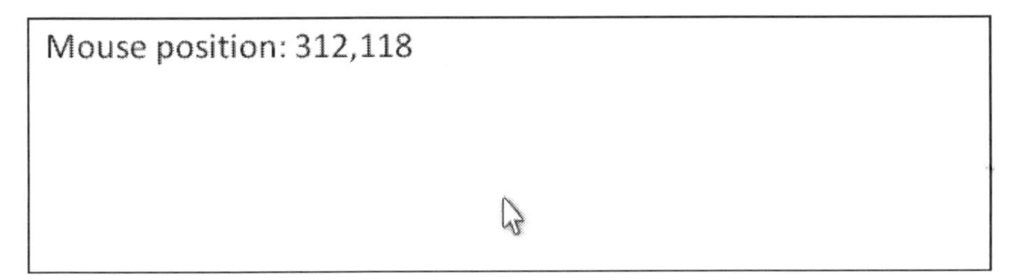

How to do it...

Follow these steps to get the canvas mouse coordinates and display them in the upper-left corner of the canvas each time the mouse cursor moves:

1. Link to the `Events` class:

```
<script src="events.js">
</script>
```

2. Define the `writeMessage()` function which writes out a message:

```
<script>
    function writeMessage(context, message){
        context.font = "18pt Calibri";
        context.fillStyle = "black";
        context.fillText(message, 10, 25);
    }
```

3. Instantiate a new `Events` object and get the canvas and context:

```
    window.onload = function(){
        var events = new Events("myCanvas");
        var canvas = events.getCanvas();
        var context = events.getContext();
```

4. When the user mouses out of the canvas, clear the canvas and then write out the message "Mouseover me!":

```
        canvas.addEventListener("mouseout", function(){
            events.clear();
            writeMessage(context, "Mouseover me!");
        }, false);
```

5. When the user moves his/her mouse in the canvas, clear the canvas, and then write out the mouse position:

```
        canvas.addEventListener("mousemove", function(){
            var mousePos = events.getMousePos();
            events.clear();

            if (mousePos !== null) {
                message = "Mouse position: " + mousePos.x + "," +
mousePos.y;
                writeMessage(context, message);
            }
        }, false);
```

6. Start listening for events:

```
    // if we don't set the stage function,
    // we'll have to manually start listening for events
        events.listen();
```

7. Write the initial message before the user begins:

```
        writeMessage(context, "Mouseover me!");
    };
</script>
```

8. Embed the canvas inside the body of the HTML document:

```
<canvas id="myCanvas" width="600" height="250" style="border:1px
solid black;">
</canvas>
```

How it works...

Once the page loads, we can instantiate an `Events` object so that we have access to the `getMousePos()` method. Next, we can attach a `mouseout` event listener to the `canvas` object which sets the event display to "Mouseover me!", and also attach a `mousemove` event listener to the `canvas` object that gets the mouse position using the `getMousePos()` method and then writes out the coordinates. Finally, we can start listening for events using the `listen()` method.

Attaching mouse event listeners to regions

In this recipe, we'll get to the meat of the `Events` class by defining regions and adding event listeners to them. We'll draw a triangle, attach a `mouseout` and `mousemove` event listener to it, we'll draw a rectangle with no event listeners, and finally we'll draw a circle and attach a `mouseover`, `mouseout`, `mousedown`, and `mouseup` event listener to try out each of the different desktop event listeners supported by the `Events` class.

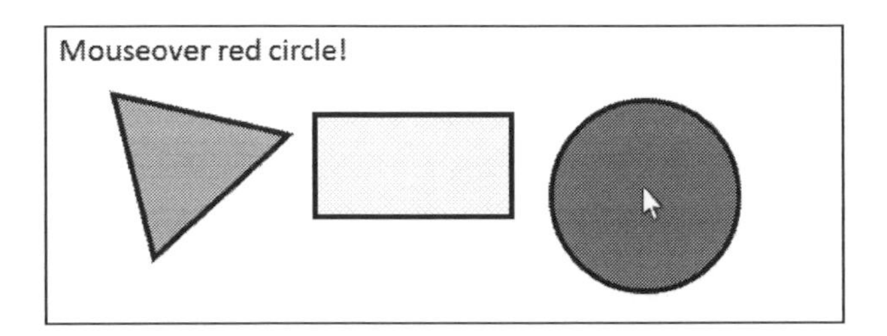

How to do it...

Follow these steps to draw a triangle, a rectangle, and a circle, and then attach mouse event listeners to each shape:

1. Link to the `Events` class:

```
<script src="events.js">
</script>
```

2. Define the `writeMessage()` function which writes out a message:

```
<script>
    function writeMessage(context, message){
        context.font = "18pt Calibri";
        context.fillStyle = "black";
        context.fillText(message, 10, 25);
    }
```

3. Instantiate a new `Events` object and get the canvas and context:

```
    window.onload = function(){
        var events = new Events("myCanvas");
        var canvas = events.getCanvas();
        var context = events.getContext();
        var message = "";
```

4. Begin defining the `stage()` function which starts by clearing the canvas:

```
        events.setStage(function(){
          this.clear();
```

5. Begin a new region with `beginRegion()` and then draw a blue triangle:

```
// draw blue triangle
this.beginRegion();
context.beginPath();
context.lineWidth = 4;
context.strokeStyle = "black";
context.fillStyle = "#00D2FF";
context.moveTo(50, 50);
context.lineTo(180, 80);
context.lineTo(80, 170);
context.closePath();
context.fill();
context.stroke();
```

6. Add `mousemove` and `mouseout` event listeners to the triangle and close the region with `closeRegion()`:

```
this.addRegionEventListener("mousemove", function(){
    var mousePos = events.getMousePos();
    var mouseX = mousePos.x - 50;
    var mouseY = mousePos.y - 50;
    message = "Triangle mouse Position: " + mouseX +
"," + mouseY;
});

this.addRegionEventListener("mouseout", function(){
    message = "Mouseout blue triangle!";
});

this.closeRegion();
```

7. Draw a yellow rectangle with no event listeners:

```
// draw yellow rectangle
// this is an example of a shape
// with no event listeners
context.beginPath();
context.lineWidth = 4;
context.strokeStyle = "black";
context.fillStyle = "yellow";
context.rect(200, 65, 150, 75);
context.fill();
context.stroke();
```

8. Begin a new region and draw a red circle:

```
            // draw red circle
            this.beginRegion();
            context.beginPath();
            context.arc(450, canvas.height / 2, 70, 0, Math.PI *
2, true);
            context.fillStyle = "red";
            context.fill();
            context.stroke();
```

9. Attach `mousedown`, `mouseup`, `mouseover`, and `mouseout` event listeners to the circle, and close the region:

```
            this.addRegionEventListener("mousedown", function(){
                message = "Mousedown red circle!";
            });
            this.addRegionEventListener("mouseup", function(){
                message = "Mouseup red circle!";
            });
            this.addRegionEventListener("mouseover", function(){
                message = "Mouseover red circle!";
            });
            this.addRegionEventListener("mouseout", function(){
                message = "Mouseout red circle!";
            });

            this.closeRegion();
```

10. Write out a message:

```
        writeMessage(context, message);
        });

    // since we set the draw stage function, the listen()
    // method is automatically called for us
    };
</script>
```

11. Embed the canvas inside the body of the HTML document:

```
<canvas id="myCanvas" width="600" height="250" style="border:1px
solid black;">
</canvas>
```

How it works...

To attach events to the three shapes in this recipe, we first need to initialize an `Events` object and then set the `stage()` function. Inside the `stage()` function, we can define a new region using `beginRegion()`, draw the blue triangle, attach events using `addRegionEventListener()`, and then close the region using `closeRegion()`. Next, we can draw the yellow rectangle without defining a region because we aren't attaching any events to it. Finally, we can define a second region, draw the red circle, attach event listeners, and then close the region, completing the `stage()` function definition.

See also...

- *Drawing a rectangle* in *Chapter 2*
- *Drawing a circle* in *Chapter 2*
- *Working with custom shapes and fill styles* in *Chapter 2*
- *Attaching touch event listeners to regions on a mobile device*

Attaching touch event listeners to regions on a mobile device

For those of you crying "What about mobile devices? Desktops and laptops are a thing of the past!" – this recipe is just for you. As Internet surfers migrate away from their giant tethered desktops and begin consuming Internet content from mobile devices, it's becoming more evident every day that the future of the Web, including canvas, will reside mostly in the mobile space.

Unlike web applications running on desktops and laptops, where user interactions are detected using the mouse from `mousedown`, `mouseup`, `mouseover`, `mouseout`, and `mousemove` events, web applications running on mobile devices are interacted with touch events from `touchstart`, `touchend`, and `touchmove` events.

In this recipe, we'll create a mobile version of the previous recipe by adding touch event listeners to the triangle and circle.

As mentioned earlier, any of the recipes in this chapter could be modified to support mobile devices by adding touch event listeners.

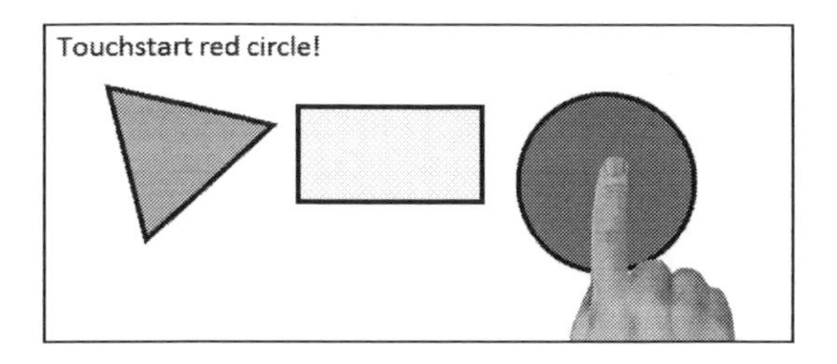

How to do it...

Follow these steps to draw a triangle, a rectangle, and a circle, and then attach mobile touch events to each shape:

1. Add a viewport meta tag inside the header tag to set the mobile device width, set the initial scale, and disable user scaling:

```
<meta name="viewport" content="width=device-width, initial-
scale=0.552, user-scalable=no"/>
```

2. Link to the `Events` class:

```
<script src="events.js">
</script>
```

3. Define the `writeMessage()` function which writes out a message:

```
<script>
    function writeMessage(context, message){
        context.font = "18pt Calibri";
        context.fillStyle = "black";
        context.fillText(message, 10, 25);
    }
```

4. Instantiate a new `Events` object and get the canvas and context:

```
    window.onload = function(){
        var events = new Events("myCanvas");
        var canvas = events.getCanvas();
        var context = events.getContext();
        var message = "";
```

5. Begin defining the `sStage()` function which starts by clearing the canvas:

```
        events.setStage(function(){
      this.clear();
```

6. Begin a new region with `beginRegion()` and then draw a blue triangle:

```
// draw blue triangle
this.beginRegion();
context.beginPath();
context.lineWidth = 4;
context.strokeStyle = "black";
context.fillStyle = "#00D2FF";
context.moveTo(50, 50);
context.lineTo(180, 80);
context.lineTo(80, 170);
context.closePath();
context.fill();
context.stroke();
```

7. Add the `touchmove` event listener to the triangle and close the region with `closeRegion()`:

```
this.addRegionEventListener("touchmove", function(){
    var touchPos = events.getTouchPos();

    if (touchPos !== null) {
        var touchX = touchPos.x - 20;
        var touchY = touchPos.y - 50;

        message = "Triangle touch position: " +
        touchX + "," + touchY;
    }
});

this.closeRegion();
```

8. Draw a yellow rectangle with no event listeners:

```
// draw yellow rectangle
// this is an example of a shape
// with no event listeners
context.beginPath();
context.lineWidth = 4;
context.strokeStyle = "black";
context.fillStyle = "yellow";
context.rect(200, 65, 150, 75);
context.fill();
context.stroke();
```

9. Begin a new region and draw a red circle:

```
            // draw red circle
            this.beginRegion();
            context.beginPath();
            context.arc(450, canvas.height / 2, 70, 0, Math.PI *
2, true);
            context.fillStyle = "red";
            context.fill();
            context.stroke();
```

10. Attach `touchstart` and `touchend` event listeners to the circle and close the region:

```
            this.addRegionEventListener("touchstart", function(){
                message = "Touchstart red circle!";
            });

            this.addRegionEventListener("touchend", function(){
                message = "Touchend red circle!";
            });

            this.closeRegion();
```

11. Write out a message:

```
        writeMessage(context, message);
        });

    // since we set the draw stage function, the listen()
    // method is automatically called for us
    };
</script>
```

12. Embed the canvas inside the body of the HTML document:

```
<canvas id="myCanvas" width="600" height="250" style="border:1px
solid black;">
</canvas>
```

How it works...

Similar to the previous recipe, in this recipe we'll attach event listeners to the triangle and the circle, except this time we'll attach touch event listeners so that the demo can be run on a mobile device.

Touch events on mobile devices are actually quite simple, and work in much the same way as desktop events. The mobile equivalent of `mousedown` is `touchstart`, the equivalent of `mouseup` is `touchend`, and the equivalent of `mousemove` is `touchmove`. As mobile devices can't detect if your finger is hovering over a region, mobile devices don't have an equivalent for `mouseover` or `mouseout`, I wouldn't be surprised if sometime in the future mobile devices *could* detect when fingers are close to the screen but not quite touching it.

To show the touch coordinates for the blue triangle, we can use the `touchmove` event listener, and to detect when the red circle is being touched or released, we can use the `touchstart` and `touchend` events.

See also...

- *Drawing a rectangle* in *Chapter 2*
- *Drawing a circle* in *Chapter 2*
- *Working with custom shapes and fill styles* in *Chapter 2*
- *Attaching mouse event listeners to regions*

Attaching event listeners to images

In this recipe, we'll attach event listeners to images. As we can only attach event listeners to paths with our `Events` class, and as images drawn on the canvas aren't classified as paths, we can create a rectangular region that overlays an image in order to attach event listeners to the rectangular region, and consequently attach event listeners to the image.

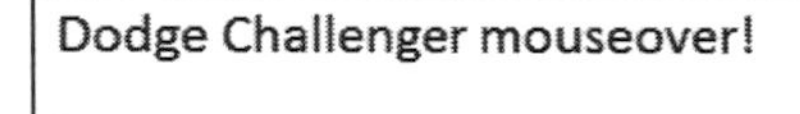

How to do it...

Follow these steps to draw two different images and then attach `mouseover`, `mouseout`, `mousedown`, and `mouseup` event listeners to them:

1. Link to the `Events` class:

```
<script src="events.js">
</script>
```

2. Define the `writeMessage()` function which writes out a message:

```
<script>
    function writeMessage(context, message){
        context.font = "18pt Calibri";
        context.fillStyle = "black";
        context.fillText(message, 10, 25);
    }
```

3. Create an image loader that loads a set of images and then calls a `callback` function whenever all of the images have loaded:

```
    /*
     * loads the images and then calls the callback function
     * with a hash of image objects when the images have loaded
     */
    function loadImages(sources, callback){
        var loadedImages = 0;
        var numImages = 0;
        var images = {};
        // get num of sources
        for (var src in sources) {
            numImages++;
        }
       // load images
        for (var src in sources) {
            images[src] = new Image();
            images[src].onload = function(){
        // call callback function() when images
        // have loaded
                if (++loadedImages >= numImages) {
                    callback(images);
                }
            };
            images[src].src = sources[src];
        }
    }
```

4. Define the `drawImages()` function which instantiates a new `Events` object and begins defining the `stage()` function:

```
function drawImages(images){
    var events = new Events("myCanvas");
    var canvas = events.getCanvas();
    var context = events.getContext();
    var message = "";

    events.setStage(function(){
  this.clear();
```

5. Begin a new region, draw the left image, define a rectangular region that represents the image path, attach event listeners to the rectangular region, and then close the region. Repeat these steps for the right image as well, and then write out a message:

```
            this.beginRegion();

            context.drawImage(images.challengerImg, 50, 70, 240,
143);
            // draw rectangular region for image
            context.beginPath();
            context.rect(50, 70, 240, 143);
            context.closePath();

            this.addRegionEventListener("mouseover", function(){
                message = "Dodge Challenger mouseover!";
            });
            this.addRegionEventListener("mouseout", function(){
                message = "Dodge Challenger mouseout!";
            });
            this.addRegionEventListener("mousedown", function(){
                message = "Dodge Challenger mousedown!";
            });
            this.addRegionEventListener("mouseup", function(){
                message = "Dodge Challenger mouseup!";
            });
            this.closeRegion();

            this.beginRegion();
            context.drawImage(images.cobraImg, 350, 50, 200, 150);
            // draw rectangular region for image
            context.beginPath();
            context.rect(350, 50, 200, 150);
            context.closePath();
```

```
            this.addRegionEventListener("mouseover", function(){
                message = "AC Cobra mouseover!";
            });
            this.addRegionEventListener("mouseout", function(){
                message = "AC Cobra mouseout!";
            });
            this.addRegionEventListener("mousedown", function(){
                message = "AC Cobra mousedown!";
            });
            this.addRegionEventListener("mouseup", function(){
                message = "AC Cobra mouseup!";
            });
            this.closeRegion();

            writeMessage(context, message);
        });
    }
```

6. When the page loads create a hash of image sources and then pass it off to the `loadImages()` function:

```
    window.onload = function(){
        var sources = {
            challengerImg: "challenger.jpg",
            cobraImg: "cobra.jpg"
        };

        loadImages(sources, drawImages);
    };
</script>
```

7. Embed the canvas inside the body of the HTML document:

```
<canvas id="myCanvas" width="600" height="250" style="border:1px
solid black;">
</canvas>
```

How it works...

Once the page loads, we can use an image loader function to load two images. When both images have loaded, the `drawImages()` function is called and an `Events` object is instantiated. Inside the `stage()` function, we can begin a new region with `beginRegion()`, draw the first image, draw a rectangular path to define the image path, attach events using `addRegionEventListener()`, and then close the region. Next, we can repeat this process to create the second image with its own set of event listeners.

See also...

- *Drawing an image* in *Chapter 3*

Dragging-and-dropping shapes

In this recipe, we'll tackle the holy grail of event listeners–drag-and-drop. Without the `Events` class or some other lightweight JavaScript library, drag-and-drop operations can be quite cumbersome to develop. We can use the `Events` class to attach a `mouseover`, `mousedown`, `mousemove`, `mouseup`, and `mouseout` event listener to the rectangle to handle different phases of the drag-and-drop operation.

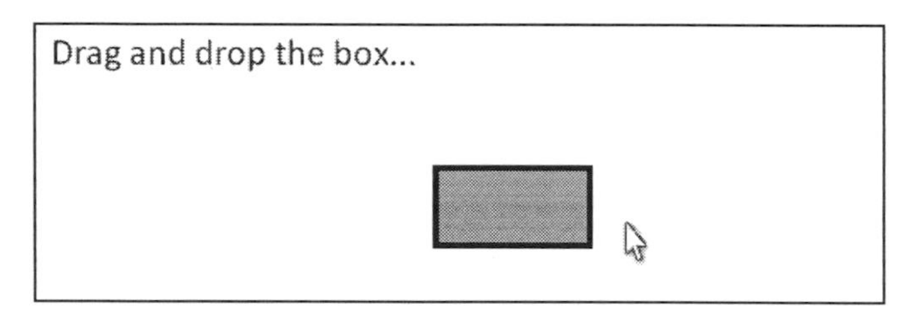

How to do it...

Follow these steps to drag-and-drop a rectangle:

1. Link to the `Events` class:

```
<script src="events.js">
</script>
```

2. Define the `writeMessage()` function which writes out a message:

```
<script>
    function writeMessage(context, message){
        context.font = "18pt Calibri";
        context.fillStyle = "black";
        context.fillText(message, 10, 25);
    }
```

3. When the page loads, instantiate a new `Events` object, define the starting position of the rectangle that will be dragged-and-dropped, and define `draggingRect`, `draggingRectOffsetX`, and `draggingRectOffsetY` for the drag-and-drop operation:

```
    window.onload = function(){
        events = new Events("myCanvas");
        var canvas = events.getCanvas();
```

```
    var context = events.getContext();

    var rectX = canvas.width / 2 - 50;
    var rectY = canvas.height / 2 - 25;
    var draggingRect = false;
    var draggingRectOffsetX = 0;
    var draggingRectOffsetY = 0;
```

4. For the `stage()` function, begin by setting the coordinates of the rectangle based on the coordinates of the mouse if the `draggingRect` Boolean is true:

```
    events.setStage(function(){
        // get the mouse position
        var mousePos = this.getMousePos();

        if (draggingRect) {
            rectX = mousePos.x - draggingRectOffsetX;
            rectY = mousePos.y - draggingRectOffsetY;
        }
```

5. Clear the canvas, write out a message, begin a new region, draw the rectangle, attach events, and then close the region:

```
        // clear the canvas
        this.clear();

        writeMessage(context, "Drag and drop the box...");

        this.beginRegion();

        // draw the box
        context.beginPath();
        context.rect(rectX, rectY, 100, 50);
        context.lineWidth = 4;
        context.strokeStyle = "black";
        context.fillStyle = "#00D2FF";
        context.fill();
        context.stroke();
        context.closePath();

        // attach event listeners
        this.addRegionEventListener("mousedown", function(){
            draggingRect = true;
            var mousePos = events.getMousePos();

            draggingRectOffsetX = mousePos.x - rectX;
```

```
                    draggingRectOffsetY = mousePos.y - rectY;
                });
                this.addRegionEventListener("mouseup", function(){
                    draggingRect = false;
                });
                this.addRegionEventListener("mouseover", function(){
                    document.body.style.cursor = "pointer";
                });
                this.addRegionEventListener("mouseout", function(){
                    document.body.style.cursor = "default";
                });

                this.closeRegion();
            });
        };
    </script>
```

6. Embed the canvas inside the body of the HTML document:

```
<canvas id="myCanvas" width="600" height="250" style="border:1px
solid black;">
</canvas>
```

How it works...

Drag-and-drop is handled with three phases:

1. Detect a `mousedown` event over a shape which begins the operation
2. Position the shape according to the mouse coordinates using the `mousemove` event listener
3. Drop the shape when the mouse button is released (`mouseup`)

Inside the `stage()` function, we can set the position of the rectangle relative to the position of the mouse if the `draggingRect` Boolean is true. We can then begin a new region with `beginRegion()`, draw the rectangle, and then attach event listeners using the `addRegionEventListener()` method. We can add a `mousedown` event listener that sets the `draggingRect` Boolean to true, and then calculates the `draggingRectOffsetX` and `draggingRectOffsetY` variables which account for the position offset between the mouse and the top-left corner of the rectangle. Next, we can add a `mouseup` event listener that sets the `draggingRect` Boolean to false, completing the drag-and-drop operation. We can also attach a `mouseover` event listener to turn the cursor into a hand to show that the element can be interacted with, and we can also attach a `mouseout` event listener to restore the cursor image back to the default pointer to indicate that the mouse cursor is no longer over the element.

See also...

- *Dragging-and-dropping images*

Dragging-and-dropping images

This recipe essentially combines the concepts from the previous two recipes to demonstrate how we can drag-and-drop an image.

How to do it...

Follow these steps to drag-and-drop an image:

1. Link to the `Events` class:

```
<script src="events.js">
</script>
```

2. Define the `writeMessage()` function which writes out a message:

```
<script>
    function writeMessage(context, message){
        context.font = "18pt Calibri";
        context.fillStyle = "black";
        context.fillText(message, 10, 25);
    }
```

3. Define the `drawImage()` function which begins by instantiating a new `Events` object and setting the initial position of the rectangular region that overlays the image:

```
    function drawImage(challengerImg){
        var events = new Events("myCanvas");
        var canvas = events.getCanvas();
        var context = events.getContext();

        var rectX = canvas.width / 2 - challengerImg.width / 2;
        var rectY = canvas.height / 2 - challengerImg.height / 2;
        var draggingRect = false;
        var draggingRectOffsetX = 0;
        var draggingRectOffsetY = 0;
```

4. Define the `stage()` function which begins by setting the position of the image based on the coordinates of the mouse if the `draggingRect` Boolean is true:

```
        events.setStage(function(){
            var mousePos = this.getMousePos();

            if (draggingRect) {
                rectX = mousePos.x - draggingRectOffsetX;
                rectY = mousePos.y - draggingRectOffsetY;
            }
```

5. Clear the canvas and write out a message:

```
            // clear the canvas
            this.clear();
            writeMessage(context, "Drag and drop the car...");
```

6. Begin a new region, draw the image, draw a rectangular region to define the image path, attach event listeners, and close the region:

```
            this.beginRegion();
            context.drawImage(challengerImg, rectX, rectY,
challengerImg.width, challengerImg.height);
            // draw rectangular region for image
            context.beginPath();
            context.rect(rectX, rectY, challengerImg.width,
challengerImg.height);
            context.closePath();

            this.addRegionEventListener("mousedown", function(){
                draggingRect = true;
                var mousePos = events.getMousePos();

                draggingRectOffsetX = mousePos.x - rectX;
                draggingRectOffsetY = mousePos.y - rectY;
            });
            this.addRegionEventListener("mouseup", function(){
                draggingRect = false;
            });
            this.addRegionEventListener("mouseover", function(){
                document.body.style.cursor = "pointer";
            });
            this.addRegionEventListener("mouseout", function(){
                document.body.style.cursor = "default";
            });

            this.closeRegion();
        });
    }
```

7. When the page loads, load the image and then call the `drawImage()` function:

```
    window.onload = function(){
        // load image
        challengerImg = new Image();
        challengerImg.onload = function(){
            drawImage(this);
        };
        challengerImg.src = "challenger.jpg";
    };
</script>
```

8. Embed the canvas inside the body of the HTML document:

```
<canvas id="myCanvas" width="600" height="250" style="border:1px
solid black;">
</canvas>
```

How it works...

To drag-and-drop an image, we can draw an invisible rectangular path on top of the image to provide a path for the image, and we can attach the `mousedown`, `mouseup`, and `mousemove` events similar to the previous recipe to handle the three phases of drag-and-drop.

When the user drags-and-drops an image, he/she is essentially dragging and dropping both the image and its corresponding rectangular path.

See also...

- *Drawing an image* in *Chapter 3*
- *Dragging-and-dropping shapes*

Creating an image magnifier

In this recipe, we'll create a really neat image magnifier by cropping out a section of a large image based on the mouse coordinates of a small image and then displaying the result on top of the small image.

How to do it...

Follow these steps to create an image magnifier that renders a magnified portion of an image when the user mouses over it:

1. Link to the `Events` class:

   ```
   <script src="events.js">
   </script>
   ```

2. Create an image loader that will load the small and large image and then call a callback function when the images have loaded:

   ```
   <script>
       /*
        * loads the images and then calls the callback function
        * with a hash of image objects  when the images have loaded
        */
       function loadImages(sources, callback){
           var loadedImages = 0;
           var numImages = 0;
           var images = {};
           // get num of sources
           for (var src in sources) {
               numImages++;
           }
           // load images
           for (var src in sources) {
               images[src] = new Image();
   ```

```
            images[src].onload = function(){
                // call callback function when images
                // have loaded
                if (++loadedImages >= numImages) {
                    callback(images);
                }
            };
            images[src].src = sources[src];
        }
    }
```

3. Define the `drawMagnifier()` function which draws the magnified image:

```
function drawMagnifier(config){
    var context = config.context;
var images = config.images;
    var mousePos = config.mousePos;
    var imageX = config.imageX;
    var imageY = config.imageY;
    var magWidth = config.magWidth;
    var magHeight = config.magHeight;
    var smallWidth = config.smallWidth;
    var smallHeight = config.smallHeight;
    var largeWidth = config.largeWidth;
    var largeHeight = config.largeHeight;

    /*
     * sourceX and sourceY assume that the rectangle we are
     * cropping out of the large image exists within the large
     * image. We'll have to make some adjustments for the
     * cases where the magnifier goes past the edges of the
     * large image
     */
    var sourceX = ((mousePos.x - imageX) *
      largeWidth / smallWidth) - magWidth / 2;
    var sourceY = ((mousePos.y - imageY) *
      largeHeight / smallHeight) - magHeight / 2;
    var destX = mousePos.x - magWidth / 2;
    var destY = mousePos.y - magHeight / 2;
    var viewWidth = magWidth;
    var viewHeight = magHeight;
    var viewX = destX;
    var viewY = destY;
    var drawMagImage = true;
```

```
        // boundary checks and adjustments for cases
        // where the magnifyer goes past the edges of the large
image
        if (sourceX < 0) {
            if (sourceX > -1 * magWidth) {
                var diffX = -1 * sourceX;
                viewX += diffX;
                viewWidth -= diffX;
                sourceX = 0;
            }
            else {
                drawMagImage = false;
            }
        }

        if (sourceX > largeWidth - magWidth) {
            if (sourceX < largeWidth) {
                viewWidth = largeWidth - sourceX;
            }
            else {
                drawMagImage = false;
            }
        }

        if (sourceY < 0) {
            if (sourceY > -1 * magHeight) {
                var diffY = -1 * sourceY;
                viewY += diffY;
                viewHeight -= diffY;
                sourceY = 0;
            }
            else {
                drawMagImage = false;
            }
        }

        if (sourceY > largeHeight - magHeight) {
            if (sourceY < largeHeight) {
                viewHeight = largeHeight - sourceY;
            }
            else {
                drawMagImage = false;
            }
        }
```

```
        // draw white magnifier background
        context.beginPath();
        context.fillStyle = "white";
        context.fillRect(destX, destY, magWidth, magHeight);

        // draw image
        if (drawMagImage) {
            context.beginPath();
            context.drawImage(images.cobraLargeImg, sourceX,
sourceY, viewWidth, viewHeight, viewX, viewY, viewWidth,
viewHeight);
        }

        // draw magnifier border
        context.beginPath();
        context.lineWidth = 2;
        context.strokeStyle = "black";
        context.strokeRect(destX, destY, magWidth, magHeight);
    }
```

4. Define the `drawImages()` function which begins by instantiating a new `Events` object and defines the magnifier properties:

```
    function drawImages(images){
        var events = new Events("myCanvas");
        var canvas = events.getCanvas();
        var context = events.getContext();

        // define magnifier dependencies
        var imageX = canvas.width / 2 - images.cobraSmallImg.width
/ 2;
        var imageY = canvas.height / 2 - images.cobraSmallImg.
height / 2;
        var magWidth = 200;
        var magHeight = 150;
        var smallWidth = images.cobraSmallImg.width;
        var smallHeight = images.cobraSmallImg.height;
        var largeWidth = images.cobraLargeImg.width;
        var largeHeight = images.cobraLargeImg.height;
```

5. Set the `stage()` function which draws the small image and then calls `drawMagnifier()` to draw the magnified image:

```
        events.setStage(function(){
            var mousePos = events.getMousePos();
            this.clear();
```

```
            context.drawImage(images.cobraSmallImg, imageX,
imageY, smallWidth, smallHeight);
            // draw border around image
            context.beginPath();
            context.lineWidth = 2;
            context.strokeStyle = "black";
            context.strokeRect(imageX, imageY, smallWidth,
smallHeight);
            context.closePath();

            if (mousePos !== null) {
                drawMagnifier({
                    context: context,
          images: images,
                    mousePos: mousePos,
                    imageX: imageX,
                    imageY: imageY,
                    magWidth: magWidth,
                    magHeight: magHeight,
                    smallWidth: smallWidth,
                    smallHeight: smallHeight,
                    largeWidth: largeWidth,
                    largeHeight: largeHeight
                });
            }
        });
```

6. Add an event listener to the canvas element which redraws the stage if the user mouses out of the canvas in order to remove the magnified image:

```
        canvas.addEventListener("mouseout", function(){
            events.stage();
        }, false);
    }
```

7. When the page loads, build a hash of image sources, and pass it on to the image loader function:

```
    window.onload = function(){
        var sources = {
            cobraSmallImg: "cobra_280x210.jpg",
            cobraLargeImg: "cobra_800x600.jpg"
        };

        loadImages(sources, drawImages);
    };
</script>
```

8. Embed the canvas inside the body of the HTML document.

```
<canvas id="myCanvas" width="600" height="250" style="border:1px
solid black;">
</canvas>
```

How it works...

To create an image magnifier, we'll need two images, one small and one large. The small image will be the image that's always visible on the canvas, and the large image will be used as a buffer image to draw the magnifier. Once the page loads, and both images are loaded, we can instantiate an `Events` object and begin defining the `stage()` function.

After drawing the small image centered on the canvas, we can draw the magnified image by calculating the `sourceX`, `sourceY`, `destX`, and `destY` parameters of the `drawImage()` method which will crop out the magnified section of the large image, and then display the result on top of the smaller image.

To get `sourceX` and `sourceY`, we can get the mouse coordinates relative to the small image by taking the difference between the mouse position and the position of the top-left corner of the small image, and then we can get the corresponding coordinates for the large image by multiplying the result by the magnification (which is the large image width divided by the small width), and then subtracting half the size of the magnified window:

```
        var sourceX = ((mousePos.x - imageX) * largeWidth /
smallWidth) - magWidth / 2;
        var sourceY = ((mousePos.y - imageY) * largeHeight /
smallHeight) - magHeight / 2;
```

To center the magnified image on the mouse cursor, we can set `destX` equal to the x position of the mouse offset by half the magnifier width, and we can set `destY` equal to the y position of the mouse offset by half the magnifier height:

```
var destX = mousePos.x - magWidth / 2;
var destY = mousePos.y - magHeight / 2;
```

See also...

- *Drawing an image* in *Chapter 3*
- *Cropping an image* in *Chapter 3*

Creating a drawing application

In this recipe, we'll create a nifty drawing application so users can draw pictures right in the browser.

How to do it...

Follow these steps to create a simple drawing application:

1. Style the toolbar, inputs, and buttons:

```
<style>
    canvas {
        border: 1px solid black;
        font-family: "Helvetica Neue", "Arial",
        "Lucida Grande", "Lucida Sans Unicode",
        "Microsoft YaHei", sans-serif;
        font-size: 13px;
        line-height: 1.5;
        color: #474747;
    }

    #toolbar {
        width: 590px;
        border: 1px solid black;
        border-bottom: 0px;
        padding: 5px;
        background-color: #f8f8f8;
    }

    input[type = 'text'] {
        width: 30px;
                    margin: 0px 5px 0px 5px;
    }
```

```
        label {
            margin-left: 40px;
        }

        label:first-of-type {
            margin-left: 0px;
        }

        input[type = 'button'] {
            float: right;
        }

        #colorSquare {
            position: relative;
            display: inline-block;
            width: 20px;
            height: 20px;
            background-color: blue;
            top: 4px;
        }
    </style>
```

2. Link to the `Events` class:

```
<script src="events.js">
</script>
```

3. Define the `addPoint()` function which adds a point to the points array:

```
    <script>
        function addPoint(events, points){
            var context = events.getContext();
            var drawingPos = events.getMousePos();

            if (drawingPos !== null) {
                points.push(drawingPos);
            }
        }
```

4. Define the `drawPath()` function which clears the canvas, redraws the canvas drawing before the path was started, and then draws the drawing path using the points in the points array:

```
        function drawPath(canvas, points, canvasImg){
            var context = canvas.getContext("2d");

            // clear canvas
```

```
                context.clearRect(0, 0, canvas.width, canvas.
height);

                // redraw canvas before path
                context.drawImage(canvasImg, 0, 0, canvas.width,
canvas.height);

                // draw patch
                context.beginPath();
                context.lineTo(points[0].x, points[0].y);
                for (var n = 1; n < points.length; n++) {
                    var point = points[n];
                    context.lineTo(point.x, point.y);
                }
                context.stroke();
            }
```

5. Define the `updateColorSquare()` function which updates the color of the toolbar color square:

```
            function updateColorSquare(){
                var red = document.getElementById("red").value;
                var green = document.getElementById("green").
value;
                var blue = document.getElementById("blue").value;

                var colorSquare = document.
getElementById("colorSquare");
                colorSquare.style.backgroundColor = "rgb(" + red +
"," + green + "," + blue + ")";
            }
```

6. Define the `getCanvasImg()` method which returns an image object of the canvas drawing:

```
            function getCanvasImg(canvas){
                var img = new Image();
                img.src = canvas.toDataURL();
                return img;
            }
```

7. When the page loads, instantiate a new `Events` object, define the `isMouseDown` flag, get the canvas image, and initialize the drawing color, and size:

```
            window.onload = function(){
                var events = new Events("myCanvas");
                var canvas = events.getCanvas();
                var context = events.getContext();
```

```
                    var isMouseDown = false;
                    var canvasImg = getCanvasImg(canvas);
                    var points = [];

                    // initialize drawing params
                    var red = document.getElementById("red").value;
                    var green = document.getElementById("green").
value;
                    var blue = document.getElementById("blue").value;
                    var size = document.getElementById("size").value;
```

8. Update the color square whenever a new color input is entered:

```
                    // attach listeners
                    document.getElementById("red").
addEventListener("keyup", function(evt){
                        updateColorSquare();
                    }, false);

                    document.getElementById("green").
addEventListener("keyup", function(evt){
                        updateColorSquare();
                    }, false);

                    document.getElementById("blue").
addEventListener("keyup", function(evt){
                        updateColorSquare();
                    }, false);
```

9. Clear the canvas when the clear button is pressed:

```
                    document.getElementById("clearButton").
addEventListener("click", function(evt){
                        events.clear();
                        points = [];
                        canvasImg = getCanvasImg(canvas);
                    }, false);
```

10. When the **Save** button is pressed, convert the canvas drawing into a data URL and open the drawing as an image in a new window:

```
                    document.getElementById("saveButton").
addEventListener("click", function(evt){
                        // open new window with saved image so user
                        // can right click and save to their computer
                        window.open(canvas.toDataURL());
                    }, false);
```

11. When the user `mousedowns` on the canvas, get the drawing position, color, and size, set the path style, add the first point to the points array, and then set the `isMouseDown` flag to true:

```
canvas.addEventListener("mousedown", function(){
    var drawingPos = events.getMousePos();

    // update drawing params
    red = document.getElementById("red").value;
    green = document.getElementById("green").
value;
    blue = document.getElementById("blue").value;
    size = document.getElementById("size").value;

    // start drawing path
    context.strokeStyle = "rgb(" + red + "," +
green + "," + blue + ")";
    context.lineWidth = size;
    context.lineJoin = "round";
    context.lineCap = "round";
    addPoint(events, points);
    isMouseDown = true;
}, false);
```

12. When the user `mouseups` from the canvas, set the `isMouseDown` flag to false, draw the path, and then save the current image drawing:

```
canvas.addEventListener("mouseup", function(){
    isMouseDown = false;
    if (points.length > 0) {
        drawPath(this, points, canvasImg);
        // reset points
        points = [];
    }
    canvasImg = getCanvasImg(this);
}, false);
```

13. When the user's mouse leaves the canvas, simulate a `mouseup` event:

```
canvas.addEventListener("mouseout", function(){
    if (document.createEvent) {
        var evt = document.
createEvent('MouseEvents');
        evt.initEvent("mouseup", true, false);
        this.dispatchEvent(evt);
    }
    else {
```

```
                    this.fireEvent("onmouseup");
                }
            }, false);
```

14. Set the `stage()` function which continuously adds new points to the current drawing path if the mouse is down and moving:

```
            events.setStage(function(){
                if (isMouseDown) {
                    addPoint(this, points);
                    drawPath(canvas, points, canvasImg);
                }
            });
        };
    </script>
```

15. Construct the toolbar and add the canvas element:

```
    <body>
        <div id="toolbar">
            <label>
                Color
            </label>
            R: <input type="text" id="red" maxlength="3"
class="short" value="0">G: <input type="text" id="green"
maxlength="3" class="short" value="0">B: <input type="text"
id="blue" maxlength="3" class="short" value="255">
            <div id="colorSquare">
            </div>
            <label>
                Size:
            </label>
            <input type="text" id="size" maxlength="3"
class="short" value="20">px<input type="button" id="clearButton"
value="Clear"><input type="button" id="saveButton" value="Save">
        </div>
        <canvas id="myCanvas" width="600" height="250">
        </canvas>
    </body>
```

How it works...

Drawing applications typically have the following core features:

- A `mousedown` event starts a drawing path, and a `mouseup` event ends a drawing path
- Line widths can be set
- Colors can be set
- The drawing can be cleared
- The drawing can be saved

Of course, if you wanted to create a Photoshop or Gimp-like drawing application on the Web, there are hundreds of other features you could add, but here we are nailing down just the basics to get started.

The first bullet in the preceding list is clearly the most important – we need to figure out a way that users can draw lines on the screen. The most straight forward way to do this is to follow these steps:

1. When the user `mousedowns` somewhere on the canvas, set the path style and add the mouse position coordinate to an array of points to define the beginning point of the drawing path.
2. When the user moves the mouse, get the mouse position and add another point to the array of points, and then redraw the path with the new point.
3. When the user `mouseups`, set a flag indicating that the path is and save the current drawing image to be used with the next drawing path.

To keep things simple, we can let the user set the line width with a text input, and we can let the user set the color with three text inputs (the red, green, and blue components of a color).

Finally, we can create a clear button that clears the canvas with the `clear()` method of the `Events` object, and we can create a save button that converts the canvas drawing into a data URL using the to `DataURL()` method of the canvas context, and then opens a new window with the data URL. From there, the user can right-click on the image to save it to their computer.

There's more...

Here are some more ideas if you're creating a more complex drawing application:

- Until the color picker input is supported by all of the major browsers, you could create a custom color picker widget that lets users choose a color graphically instead of inputting the red, green, and blue components of the color that they want
- You could create a slider bar using the HTML5 range input for the paint brush size
- You could create layer support by dynamically creating a new canvas element for each layer. Similar to Photoshop and Gimp, you could provide an ability to delete layers and merge layers
- If your application supports layering, you could also add an opacity control for each layer
- You could enhance the save feature by saving the drawing in local storage or in an offline database (see *Converting a canvas drawing into a data URL* in *Chapter 3*)
- Provide pre-built drawing shapes such as lines, rectangles, and circles
- Allow shapes to be scaled and rotated
- Allow users to import images into their drawings
- The list goes on...

Hopefully this recipe further sparks your interest in canvas and gets you thinking about other possibilities. I think it's safe to say that someone will eventually create a full-blown image editing web application powered entirely by canvas and give Adobe a run for their money. Maybe it will be you!

See also...

- *Drawing a spiral* in *Chapter 1*
- *Converting a canvas drawing into a data URL in Chapter 3*
- *Saving a canvas drawing as an image in Chapter 3*
- *Working with canvas mouse coordinates*

7
Creating Graphs and Charts

In this chapter, we will cover:

- Creating a pie chart
- Creating a bar chart
- Graphing equations
- Plotting data points with a line chart

Introduction

By now you may have noticed that *Chapters 1* to *4* cover HTML5 canvas basics, *Chapters 5* and *6* cover advanced topics, while *Chapters 7* and *8* cover real life implementations. After all, what good is it to learn about the canvas if we aren't able to produce something useful? This chapter focuses on doing just that by creating some real life canvas applications by creating a pie chart, a bar chart, graphs, and a line chart. In contrast to the previous chapters, this chapter contains only four recipes because each recipe provides a complete, easily configurable, and production-ready product. Let's get started!

Creating a pie chart

Pie charts are probably one of the most common data visualizations because they quickly give users a sense of the relative weights of data elements. In this recipe, we'll create a configurable Pie Chart class that takes in an array of data elements and produces a pie chart. Furthermore, we'll construct the Pie Chart drawing methods in such a way that the pie chart and label automatically fills up as much of the canvas as possible.

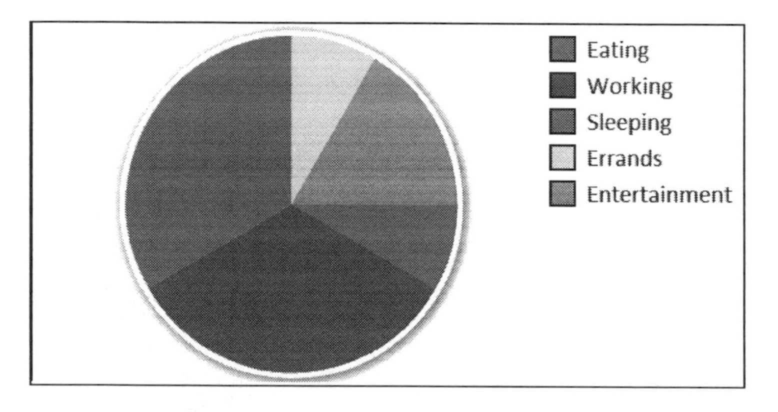

How to do it...

Follow these steps to create a Pie Chart class that can automatically position and size a pie chart and a legend from an array of data:

1. Define the constructor for the `PieChart` class which draws the pie chart:

```
/*
 * PieChart constructor
 */
function PieChart(canvasId, data){
  // user defined properties
  this.canvas = document.getElementById(canvasId);
  this.data = data;

  // constants
  this.padding = 10;
  this.legendBorder = 2;
  this.pieBorder = 5;
  this.colorLabelSize = 20;
  this.borderColor = "#555";
  this.shadowColor = "#777";
  this.shadowBlur = 10;
  this.shadowX = 2;
```

```
    this.shadowY = 2;
    this.font = "16pt Calibri";

        // relationships
        this.context = this.canvas.getContext("2d");
        this.legendWidth = this.getLegendWidth();
        this.legendX = this.canvas.width - this.legendWidth;
        this.legendY = this.padding;
        this.pieAreaWidth = (this.canvas.width - this.legendWidth);
        this.pieAreaHeight = this.canvas.height;
        this.pieX = this.pieAreaWidth / 2;
        this.pieY = this.pieAreaHeight / 2;
        this.pieRadius = (Math.min(this.pieAreaWidth,
        this.pieAreaHeight) / 2) - (this.padding);

        // draw pie chart
        this.drawPieBorder();
        this.drawSlices();
        this.drawLegend();
}
```

2. Define the `getLegendWidth()` method which returns the width of the legend by taking into account the text length of the longest label:

```
/*
 * gets the legend width based on the size
 * of the label text
 */
PieChart.prototype.getLegendWidth = function(){
    /*
     * loop through all labels and determine which
     * label is the longest.  Use this information
     * to determine the label width
     */
    this.context.font = this.font;
    var labelWidth = 0;

    for (var n = 0; n < this.data.length; n++) {
        var label = this.data[n].label;
        labelWidth = Math.max(labelWidth, this.context.
measureText(label).width);
    }

    return labelWidth + (this.padding * 2) + this.legendBorder +
this.colorLabelSize;
};
```

3. Define the `drawPieBorder()` method which draws a border around the pie chart:

```
PieChart.prototype.drawPieBorder = function(){
    var context = this.context;
    context.save();
    context.fillStyle = "white";
    context.shadowColor = this.shadowColor;
    context.shadowBlur = this.shadowBlur;
    context.shadowOffsetX = this.shadowX;
    context.shadowOffsetY = this.shadowY;
    context.beginPath();
    context.arc(this.pieX, this.pieY, this.pieRadius + this.
pieBorder, 0, Math.PI * 2, false);
    context.fill();
    context.closePath();
    context.restore();
};
```

4. Define the `drawSlices()` method which loops over the data and draws a slice of the pie for each data element:

```
/*
 * draws the slices for the pie chart
 */
PieChart.prototype.drawSlices = function(){
    var context = this.context;
    context.save();
    var total = this.getTotalValue();
    var startAngle = 0;
    for (var n = 0; n < this.data.length; n++) {
        var slice = this.data[n];

        // draw slice
        var sliceAngle = 2 * Math.PI * slice.value / total;
        var endAngle = startAngle + sliceAngle;

        context.beginPath();
        context.moveTo(this.pieX, this.pieY);
        context.arc(this.pieX, this.pieY, this.pieRadius,
startAngle, endAngle, false);
        context.fillStyle = slice.color;
        context.fill();
        context.closePath();
        startAngle = endAngle;
    }
  context.restore();
};
```

5. Define the `getTotalValue()` method which is used to get the sum of the data values:

```
/*
 * gets the total value of the labels by looping through
 * the data and adding up each value
 */
PieChart.prototype.getTotalValue = function(){
    var data = this.data;
    var total = 0;

    for (var n = 0; n < data.length; n++) {
        total += data[n].value;
    }

    return total;
};
```

6. Define the `drawLegend()` method which draws a legend:

```
/*
 * draws the legend
 */
PieChart.prototype.drawLegend = function(){
    var context = this.context;
    context.save();
    var labelX = this.legendX;
    var labelY = this.legendY;

    context.strokeStyle = "black";
    context.lineWidth = this.legendBorder;
    context.font = this.font;
    context.textBaseline = "middle";

    for (var n = 0; n < this.data.length; n++) {
        var slice = this.data[n];

        // draw legend label
        context.beginPath();
        context.rect(labelX, labelY, this.colorLabelSize, this.
colorLabelSize);
        context.closePath();
        context.fillStyle = slice.color;
        context.fill();
        context.stroke();
```

```
            context.fillStyle = "black";
            context.fillText(slice.label, labelX + this.colorLabelSize
    + this.padding, labelY + this.colorLabelSize / 2);

            labelY += this.colorLabelSize + this.padding;
        }
      context.restore();
    };
```

7. When the page loads, build the data and instantiate a `PieChart` object:

```
window.onload = function(){
    var data = [{
        label: "Eating",
        value: 2,
        color: "red"
    }, {
        label: "Working",
        value: 8,
        color: "blue"
    }, {
        label: "Sleeping",
        value: 8,
        color: "green"
    }, {
        label: "Errands",
        value: 2,
        color: "yellow"
    }, {
        label: "Entertainment",
        value: 4,
        color: "violet"
    }];

    new PieChart("myCanvas", data);
};
```

8. Embed the canvas tag inside the body of the HTML document:

```
<canvas id="myCanvas" width="600" height="300" style="border:1px
solid black;">
</canvas>
```

See also...

- *Drawing an arc* in *Chapter 1*
- *Working with text* in *Chapter 1*
- *Drawing a rectangle* in *Chapter 2*

How it works...

Before diving into how the code works, let's first take a step back and think about what a `PieChart` object should do. As a developer, we would need to pass in the canvas ID so the object knows where to draw, and also an array of data elements so it knows what to draw.

The `PieChart` element is rendered with the `drawSlices()` and `drawPieBorder()` methods. The `drawSlices()` method performs these steps:

1. Loops through the data elements.
2. Calculates the angle of each data value by multiplying 2π by the value fraction of the total value.
3. Draws an arc using the `arc()` method for each slice.
4. Fills each slice with the data element color.

Once the pie chart is rendered, we can draw the legend with the `drawLegend()` method. This method performs these steps:

1. Loops through the data elements.
2. Draws a box using `rect()` for each element.
3. Strokes and fills each box with the data element color using `stroke()` and `fill()`.
4. Writes the corresponding label using `fillText()` for each element.

Once the page loads, we can create an array of data elements that identify our daily activities with the corresponding number of hours for each activity and then instantiate a new PieChart object by passing in the data array.

In this recipe, we've created artificial data by hard coding an array of data elements. In real life, however, it's more likely that our data will be provided via JSON or XML, for example.

Creating a bar chart

Right behind pie charts, bar charts are another popular tool for visualizing data. In this recipe, we'll create a configurable Bar Chart class that takes in an array of data elements and creates a simple bar chart. We'll reuse the data structure from the previous recipe to compare the results. Like the Pie Chart class, the bar chart drawing methods also automatically scale the chart to fill up the canvas.

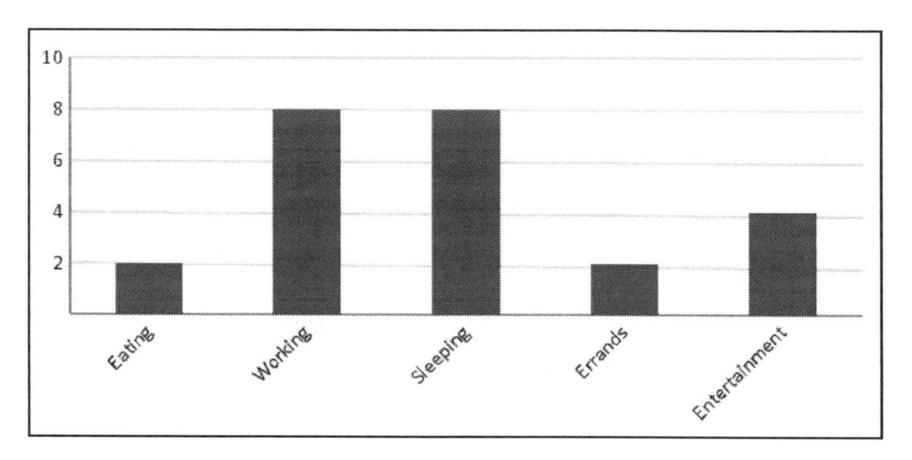

How to do it...

Follow these steps to create a Bar Chart class that can automatically position and size a bar chart from an array of data:

1. Define the `BarChart` constructor which draws the chart:

```
/*
 * BarChart constructor
 */
function BarChart(config){
    // user defined properties
    this.canvas = document.getElementById(config.canvasId);
    this.data = config.data;
    this.color = config.color;
    this.barWidth = config.barWidth;
    this.gridLineIncrement = config.gridLineIncrement;
    /*
     * adjust max value to highest possible value divisible
     * by the grid line increment value and less than
     * the requested max value
```

```
     */
    this.maxValue = config.maxValue - Math.floor(config.maxValue %
this.gridLineIncrement);
    this.minValue = config.minValue;

    // constants
    this.font = "12pt Calibri";
    this.axisColor = "#555";
    this.gridColor = "#aaa";
    this.padding = 10;

    // relationships
    this.context = this.canvas.getContext("2d");
    this.range = this.maxValue - this.minValue;
    this.numGridLines = this.numGridLines = Math.round(this.range
/ this.gridLineIncrement);
    this.longestValueWidth = this.getLongestValueWidth();
    this.x = this.padding + this.longestValueWidth;
    this.y = this.padding * 2;
    this.width = this.canvas.width - (this.longestValueWidth +
this.padding * 2);
    this.height = this.canvas.height - (this.getLabelAreaHeight()
+ this.padding * 4);

    // draw bar chart
    this.drawGridlines();
    this.drawYAxis();
    this.drawXAxis();
    this.drawBars();
    this.drawYVAlues();
    this.drawXLabels();
}
```

2. Define the `getLabelAreaHeight()` method which determines the label area height (the labels below the x axis):

```
/*
 * gets the label height by finding the max label width and
 * using trig to figure out the projected height since
 * the text will be rotated by 45 degrees
 */
BarChart.prototype.getLabelAreaHeight = function(){
    this.context.font = this.font;
    var maxLabelWidth = 0;

    /*
```

```
         * loop through all labels and determine which
         * label is the longest.  Use this information
         * to determine the label width
         */
        for (var n = 0; n < this.data.length; n++) {
            var label = this.data[n].label;
            maxLabelWidth = Math.max(maxLabelWidth, this.context.
    measureText(label).width);
        }

        /*
         * return y component of the labelWidth which
         * is at a 45 degree angle:
         *
         * a^2 + b^2 = c^2
         * a = b
         * c = labelWidth
         * a = height component of right triangle
         * solve for a
         */
        return Math.round(maxLabelWidth / Math.sqrt(2));
    };
```

3. Define the `getLongestValueWidth()` method which returns the longest value text width:

```
BarChart.prototype.getLongestValueWidth = function(){
    this.context.font = this.font;
    var longestValueWidth = 0;
    for (var n = 0; n <= this.numGridLines; n++) {
        var value = this.maxValue - (n * this.gridLineIncrement);
        longestValueWidth = Math.max(longestValueWidth, this.
context.measureText(value).width);

    }
    return longestValueWidth;
};
```

4. Define the `drawXLabels()` method which draws the x axis labels:

```
BarChart.prototype.drawXLabels = function(){
    var context = this.context;
    context.save();
    var data = this.data;
    var barSpacing = this.width / data.length;

    for (var n = 0; n < data.length; n++) {
```

```
        var label = data[n].label;
        context.save();
        context.translate(this.x + ((n + 1 / 2) * barSpacing),
this.y + this.height + 10);
        context.rotate(-1 * Math.PI / 4); // rotate 45 degrees
        context.font = this.font;
        context.fillStyle = "black";
        context.textAlign = "right";
        context.textBaseline = "middle";
        context.fillText(label, 0, 0);
        context.restore();
    }
    context.restore();
};
```

5. Define the `drawYValues()` method which draws the y axis values:

```
BarChart.prototype.drawYVAlues = function(){
    var context = this.context;
    context.save();
    context.font = this.font;
    context.fillStyle = "black";
    context.textAlign = "right";
    context.textBaseline = "middle";

    for (var n = 0; n <= this.numGridLines; n++) {
        var value = this.maxValue - (n * this.gridLineIncrement);
        var thisY = (n * this.height / this.numGridLines) +
this.y;
        context.fillText(value, this.x - 5, thisY);
    }

    context.restore();
};
```

6. Define the `drawBars()` method which loops through all of the data elements and draws a bar for each one:

```
BarChart.prototype.drawBars = function(){
    var context = this.context;
    context.save();
    var data = this.data;
    var barSpacing = this.width / data.length;
    var unitHeight = this.height / this.range;

    for (var n = 0; n < data.length; n++) {
        var bar = data[n];
```

```
        var barHeight = (data[n].value - this.minValue) *
unitHeight;

        /*
         * if bar height is less than zero, this means that its
         * value is less than the min value.  Since we don't want
to draw
         * bars below the x-axis, only draw bars whose height is
greater
         * than zero
         */
        if (barHeight > 0) {
            context.save();
            context.translate(Math.round(this.x + ((n + 1 / 2) *
barSpacing)), Math.round(this.y + this.height));
            /*
             * for convenience, we can draw the bars upside down
             * starting at the x-axis and then flip
             * them back into the correct orientation using
             * scale(1, -1).  This is a great example of how
             * transformations can help reduce computations
             */
            context.scale(1, -1);

            context.beginPath();
            context.rect(-this.barWidth / 2, 0, this.barWidth,
barHeight);
            context.fillStyle = this.color;
            context.fill();
            context.restore();
        }
    }
    context.restore();
};
```

7. Define the `drawGridlines()` method which draws horizontal gridlines on the bar chart:

```
BarChart.prototype.drawGridlines = function(){
    var context = this.context;
    context.save();
    context.strokeStyle = this.gridColor;
    context.lineWidth = 2;

    // draw y axis grid lines
    for (var n = 0; n < this.numGridLines; n++) {
```

```
            var y = (n * this.height / this.numGridLines) + this.y;
            context.beginPath();
            context.moveTo(this.x, y);
            context.lineTo(this.x + this.width, y);
            context.stroke();
        }
        context.restore();
    };
```

8. Define the `drawXAxis()` method which draws the x axis:

```
BarChart.prototype.drawXAxis = function(){
    var context = this.context;
    context.save();
    context.beginPath();
    context.moveTo(this.x, this.y + this.height);
    context.lineTo(this.x + this.width, this.y + this.height);
    context.strokeStyle = this.axisColor;
    context.lineWidth = 2;
    context.stroke();
    context.restore();
};
```

9. Define the `drawYAxis()` method which draws the y axis:

```
BarChart.prototype.drawYAxis = function(){
    var context = this.context;
    context.save();
    context.beginPath();
    context.moveTo(this.x, this.y);
    context.lineTo(this.x, this.height + this.y);
    context.strokeStyle = this.axisColor;
    context.lineWidth = 2;
    context.stroke();
    context.restore();
};
```

10. When the page loads, build the data and instantiate a new `BarChart` object:

```
window.onload = function(){
    var data = [{
        label: "Eating",
        value: 2
    }, {
        label: "Working",
        value: 8
    }, {
```

```
            label: "Sleeping",
            value: 8
        }, {
            label: "Errands",
            value: 2
        }, {
            label: "Entertainment",
            value: 4
        }];

        new BarChart({
            canvasId: "myCanvas",
            data: data,
            color: "blue",
            barWidth: 50,
            minValue: 0,
            maxValue: 10,
            gridLineIncrement: 2
        });
    };
```

11. Embed the canvas inside the body of the HTML document:

```
<canvas id="myCanvas" width="600" height="300" style="border:1px
solid black;">
</canvas>
```

How it works...

In contrast to a pie chart, a bar chart will need a bit more configuration to make it truly generic. For our implementation of the `BarChart` class, we'll need to pass in the canvas id, an array of data elements, the bar colors, the bar widths, the grid line increment which is the number of units between grid lines, the max value and the min value. The `BarChart` constructor uses six methods to render the bar chart—`drawGridlines()`, `drawYAxis()`, `drawXAxis()`, `drawBars()`, `drawYValues()`, and `drawXLabels()`.

The key to the `BarChart` class is the `drawBars()` method that iterates over all of the data elements, and then draws a rectangle for each one. The easiest way to draw each bar is to first invert the context vertically (so that positive values of y go up and not down), position the cursor on the x axis, and then draw a rectangle downwards whose height is equal to the value of the data element. As the context is inverted vertically, the bar will actually rise upwards.

See also...

- *Working with text* in *Chapter 1*
- *Drawing a rectangle* in *Chapter 2*
- *Translating the canvas context* in *Chapter 4*
- *Rotating the canvas context* in *Chapter 4*
- *Creating a mirror transform* in *Chapter 4*

Graphing equations

In this recipe, we'll create a configurable Graph class that draws the x and y axis with tick marks and values, and then we'll construct a method called `drawEquation()` that allows us to graph f(x) functions. We'll instantiate a Graph object and then draw a sine wave, a parabolic equation, and a linear equation.

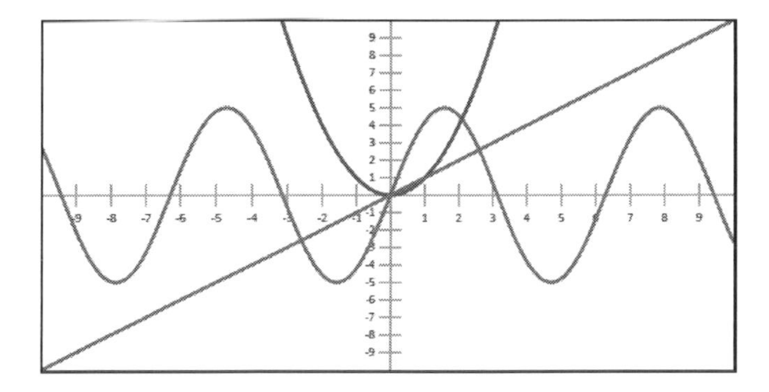

How to do it...

Follow these steps to create a Graph class that can draw an x and y axis with values, and also graph multiple f(x) equations:

1. Define the constructor for the `Graph` class that draws the x and y axis:

```
function Graph(config){
    // user defined properties
    this.canvas = document.getElementById(config.canvasId);
    this.minX = config.minX;
    this.minY = config.minY;
    this.maxX = config.maxX;
    this.maxY = config.maxY;
    this.unitsPerTick = config.unitsPerTick;
```

```
    // constants
    this.axisColor = "#aaa";
    this.font = "8pt Calibri";
    this.tickSize = 20;

    // relationships
    this.context = this.canvas.getContext("2d");
    this.rangeX = this.maxX - this.minX;
    this.rangeY = this.maxY - this.minY;
    this.unitX = this.canvas.width / this.rangeX;
    this.unitY = this.canvas.height / this.rangeY;
    this.centerY = Math.round(Math.abs(this.minY / this.rangeY) *
this.canvas.height);
    this.centerX = Math.round(Math.abs(this.minX / this.rangeX) *
this.canvas.width);
    this.iteration = (this.maxX - this.minX) / 1000;
    this.scaleX = this.canvas.width / this.rangeX;
    this.scaleY = this.canvas.height / this.rangeY;

    // draw x and y axis
    this.drawXAxis();
    this.drawYAxis();
}
```

2. Define the `drawXAxis()` method which draws the x axis:

```
Graph.prototype.drawXAxis = function(){
    var context = this.context;
    context.save();
    context.beginPath();
    context.moveTo(0, this.centerY);
    context.lineTo(this.canvas.width, this.centerY);
    context.strokeStyle = this.axisColor;
    context.lineWidth = 2;
    context.stroke();

    // draw tick marks
    var xPosIncrement = this.unitsPerTick * this.unitX;
    var xPos, unit;
    context.font = this.font;
    context.textAlign = "center";
    context.textBaseline = "top";

    // draw left tick marks
    xPos = this.centerX - xPosIncrement;
```

```
    unit = -1 * this.unitsPerTick;
    while (xPos > 0) {
        context.moveTo(xPos, this.centerY - this.tickSize / 2);
        context.lineTo(xPos, this.centerY + this.tickSize / 2);
        context.stroke();
        context.fillText(unit, xPos, this.centerY + this.tickSize
/ 2 + 3);
        unit -= this.unitsPerTick;
        xPos = Math.round(xPos - xPosIncrement);
    }
    // draw right tick marks
    xPos = this.centerX + xPosIncrement;
    unit = this.unitsPerTick;
    while (xPos < this.canvas.width) {
        context.moveTo(xPos, this.centerY - this.tickSize / 2);
        context.lineTo(xPos, this.centerY + this.tickSize / 2);
        context.stroke();
        context.fillText(unit, xPos, this.centerY + this.tickSize
/ 2 + 3);
        unit += this.unitsPerTick;
        xPos = Math.round(xPos + xPosIncrement);
    }
    context.restore();
};
```

3. Define the `drawYAxis()` method which draws the y axis:

```
Graph.prototype.drawYAxis = function(){
    var context = this.context;
    context.save();
    context.beginPath();
    context.moveTo(this.centerX, 0);
    context.lineTo(this.centerX, this.canvas.height);
    context.strokeStyle = this.axisColor;
    context.lineWidth = 2;
    context.stroke();

    // draw tick marks
    var yPosIncrement = this.unitsPerTick * this.unitY;
    var yPos, unit;
    context.font = this.font;
    context.textAlign = "right";
    context.textBaseline = "middle";

    // draw top tick marks
```

```
        yPos = this.centerY - yPosIncrement;
        unit = this.unitsPerTick;
        while (yPos > 0) {
            context.moveTo(this.centerX - this.tickSize / 2, yPos);
            context.lineTo(this.centerX + this.tickSize / 2, yPos);
            context.stroke();
            context.fillText(unit, this.centerX - this.tickSize / 2 -
    3, yPos);
            unit += this.unitsPerTick;
            yPos = Math.round(yPos - yPosIncrement);
        }

        // draw bottom tick marks
        yPos = this.centerY + yPosIncrement;
        unit = -1 * this.unitsPerTick;
        while (yPos < this.canvas.height) {
            context.moveTo(this.centerX - this.tickSize / 2, yPos);
            context.lineTo(this.centerX + this.tickSize / 2, yPos);
            context.stroke();
            context.fillText(unit, this.centerX - this.tickSize / 2 -
    3, yPos);
            unit -= this.unitsPerTick;
            yPos = Math.round(yPos + yPosIncrement);
        }
        context.restore();
    };
```

4. Define the `drawEquation()` method which takes in a function f(x) and then draws the equation by looping through incremental values of x from `minX` to `maxX`:

```
Graph.prototype.drawEquation = function(equation, color,
thickness){
    var context = this.context;
    context.save();
    context.save();
    this.transformContext();

    context.beginPath();
    context.moveTo(this.minX, equation(this.minX));

    for (var x = this.minX + this.iteration; x <= this.maxX; x +=
this.iteration) {
        context.lineTo(x, equation(x));
    }

    context.restore();
```

```
        context.lineJoin = "round";
        context.lineWidth = thickness;
        context.strokeStyle = color;
        context.stroke();
        context.restore();
    };
```

5. Define the `transformContext()` method which translates the context to the center of the graph, stretches the graph to fit the canvas, and then inverts the y axis:

```
Graph.prototype.transformContext = function(){
    var context = this.context;

    // move context to center of canvas
    this.context.translate(this.centerX, this.centerY);

    /*
     * stretch grid to fit the canvas window, and
     * invert the y scale so that increments
     * as you move upwards
     */
    context.scale(this.scaleX, -this.scaleY);
};
```

6. When the page loads, instantiate a new `Graph` object, and then draw three equations using the `drawEquation()` method:

```
window.onload = function(){
    var myGraph = new Graph({
        canvasId: "myCanvas",
        minX: -10,
        minY: -10,
        maxX: 10,
        maxY: 10,
        unitsPerTick: 1
    });

    myGraph.drawEquation(function(x){
        return 5 * Math.sin(x);
    }, "green", 3);

    myGraph.drawEquation(function(x){
        return x * x;
    }, "blue", 3);

    myGraph.drawEquation(function(x){
        return 1 * x;
    }, "red", 3);
};
```

7. Embed the canvas inside the body of the HTML document:

```
<canvas id="myCanvas" width="600" height="300" style="border:1px
solid black;">
</canvas>
```

How it works...

Our `Graph` class only requires six parameters, the `canvasId`, `minX`, `minY`, `maxX`, `maxY`, and `unitsPerTick`. When instantiated, it draws the x axis with the `drawXAxis()` method and the y axis with the `drawYAxis()` method.

The real gem of the `Graph` object is the `drawEquation()` method that takes in an equation f(x), a line color, and a line thickness. Although the method is relatively short (about 20 lines of code), it's actually quite powerful. Here's how it works:

1. First, call the `transformContext()` method which positions the canvas context, scales the context to fit the canvas, and inverts the y axis with the `scale()` method by multiplying the y component by -1. This makes the drawing process much simpler because increasing y values will go upwards and not downwards (remember that by default, y increases as you move downwards).
2. Once the canvas context has been prepared, use the `equation` function to determine the y value when x equals `minX`, that is, f(minX).
3. Move the drawing cursor with `moveTo()`.
4. With a `for` loop, slightly increment the x value and determine the corresponding y value using the equation f(x) for each iteration.
5. Draw a line from the last point to the current point with `lineTo()`.
6. Continue looping until x equals `maxX`.

As the lines drawn are extremely small with each iteration, they are invisible to the human eye, resulting in the illusion of smooth curves.

When the page loads, we can instantiate a new `Graph` object, and then graph a green sine wave, a blue parabolic equation, and a red linear equation by calling the `drawEquation()` method.

See also...

- *Drawing a line* in *Chapter 1*
- *Working with text* in *Chapter 1*
- *Translating the canvas context* in *Chapter 4*
- *Scaling the canvas context* in *Chapter 4*
- *Creating a mirror transform* in *Chapter 4*

Plotting data points with a line chart

If you've ever taken a science class, you're probably familiar with generating line charts based on a set of data for your experiments. Line charts are probably one of the most useful data visualizations when communicating data trends. In this recipe, we'll create a configurable Line Chart class which takes in an array of data elements and plots each point while connecting the points with line segments.

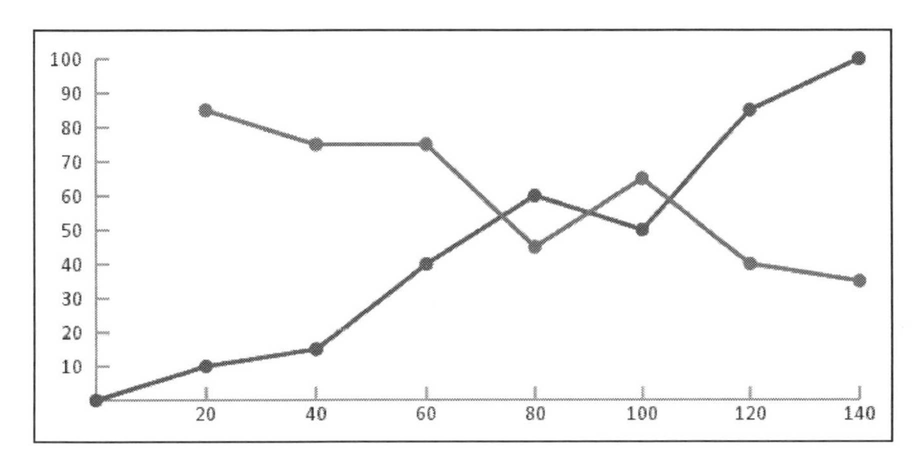

How to do it...

Follow these steps to create a Line Chart class that can automatically position and size a line chart from an array of data:

1. Define the constructor for the `LineChart` class that draws the x and y axis:

```
function LineChart(config){
    // user defined properties
    this.canvas = document.getElementById(config.canvasId);
    this.minX = config.minX;
    this.minY = config.minY;
    this.maxX = config.maxX;
    this.maxY = config.maxY;
    this.unitsPerTickX = config.unitsPerTickX;
    this.unitsPerTickY = config.unitsPerTickY;

    // constants
    this.padding = 10;
    this.tickSize = 10;
    this.axisColor = "#555";
    this.pointRadius = 5;
```

```
    this.font = "12pt Calibri";
    /*
     * measureText does not provide a text height
     * metric, so we'll have to hardcode a text height
     * value
     */
    this.fontHeight = 12;
    // relationships
    this.context = this.canvas.getContext("2d");
    this.rangeX = this.maxX - this.minY;
    this.rangeY = this.maxY - this.minY;
    this.numXTicks = Math.round(this.rangeX / this.unitsPerTickX);
    this.numYTicks = Math.round(this.rangeY / this.unitsPerTickY);
    this.x = this.getLongestValueWidth() + this.padding * 2;
    this.y = this.padding * 2;
    this.width = this.canvas.width - this.x - this.padding * 2;
    this.height = this.canvas.height - this.y - this.padding -
this.fontHeight;
    this.scaleX = this.width / this.rangeX;
    this.scaleY = this.height / this.rangeY;

    // draw x y axis and tick marks
    this.drawXAxis();
    this.drawYAxis();
}
```

2. Define the `getLongestValueWidth()` method which returns the length in pixels of the longest value text:

```
LineChart.prototype.getLongestValueWidth = function(){
    this.context.font = this.font;
    var longestValueWidth = 0;
    for (var n = 0; n <= this.numYTicks; n++) {
        var value = this.maxY - (n * this.unitsPerTickY);
        longestValueWidth = Math.max(longestValueWidth, this.
context.measureText(value).width);
    }
    return longestValueWidth;
};
```

3. Define the `drawXAxis()` method which draws the x axis and the labels:

```
LineChart.prototype.drawXAxis = function(){
    var context = this.context;
    context.save();
    context.beginPath();
    context.moveTo(this.x, this.y + this.height);
```

```
        context.lineTo(this.x + this.width, this.y + this.height);
        context.strokeStyle = this.axisColor;
        context.lineWidth = 2;
        context.stroke();

        // draw tick marks
        for (var n = 0; n < this.numXTicks; n++) {
            context.beginPath();
            context.moveTo((n + 1) * this.width / this.numXTicks +
    this.x, this.y + this.height);
            context.lineTo((n + 1) * this.width / this.numXTicks +
    this.x, this.y + this.height - this.tickSize);
            context.stroke();
        }

        // draw labels
        context.font = this.font;
        context.fillStyle = "black";
        context.textAlign = "center";
        context.textBaseline = "middle";

        for (var n = 0; n < this.numXTicks; n++) {
            var label = Math.round((n + 1) * this.maxX / this.
    numXTicks);
            context.save();
            context.translate((n + 1) * this.width / this.numXTicks +
    this.x, this.y + this.height + this.padding);
            context.fillText(label, 0, 0);
            context.restore();
        }
        context.restore();
    };
```

4. Define the `drawYAxis()` method which draws the y axis and the values:

```
    LineChart.prototype.drawYAxis = function(){
        var context = this.context;
        context.save();
        context.save();
        context.beginPath();
        context.moveTo(this.x, this.y);
        context.lineTo(this.x, this.y + this.height);
        context.strokeStyle = this.axisColor;
        context.lineWidth = 2;
        context.stroke();
        context.restore();
```

```
    // draw tick marks
    for (var n = 0; n < this.numYTicks; n++) {
        context.beginPath();
        context.moveTo(this.x, n * this.height / this.numYTicks +
this.y);
        context.lineTo(this.x + this.tickSize, n * this.height /
this.numYTicks + this.y);
        context.stroke();
    }

    // draw values
    context.font = this.font;
    context.fillStyle = "black";
    context.textAlign = "right";
    context.textBaseline = "middle";

    for (var n = 0; n < this.numYTicks; n++) {
        var value = Math.round(this.maxY - n * this.maxY / this.
numYTicks);
        context.save();
        context.translate(this.x - this.padding, n * this.height /
this.numYTicks + this.y);
        context.fillText(value, 0, 0);
        context.restore();
    }
    context.restore();
};
```

5. Define the `drawLine()` method which loops through the data points and draws line segments connecting each data point:

```
LineChart.prototype.drawLine = function(data, color, width){
    var context = this.context;
    context.save();
    this.transformContext();
    context.lineWidth = width;
    context.strokeStyle = color;
    context.fillStyle = color;
    context.beginPath();
    context.moveTo(data[0].x * this.scaleX, data[0].y * this.
scaleY);

    for (var n = 0; n < data.length; n++) {
        var point = data[n];

        // draw segment
```

```
        context.lineTo(point.x * this.scaleX, point.y * this.
scaleY);
        context.stroke();
        context.closePath();
        context.beginPath();
        context.arc(point.x * this.scaleX, point.y * this.scaleY,
this.pointRadius, 0, 2 * Math.PI, false);
        context.fill();
        context.closePath();

        // position for next segment
        context.beginPath();
        context.moveTo(point.x * this.scaleX, point.y * this.
scaleY);
    }
    context.restore();
};
```

6. Define the `transformContext()` method which translates the context and then inverts the context vertically:

```
LineChart.prototype.transformContext = function(){
    var context = this.context;

    // move context to center of canvas
    this.context.translate(this.x, this.y + this.height);

    // invert the y scale so that that increments
    // as you move upwards
    context.scale(1, -1);
};
```

7. When the page loads, instantiate a `LineChart` object, create a data set for the blue line, plot the line using `drawLine()`, define another data set for the red line, and then plot the red line:

```
window.onload = function(){
    var myLineChart = new LineChart({
        canvasId: "myCanvas",
        minX: 0,
        minY: 0,
        maxX: 140,
        maxY: 100,
        unitsPerTickX: 10,
        unitsPerTickY: 10
    });
```

```
var data = [{
    x: 0,
    y: 0
}, {
    x: 20,
    y: 10
}, {
    x: 40,
    y: 15
}, {
    x: 60,
    y: 40
}, {
    x: 80,
    y: 60
}, {
    x: 100,
    y: 50
}, {
    x: 120,
    y: 85
}, {
    x: 140,
    y: 100
}];

myLineChart.drawLine(data, "blue", 3);

var data = [{
    x: 20,
    y: 85
}, {
    x: 40,
    y: 75
}, {
    x: 60,
    y: 75
}, {
    x: 80,
    y: 45
}, {
    x: 100,
    y: 65
}, {
```

```
            x: 120,
            y: 40
        }, {
            x: 140,
            y: 35
        }];

        myLineChart.drawLine(data, "red", 3);
    };
```

8. Embed the canvas inside the body of the HTML document:

```
<canvas id="myCanvas" width="600" height="300" style="border:1px
solid black;">
</canvas>
```

How it works...

To start off, we'll need to configure the `LineChart` object with seven properties, including the `canvasId`, `minX`, `minY`, `maxX`, `maxY`, `unitsPerTickX`, and `unitsPerTickY`. When the `LineChart` object is instantiated, we'll render the x axis and the y axis.

Most of the interesting stuff happens in the `drawLine()` method, which requires an array of data elements, a line color, and a line thickness. Here's how it works:

1. Use `transformContext()` to translate, scale, and invert the context.
2. Position the drawing cursor at the first data point from the data array with the `moveTo()` method.
3. Loop through all of the data elements, draw a line from the previous point to the current point, and then draw a small circle at the current position using the `arc()` method.

Once the page loads, we can instantiate the `LineChart` object, create an array of data points for the blue line, draw the line using the `drawLine()` method, create another array of data points for the red line, and then draw the red line.

See also...

- *Drawing a line* in *Chapter 1*
- *Working with text* in *Chapter 1*
- *Drawing a circle* in *Chapter 2*
- *Translating the canvas context* in *Chapter 4*

8
Saving the World with Game Development

In this chapter, we will cover:

- Creating sprite sheets for the hero and enemies
- Creating level images and boundary maps
- Creating an Actor class for the hero and enemies
- Creating a Level class
- Creating a Health Bar class
- Creating a Controller class
- Creating a Model class
- Creating a View class
- Setting up the HTML document and starting the game

Introduction

I wouldn't be surprised if some of you bought this book solely for this chapter—after all, what fun is it to master the HTML5 canvas without being able to create your own video games? Of all the chapters in this book, this chapter was by far my favorite (with the next chapter being a close second). We might not actually be able to save the world with game development, but it sure is fun to create our own virtual worlds and save those instead. In this chapter, we're going to pull all of our new found knowledge together to create Canvas Hero, a side-scroller action game starring the Canvas Hero, who can run, jump, levitate, and punch through a futuristic world full of menacing bad guys. Here are some of the features of the game:

- The hero can run left, run right, jump, and punch to attack
- The level will look futuristic

- The level will be full of enemies running around looking for trouble
- The level will have a foreground image that moves to the left and to the right as the player moves, and will also have a stationary background image to create depth
- The player can jump high enough to jump over bad guys and avoid getting punched
- When either the player or the enemies are hit, they will flash white to show that they have sustained damage
- Gravity will act on the player at all times
- The player cannot fall through the floor, run through walls, or jump through the ceiling
- Although the hero can jump very high, there will be strategically placed levitation pods throughout the level to give the player a vertical boost so that he can reach high-up platforms
- The game is over when the player's health drops to zero or if the player falls into a hole
- The player wins the game when all of the bad guys have been defeated

And here are a few screenshots to give you an idea of what the game will look like when we're done:

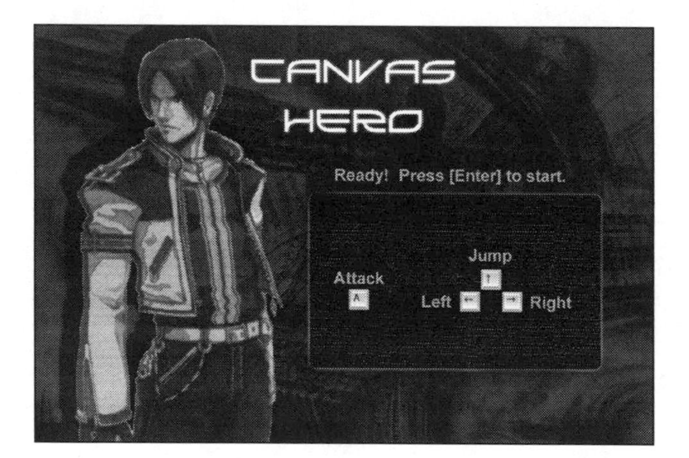

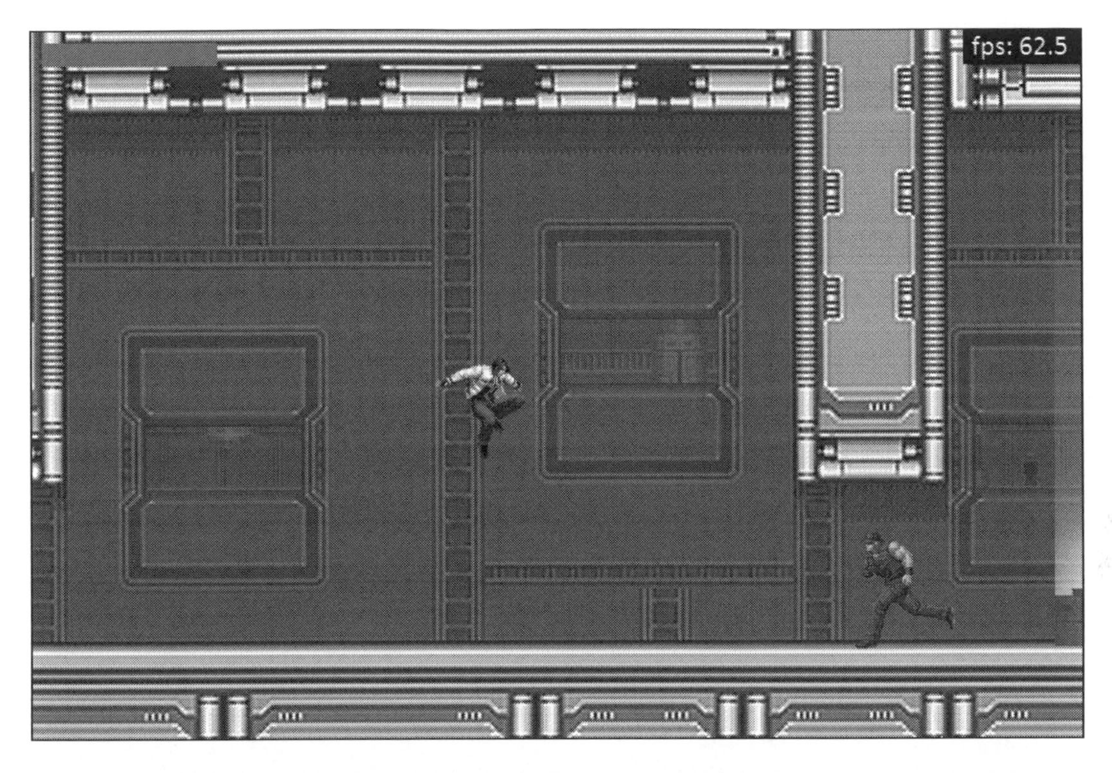
fps: 62.5

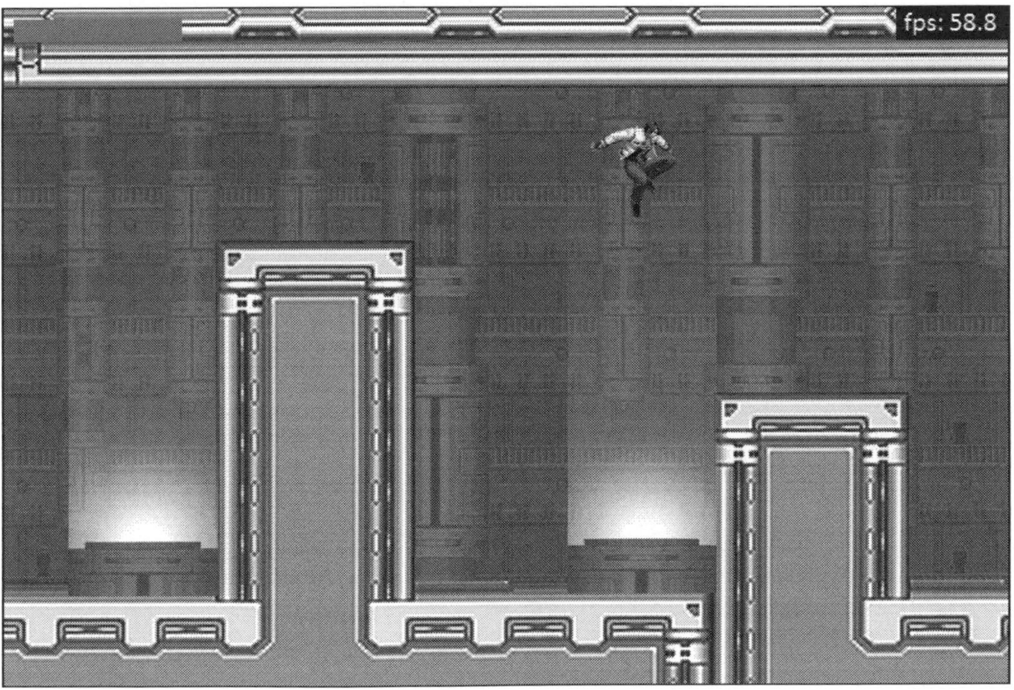
fps: 58.8

The first two recipes of this chapter cover techniques for creating the sprite sheets for the hero and bad guys as well as the level image and boundary map image. The next three recipes cover steps for creating classes for the hero, bad guys, level, and health bar objects. Recipes after that cover the **MVC** (**model**, **view**, **controller**) architecture of the game, and the last recipe will cover the HTML markup. Let's get started!

Creating sprite sheets for the heroes and enemies

Sprite sheets are image files that contain snapshots of different motions for different players and enemies that will appear in the game. Sprite sheets are an alternative to working with dozens or hundreds of individual images which can impact the initial loading time and also become a nightmare for graphic artists to maintain. Canvas Hero contains a sprite sheet for the hero, a sprite sheet for the bad guys, and also a set of white sprite sheets used when either the hero or the bad guys sustain damage.

Getting ready...

Before we get started, it's worth noting that even the most talented of game artists can spend more time creating game graphics than the time it takes to code a game, which is something that's often times overlooked. For Canvas Hero, we can make life easier for ourselves by downloading some sprites from my favorite sprite resource, `http://www.spriters-resource.com`, which is a free website containing a huge collection of sprite sheets and level images of classic old-school games.

How to do it

Once we find suitable sprite sheets for the hero and the bad guys, we can crop out the sprites we need and then put together a sprite sheet using Adobe Photoshop, Gimp, or some other image editing software. Here's the finished hero sprite sheet:

As you can see, the hero sprite sheet contains four motions, one for standing, one for jumping, one for running, and one for punching (from top to bottom). When creating a sprite sheet, it's important that all of the sprite images fit inside a defined sprite size. For Canvas Hero, each sprite image fits inside a square that's 144 x 144 px. We should also ensure that each sprite image is facing the same direction because we can programmatically flip these images horizontally when we want to render a sprite that's facing the other direction.

Likewise, we can use this same process to create a sprite sheet for the bad guys as well:

You'll notice that the bad guy sprite sheet is much simpler than the hero sprite sheet, simply because their movements are limited to running around and fighting (they never stand still or jump). For consistency, we can make the bad guy sprites 144 x 144 px as well.

Creating level images and boundary maps

Now that we have sprite sheets for the hero and the bad guys, it's time to create a virtual world for them to live in. In Canvas Hero, our virtual world will be a single level that moves left and right as the player moves through it, which will contain walls, a ceiling, a floor, platforms, and holes. In this recipe, we'll go over the steps for making a level image as well as a boundary map image that graphically contains information about the bounds of the level and also identifies special zones with different colors.

How to do it...

To create the level image for Canvas Hero, we can use some prebuilt graphics downloaded from `http://www.spriters-resource.com` and add in new platforms, holes, and levitators using Photoshop, Gimp, or some other image editor of your choice. To keep the level somewhat small in size, we can create a foreground level image that's 6944 x 600 px. The canvas, which is 900 x 600 px, will act as a viewing window to the level. Here's a snapshot of a portion of the level which contains a transparent foreground and a couple of levitator pods:

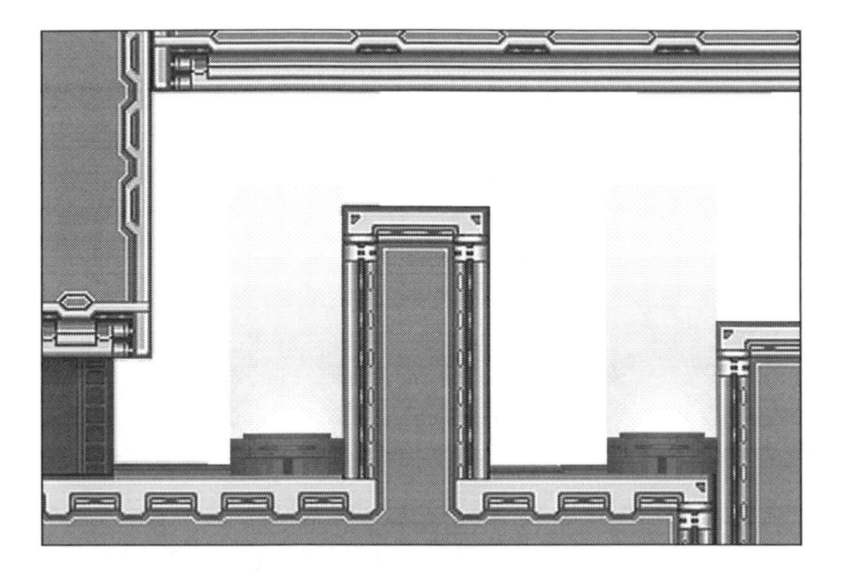

Next, we can create a background image to create the illusion of depth. Here's the finished background image for Canvas Hero:

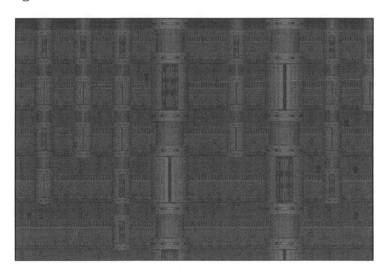

And here's how the foreground and background images look together:

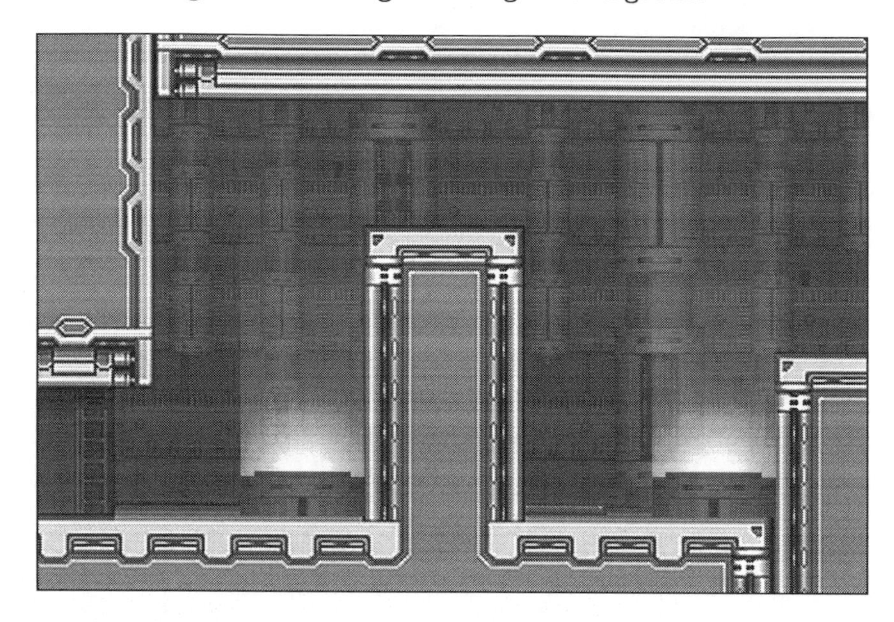

Once we have the foreground and background images completed, our next step is to create a boundary map. A boundary map is a graphical way to bound the player inside certain areas and also define special zones.

To create the boundary map for Canvas Hero, we can start with a black background juxtaposed on top of the level image, and then draw magenta rectangles where the actors can run freely, and also add cyan rectangles to represent levitation zones. Keeping the background image a solid color helps reduce the boundary map image size and cuts down on the image loading time. The following image is a section of the boundary map that corresponds to the preceding image:

How it works...

To better understand how boundary maps work, let's walk through the player's steps as he navigates through the preceding screen from left to right. Also keep in mind that the player's x ,y position is in the center of the sprite image which is about level with the hero's hip:

- Starting from the left, notice that the magenta portion, RGB (255, 0, 255), of the boundary map is extremely thin (only about 10 px or so). This region corresponds to the small space that the player can reside beneath the low hanging ceiling above his head. If the player were to jump while in this region, his vertical ascent would be prevented.
- Once the hero walks past the low hanging ceiling, he'll come up to a levitation pod. Notice that there is plenty of vertical magenta space for him to jump upwards and into the levitation zone, which is cyan, RGB (0, 255, 255).
- Once the player is inside of a cyan zone, he'll begin to float upwards until he can reach the platform in the middle of the screen.
- When the player is on the platform, the ceiling is right above his head which prevents him from jumping.
- The player can continue walking to the right and then fall off the platform towards the ground.
- Once on the ground, the player can jump into a second levitation zone identified by the cyan rectangle, which boosts him up onto the next platform.

There's more...

There's more to it!

Boundary map alternative

If you'd rather not use a boundary map to define the level boundaries, you might consider constructing a large array of boundary points that define zones in space where the player can reside. The downside of this approach is that as the levels become large and complex, maintenance of the array can be quite time consuming. Additionally, this method can incur a significant performance overhead by constantly looping through the array and performing boundary calculations for each animation frame.

Level image alternatives

To keep this chapter as simple as possible, we chose to create the level with one large image. This image, unfortunately, is the main bottleneck when loading the game. Although the other images are small in size, including the boundary map, the level image is about 1.6 MB and can take a few seconds to load. If your levels are large, or you're simply trying to make the game load as fast as possible, you might consider one of these alternatives:

- **Lazy Loader**—A lazy loader will request sections of the level based on the player's location such that only the visible and surrounding blocks of a level are downloaded rather than downloading the entire level image at once. The upside of this approach is an improved initial loading time, and the downside of this approach is that you have to programmatically manage which sections of the level are downloaded at which times.
- **Tiled Layout**—A tiled layout is a level that's constructed from tile images. In other words, you could create small tiled images (say 30 x 30 px) that make up the textures for the floor, the walls, the ceilings, the levitator pods, and so on, and then use those images to build the level. The upside of this approach is that there's virtually no loading time since the images are so small, and the downside is that the levels can start to look a little redundant and uninteresting .

Creating an Actor class for the hero and enemies

Now that we have all the main images set up and ready to go, it's time for the fun part (at least in my opinion) as we bring our virtual world to life with JavaScript and HTML5 canvas. Our first order of business is to create an Actor class which contains properties and methods for both the hero and the bad guys. In other words, both the hero and the bad guys will be instances of the Actor class. The Actor class will be responsible for directing the actors with methods such as `moveRight()` and `moveLeft()`, and is also responsible for rendering the actors by animating them with sprite sheets.

How to do it...

Follow these steps to create an Actor class which can be used to instantiate the hero or the bad guys:

1. Define the `Actor` constructor:

```
/*
 * Actor class should have no knowledge
 * of the Level or HealthBar classes to
 * keep it decoupled
 */
function Actor(config){
```

```
        this.controller = config.controller;
        this.normalSpriteSheet = config.normalSpriteSheet;
        this.hitSpriteSheet = config.hitSpriteSheet;
        this.x = config.x; // absolute x
        this.y = config.y; // absolute y
        this.playerSpeed = config.playerSpeed; // px / s
        this.motions = config.motions;
        this.startMotion = config.startMotion;
        this.facingRight = config.facingRight;
        this.moving = config.moving;
        this.spriteInterval = config.spriteInterval; // ms
        this.maxHealth = config.maxHealth;
        this.attackRange = config.attackRange;
        this.minAttackInterval = config.minAttackInterval;

        this.SPRITE_SIZE = 144;
        this.FADE_RATE = 1; // full fade in 1s
        this.spriteSheet = this.normalSpriteSheet;
        this.vx = 0;
        this.vy = 0;
        this.spriteSeq = 0;
        this.motion = this.startMotion;
        this.lastMotion = this.motion;
        this.airborne = false;
        this.attacking = false;
        this.canAttack = true;
        this.health = this.maxHealth;
        this.alive = true;
        this.opacity = 1;
        this.timeSinceLastSpriteFrame = 0;
    }
```

2. Define the `attack()` method which triggers an attack:

```
Actor.prototype.attack = function(){
    this.attacking = true;
    this.canAttack = false;
    var that = this;
    setTimeout(function(){
        that.canAttack = true;
    }, this.minAttackInterval);
};
```

3. Define the `stop()` method which stops the actor from moving:

```
Actor.prototype.stop = function(){
    this.moving = false;
};
```

4. Define the `isFacingRight()` method:

```
Actor.prototype.isFacingRight = function(){
    return this.facingRight;
};
```

5. Define the `moveRight()` method:

```
Actor.prototype.moveRight = function(){
    this.moving = true;
    this.facingRight = true;
};
```

6. Define the `moveLeft()` method:

```
Actor.prototype.moveLeft = function(){
    this.moving = true;
    this.facingRight = false;
};
```

7. Define the `jump()` method which triggers the actor to jump:

```
Actor.prototype.jump = function(){
    if (!this.airborne) {
        this.airborne = true;
        this.vy = -1;
    }
};
```

8. Define the `draw()` method:

```
Actor.prototype.draw = function(pos){
    var context = this.controller.view.context;
    var sourceX = this.spriteSeq * this.SPRITE_SIZE;
    var sourceY = this.motion.index * this.SPRITE_SIZE;

    context.save();
    context.translate(pos.x, pos.y);

    if (this.facingRight) {
        context.translate(this.SPRITE_SIZE, 0);
        context.scale(-1, 1);
    }
```

```
    context.globalAlpha = this.opacity;
    context.drawImage(this.spriteSheet, sourceX, sourceY, this.
SPRITE_SIZE, this.SPRITE_SIZE, 0, 0, this.SPRITE_SIZE, this.
SPRITE_SIZE);
    context.restore();
};
```

9. Define the `fade()` method which fades the actor when he's defeated:

```
Actor.prototype.fade = function(){
  var opacityChange = this.controller.anim.getTimeInterval() *
this.FADE_RATE / 1000;
    this.opacity -= opacityChange;
    if (this.opacity < 0) {
        this.opacity = 0;
    }
};
```

10. Define the `updateSpriteMotion()` method:

```
Actor.prototype.updateSpriteMotion = function(){
  // if attack sequence has finished, set attacking = false
    if (this.attacking && this.spriteSeq == this.motion.numSprites
- 1) {
        this.attacking = false;
    }

    if (this.attacking) {
        this.motion = this.motions.ATTACKING;
    }
    else {
        if (this.airborne) {
            this.motion = this.motions.AIRBORNE;
        }
        else {
            this.vy = 0;
            if (this.moving) {
                this.motion = this.motions.RUNNING;
            }
            else {
                this.motion = this.motions.STANDING;
            }
        }
    }
};
```

11. Define the `updateSpriteSeqNum()` method which increments or resets the sprite sequence number for each sprite interval:

```
Actor.prototype.updateSpriteSeqNum = function() {
    var anim = this.controller.anim;
    this.timeSinceLastSpriteFrame += anim.getTimeInterval();

    if (this.timeSinceLastSpriteFrame > this.spriteInterval) {
        if (this.spriteSeq < this.motion.numSprites - 1) {
            this.spriteSeq++;
        }
        else {
            if (this.motion.loop) {
                this.spriteSeq = 0;
            }
        }

        this.timeSinceLastSpriteFrame = 0;
    }

    if (this.motion != this.lastMotion) {
        this.spriteSeq = 0;
        this.lastMotion = this.motion;
    }
};
```

12. Define the `damage()` method which decrements the actor's health and sets the sprite sheet to the hit sprite sheet, causing the actor to flash white for a brief moment:

```
Actor.prototype.damage = function(){
    this.health = this.health <= 0 ? 0 : this.health - 1;

    this.spriteSheet = this.hitSpriteSheet;
    var that = this;
    setTimeout(function(){
        that.spriteSheet = that.normalSpriteSheet;
    }, 200);
};
```

13. Define the `getCenter()` method which returns the position of the center of the actor:

```
Actor.prototype.getCenter = function(){
    return {
        x: Math.round(this.x) + this.SPRITE_SIZE / 2,
        y: Math.round(this.y) + this.SPRITE_SIZE / 2
    };
};
```

How it works...

The idea of the `Actor` class is to create a class that can be used to instantiate both the hero and the bad guys. It includes methods for controlling the actor, such as `moveRight()`, `moveLeft()`, `jump()`, and `attack()`, that either the game engine can call or a human player can call. The game engine will use these methods to control the bad guys, and a human player will use these methods to control the hero by pressing keys on the keyboard.

In addition to controls, the `Actor` class also manages the sprite animation by updating the sprite motion with the `updateSpriteMotion()` method and also increments or cycles the sprite sequence number with the `updateSpriteSeqNum()` method.

Finally, the `draw()` method picks out the sprite image corresponding to the actor's motion, flips the image horizontally if the actor is facing to the right, and then draws the actor on the screen using the `drawImage()` method of the canvas context.

See also...

- *Cropping an image* in *Chapter 3*
- *Translating the canvas context* in *Chapter 4*
- *Creating a mirror transform* in *Chapter 4*

Creating a Level class

In this recipe, we'll create a Level class which will be used to render the level and provide an API to the boundary map.

How to do it...

Follow these steps to create a Level class:

1. Define the `Level` constructor:

```
/*
 * Level class should have no knowledge
 * of the Actor or HealthBar classes to
 * keep it decoupled
 */
function Level(config){
  this.controller = config.controller;
    this.x = config.x;
    this.y = config.y;
    this.leftBounds = config.leftBounds;
    this.rightBounds = config.rightBounds;
  this.boundsData = null;
```

```
        this.GRAVITY = 3; // px / second^2
        this.MID_RGB_COMPONENT_VALUE = 128;
        this.LEVEL_WIDTH = 6944;

        this.setBoundsData();
    }
```

2. Define the `setBoundsData()` method which extracts the zone data from the boundary map image:

```
Level.prototype.setBoundsData = function(){
  var controller = this.controller;
  var canvas = controller.view.canvas;
  var context = controller.view.context;
    canvas.width = 6944;
    context.drawImage(controller.images.levelBounds, 0, 0);
    imageData = context.getImageData(0, 0, 6944, 600);
    this.boundsData = imageData.data;
    canvas.width = 900;
};
```

3. Define the `draw()` method which draws the background image and the level image:

```
Level.prototype.draw = function(){
  var context = this.controller.view.context;
    context.drawImage(this.controller.images.background, 0, 0);
    context.drawImage(this.controller.images.level, this.x,
this.y);
};
```

4. Define the `getZoneInfo()` method which returns zone information about a point in the boundary map:

```
Level.prototype.getZoneInfo = function(pos){
  var x = pos.x;
  var y = pos.y;
    var red = this.boundsData[((this.LEVEL_WIDTH * y) + x) * 4];
    var green = this.boundsData[((this.LEVEL_WIDTH * y) + x) * 4 +
1];
    var blue = this.boundsData[((this.LEVEL_WIDTH * y) + x) * 4 +
2];

    var inBounds = false;
    var levitating = false;

    /*
     * COLOR KEY
```

```
         *
         * PINK: 255 0   255
         * CYAN: 0   255 255
         *
         * COLOR NOTATION
         *
         * PINK: player is in bounds and can jump
         * CYAN: player is in bounds and is levitating
         */
      var mid = this.MID_RGB_COMPONENT_VALUE;
        if ((red > mid && green < mid && blue > mid) || (red < mid &&
    green > mid && blue > mid)) {
            inBounds = true;
        }
        if (red < mid && green > mid && blue > mid) {
            levitating = true;
        }

        return {
            inBounds: inBounds,
            levitating: levitating
        };
    };
```

How it works...

Most of the heavy lifting in the `Level` class is done in the `setBoundsData()` method and the `getZoneInfo()` method. The `setBoundsData()` method takes the boundary map image and converts it into an array of pixel data using the `getImageData()` method of the canvas context. The `getZoneInfo()` method is used to access a point in the boundary map and then return the corresponding zone information.

For Canvas Hero, the zone information object contains two flags: `inBounds` and `levitating`. If the corresponding pixel in the boundary map is cyan, then this point corresponds to a zone that's in bounds and is also inside a levitation zone. If the corresponding pixel in the boundary map is magenta, then this point corresponds to a zone that's in bounds but not in a levitation zone. Finally, if the corresponding pixel in the boundary map is black, this means that the point is not in bounds or in a levitation zone.

See also...

- *Drawing an image* in *Chapter 3*
- *Getting image data* in *Chapter 3*

Creating a Health Bar class

In this recipe, we'll create a Health Bar class which is used to update and render the hero's health display.

How to do it...

Follow these steps to create a health bar class:

1. Define the `HealthBar` constructor:

```
/*
 * HealthBar class should have no knowledge
 * of the Actor or Level classes to
 * keep it decoupled
 */
function HealthBar(config){
  this.controller = config.controller;
    this.maxHealth = config.maxHealth;
    this.x = config.x;
    this.y = config.y;
    this.maxWidth = config.maxWidth;
    this.height = config.height;

    this.health = this.maxHealth;
}
```

2. Define the `setHealth()` method which sets the health value:

```
HealthBar.prototype.setHealth = function(health){
    this.health = health;
};
```

3. Define the `draw()` method which draws the health bar:

```
HealthBar.prototype.draw = function(){
  var context = this.controller.view.context;
    context.beginPath();
    context.rect(this.x, this.y, this.maxWidth, this.height);
    context.fillStyle = "black";
    context.fill();
    context.closePath();

    context.beginPath();
    var width = this.maxWidth * this.health / this.maxHealth;
    context.rect(this.x, this.y, width, this.height);
```

```
        context.fillStyle = "red";
        context.fill();
        context.closePath();
    };
```

How it works...

The `HealthBar` object has a simple constructor that initializes the position and size of the health bar, and it also contains two methods, `setHealth()` and `draw()`. The `setHealth()` method sets the `health` property of the `HealthBar` object, and the `draw()` method draws the health bar using the `rect()` method of the canvas context.

Creating a Controller class

Now that we have all of the images and classes for the objects in the game, our next order of business is to build the game engine. Canvas Hero is built with a standard MVC architecture, which separates the data, the presentation, and the control methods. In this recipe, we'll create a Controller class which is responsible for instantiating the model and view, initializing the game, controlling the game state, and managing keyboard events.

How to do it...

Follow these steps to create the controller for Canvas Hero:

1. Define the `Controller` constructor:

```
/*
 * Game controller
 *
 * The controller is responsible for instantiating
 * the view and the model, initializing the game,
 * controlling the game state, and managing keyboard events
 */
function Controller(canvasId){
    this.imageSources = {
        levelBounds: "img/level_bounds.png",
        level: "img/level.png",
        heroSprites: "img/hero_sprites.png",
        heroHitSprites: "img/hero_hit_sprites.png",
        badGuySprites: "img/bad_guy_sprites.png",
        badGuyHitSprites: "img/bad_guy_hit_sprites.png",
        background: "img/background.png",
        readyScreen: "img/readyScreen.png",
        gameoverScreen: "img/gameoverScreen.png",
```

```
        winScreen: "img/winScreen.png"
    };
    this.images = {};

    this.states = {
        INIT: "INIT",
        READY: "READY",
        PLAYING: "PLAYING",
        WON: "WON",
        GAMEOVER: "GAMEOVER"
    };

  this.keys = {
    ENTER: 13,
    UP: 38,
    LEFT: 37,
    RIGHT: 39,
    A: 65
  };

  this.anim = new Animation(canvasId);
    this.state = this.states.INIT;
    this.model = new Model(this);
    this.view = new View(this);
  this.avgFps = 0;
  this.leftKeyup = true;
  this.rightKeyup = true;
    this.addKeyboardListeners();
    this.loadImages();
}
```

2. Define the `loadImages()` method which loads all of the game images and then calls `initGame()` when they've all loaded:

```
Controller.prototype.loadImages = function(){
  /*
   * we need to load the loading image first
   * so go ahead and insert it into the dom
   * and them load the rest of the images
   */
  this.view.canvas.style.background = "url('img/loadingScreen.
png')";

    var that = this;
    var loadedImages = 0;
```

```
        var numImages = 0;
        for (var src in this.imageSources) {
            numImages++;
        }
        for (var src in this.imageSources) {
            this.images[src] = new Image();
            this.images[src].onload = function(){
                if (++loadedImages >= numImages) {
                    that.initGame();
                }
            };
            this.images[src].src = this.imageSources[src];
        }
    };
```

3. Define the `addKeyboardListeners()` method which attaches keyboard event listeners to the game:

```
    Controller.prototype.addKeyboardListeners = function(){
        var that = this;
        document.onkeydown = function(evt){
            that.handleKeydown(evt);
        };
        document.onkeyup = function(evt){
            that.handleKeyup(evt);
        };
    };
```

4. Define the `handleKeyUp()` method which is fired when a key is released:

```
    Controller.prototype.handleKeyup = function(evt){
        keycode = ((evt.which) || (evt.keyCode));

        switch (keycode) {
            case this.keys.LEFT:
                this.leftKeyup = true;
                if (this.leftKeyup && this.rightKeyup) {
                    this.model.hero.stop();
                }
                break;

            case this.keys.UP:
                break;

            case this.keys.RIGHT:
                this.rightKeyup = true;
```

```
                if (this.leftKeyup && this.rightKeyup) {
                    this.model.hero.stop();
                }
                break;
        }
    };
```

5. Define the `handleKeyDown()` method which is fired when a key is pressed down:

```
    Controller.prototype.handleKeydown = function(evt){
        var that = this;
        keycode = ((evt.which) || (evt.keyCode));
        switch (keycode) {
            case this.keys.ENTER: // enter
                if (this.state == this.states.READY) {
                    this.state = this.states.PLAYING;
                    // start animation
                    this.anim.start();
                }
                else if (this.state == this.states.GAMEOVER || this.
    state == this.states.WON) {
                    this.resetGame();
                    this.state = this.states.PLAYING;
                }
                break;
            case this.keys.LEFT:
                this.leftKeyup = false;
                this.model.hero.moveLeft();
                break;

            case this.keys.UP:
                this.model.hero.jump();
                break;

            case this.keys.RIGHT:
                this.rightKeyup = false;
                this.model.hero.moveRight();
                break;

            case this.keys.A: // attack
              var model = this.model;
          var hero = model.hero;
                hero.attack();
                setTimeout(function(){
                    for (var n = 0; n < model.badGuys.length; n++) {
```

```
                        (function(){
                            var badGuy = model.badGuys[n];
                            if (model.nearby(hero, badGuy)
                 && ((badGuy.x - hero.x > 0 && hero.isFacingRight())
|| (hero.x - badGuy.x > 0 && !hero.isFacingRight()))) {
                                badGuy.damage();
                            }
                        })();
                    }
                }, 200);
                break;
        }
};
```

6. Define the `initGame()` method which initializes the game:

```
Controller.prototype.initGame = function(){
  var model = this.model;
  var view = this.view;
    model.initLevel();
    model.initHero();
    model.initBadGuys();
    model.initHealthBar();

    // set stage method
    this.anim.setStage(function(){
        model.updateStage();
        view.stage();
    });

    // game is now ready to play
    this.state = this.states.READY;
    view.drawScreen(this.images.readyScreen);
};
```

7. Define the `resetGame()` method which resets the game by reinitializing the game objects:

```
Controller.prototype.resetGame = function(){
    var model = this.model;
    model.level = null;
    model.hero = null;
    model.healthBar = null;
    model.badGuys = [];

    model.initLevel();
```

```
        model.initHero();
        model.initBadGuys();
        model.initHealthBar();
    };
```

How it works...

The most important role of a game controller is to control the flow of the game through game states. In Canvas Hero, the first game state is the loading state. This is the state where the player can read about how to play the game as the game loads. Once the game has finished loading, the controller is responsible for changing the game state to the ready state. While in this state, the game waits for the user to press enter to continue. Once the user presses enter, the controller now changes the game state to the play game state.

At this moment, the actual game begins and the user has full control over the hero. If the player's health drops to zero, or if the player falls into a hole, the controller will change the game state to the game over state. If, on the other hand, the player succeeds in defeating all of the enemies, the controller changes the game state to the win state, congratulating the hero on his awesome feat. Take a look at the following state machine:

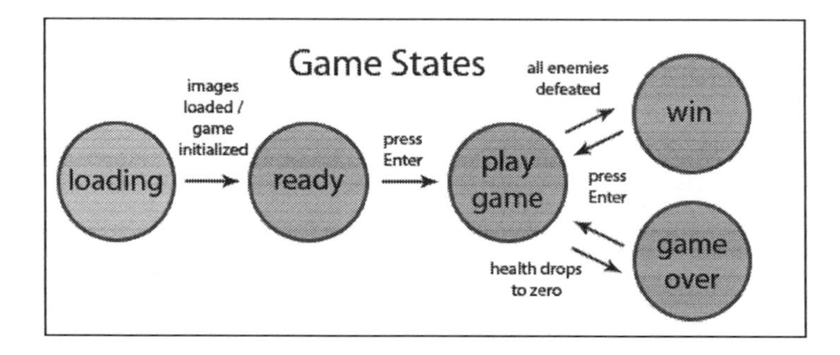

In addition to controlling the game state, the controller is also responsible for managing keyboard events. The keyboard events are attached with the `addKeyboardListeners()` method.

Creating a Model class

In this recipe, we'll create a Model class which is responsible for initializing and updating the hero, the bad guys, the level, and the health bar. These objects can be seen as the "data" of our game.

How to do it...

Follow these steps to create the model for Canvas Hero:

1. Define the `Model` constructor:

```
/*
 * Game model
 *
 * The model is responsible for initializing and
 * updating the hero, level, bad guys, and health bar
 */
function Model(controller){
    this.controller = controller;
    this.healthBar = null;
    this.hero = null;
    this.level = null;
    this.badGuys = []; // array of bad guys
    this.heroCanvasPos = {};
}
```

2. Define the `removeDefeatedBadGuys()` method which loops through the bad guy array and then removes the ones that are no longer alive:

```
Model.prototype.removeDefeatedBadGuys = function(){
    for (var n = 0; n < this.badGuys.length; n++) {
        var badGuy = this.badGuys[n];
        if (!badGuy.alive && badGuy.opacity == 0) {
            this.badGuys.splice(n, 1);
        }
    }
};
```

3. Define the `updateBadGuys()` method:

```
Model.prototype.updateBadGuys = function(){
    var that = this;
    for (var n = 0; n < this.badGuys.length; n++) {
        var badGuy = this.badGuys[n];
        if (badGuy.alive
      && this.hero.alive
      && !badGuy.attacking
      && badGuy.canAttack
      && this.nearby(this.hero, badGuy)
      && ((badGuy.x - this.hero.x > 0 && !badGuy.isFacingRight())
|| (this.hero.x - badGuy.x > 0 && badGuy.isFacingRight()))) {
      badGuy.attack();
```

```
                setTimeout(function(){
                    that.hero.damage();
                }, 200);
            }
            this.updateActor(badGuy);
        }
    };
```

4. Define the `updateStage()` method which updates all of the game objects for each animation frame:

```
Model.prototype.updateStage = function(){
    var controller = this.controller;
    var canvas = controller.view.canvas;
    if (controller.state == controller.states.PLAYING) {
        this.removeDefeatedBadGuys();

        // if hero dies then set state to GAMEOVER
        if (!this.hero.alive && controller.state == controller.
states.PLAYING) {
            controller.state = controller.states.GAMEOVER;
        }

        // if all bad guys defeated, change state to WON
        if (this.badGuys.length == 0) {
            controller.state = controller.states.WON;
        }

        // move bad guys around
        this.moveBadGuys();

        // update level position
        this.updateLevel();

    /*
     * update bad guys and also see
     * if they can attack the hero
     */
        this.updateBadGuys();

        // update hero
        var oldHeroX = this.hero.x;
        this.updateActor(this.hero);
        this.updateHeroCanvasPos(oldHeroX);
```

```
        // update health bar
        this.healthBar.setHealth(this.hero.health);

        // if hero falls into a hole set health to zero
        if (this.hero.y > canvas.height - this.hero.spriteSize * 2
/ 3) {
            this.hero.health = 0;
        }

        // update avg fps
        var anim = controller.anim;
        if (anim.getFrame() % 20 == 0) {
            this.controller.avgFps = Math.round(anim.getFps() *
10) / 10;
        }
    }
};
```

5. Define the `initHealthBar()` method which initializes the health bar:

```
Model.prototype.initHealthBar = function(){
    this.healthBar = new HealthBar({
        controller: this.controller,
        maxHealth: this.hero.maxHealth,
        x: 10,
        y: 10,
        maxWidth: 150,
        height: 20
    });
};
```

6. Define the `initLevel()` method which initializes the level:

```
Model.prototype.initLevel = function(){
    this.level = new Level({
        controller: this.controller,
        x: 0,
        y: 0,
        leftBounds: 100,
        rightBounds: 500
    });
};
```

7. Define the `initHero()` method which initializes the hero:

```
Model.prototype.initHero = function(){
    // initialize Hero
    var heroMotions = {
        STANDING: {
            index: 0,
            numSprites: 5,
            loop: true
        },
        AIRBORNE: {
            index: 1,
            numSprites: 5,
            loop: false
        },
        RUNNING: {
            index: 2,
            numSprites: 6,
            loop: true
        },
        ATTACKING: {
            index: 3,
            numSprites: 5,
            loop: false
        }
    };

    this.hero = new Actor({
        controller: this.controller,
        normalSpriteSheet: this.controller.images.heroSprites,
        hitSpriteSheet: this.controller.images.heroHitSprites,
        x: 30,
        y: 381,
        playerSpeed: 300,
        motions: heroMotions,
        startMotion: heroMotions.STANDING,
        facingRight: true,
        moving: false,
        spriteInterval: 90,
        maxHealth: 3,
        attackRange: 100,
        minAttackInterval: 200
    });

    this.heroCanvasPos = {
```

```
        x: this.hero.x,
        y: this.hero.y
    };
};
```

8. Define the `initBadGuys()` method which initializes an array of bad guys:

```
Model.prototype.initBadGuys = function(){
    // notice that AIRBORNE and RUNNING
    // both use the same sprite animation
    var badGuyMotions = {
        RUNNING: {
            index: 0,
            numSprites: 6,
            loop: true
        },
        AIRBORNE: {
            index: 0,
            numSprites: 4,
            loop: false
        },
        ATTACKING: {
            index: 1,
            numSprites: 4,
            loop: false
        }
    };

    var badGuyStartConfig = [{
        x: 600,
        facingRight: true
    }, {
        x: 1460,
        facingRight: true
    }, {
        x: 2602,
        facingRight: true
    }, {
        x: 3000,
        facingRight: true
    }, {
        x: 6402,
        facingRight: true
    }, {
        x: 6602,
```

```
            facingRight: true
        }];

        for (var n = 0; n < badGuyStartConfig.length; n++) {
            this.badGuys.push(new Actor({
                controller: this.controller,
                normalSpriteSheet: this.controller.images.
badGuySprites,
                hitSpriteSheet: this.controller.images.
badGuyHitSprites,
                x: badGuyStartConfig[n].x,
                y: 381,
                playerSpeed: 100,
                motions: badGuyMotions,
                startMotion: badGuyMotions.RUNNING,
                facingRight: badGuyStartConfig[n].facingRight,
                moving: true,
                spriteInterval: 160,
                maxHealth: 3,
                attackRange: 100,
                minAttackInterval: 2000
            }));
        }
};
```

9. Define the `moveBadGuys()` method which serves as a simple AI engine:

```
Model.prototype.moveBadGuys = function(){
    var level = this.level;
    for (var n = 0; n < this.badGuys.length; n++) {
        var badGuy = this.badGuys[n];

        if (badGuy.alive) {
            if (badGuy.isFacingRight()) {
                badGuy.x += 5;
                if (!level.getZoneInfo(badGuy.getCenter()).
inBounds) {
                    badGuy.facingRight = false;
                }
                badGuy.x -= 5;
            }

            else {
                badGuy.x -= 5;
                if (!level.getZoneInfo(badGuy.getCenter()).
inBounds) {
```

```
                    badGuy.facingRight = true;
                }
                badGuy.x += 5;
            }
        }
    }
};
```

10. Define the `updateLevel()` method:

```
Model.prototype.updateLevel = function(){
    var hero = this.hero;
    var level = this.level;
    level.x = -hero.x + this.heroCanvasPos.x;
};
```

11. Define the `updateHeroCanvasPos()` method which updates the position of the hero relative to the canvas:

```
Model.prototype.updateHeroCanvasPos = function(oldHeroX){
    this.heroCanvasPos.y = this.hero.y;
    var heroDiffX = this.hero.x - oldHeroX;
    var newHeroCanvasPosX = this.heroCanvasPos.x + heroDiffX;
    // if moving right and not past right bounds
    if (heroDiffX > 0 && newHeroCanvasPosX < this.level.
rightBounds) {
        this.heroCanvasPos.x += heroDiffX;
    }
    // if moving left and not past left bounds
    if (heroDiffX < 0 && newHeroCanvasPosX > this.level.
leftBounds) {
        this.heroCanvasPos.x += heroDiffX;
    }

  if (this.hero.x < this.level.leftBounds) {
    this.heroCanvasPos.x = this.hero.x;
  }
};
```

12. Define the `updateActor()` method:

```
Model.prototype.updateActor = function(actor){
    if (actor.alive) {
        if (actor.health <= 0 || actor.y + actor.SPRITE_SIZE >
this.controller.view.canvas.height) {
            actor.alive = false;
        }
        else {
```

```
        this.updateActorVY(actor);
        this.updateActorY(actor);
        this.updateActorX(actor);

              actor.updateSpriteMotion();
        actor.updateSpriteSeqNum();
          }
      }
      else {
          if (actor.opacity > 0) {
              actor.fade();
          }
      }
};
```

13. Define the `updateActorVY()` method which uses the downward force of gravity and the upward force of the levitation pods to update the vertical velocity of an actor:

```
Model.prototype.updateActorVY = function(actor) {
  var anim = this.controller.anim;
  var level = this.level;

    // apply gravity (+y)
    var gravity = this.controller.model.level.GRAVITY;
    var speedIncrementEachFrame = gravity * anim.getTimeInterval()
/ 1000; // pixels / second
    actor.vy += speedIncrementEachFrame;

    // apply levitation (-y)
    if (level.getZoneInfo(actor.getCenter()).levitating) {
        actor.vy = (65 - actor.y) / 200;
    }
};
```

14. Define the `updateActorY()` method which updates the y position of the actor based on his vertical velocity:

```
Model.prototype.updateActorY = function(actor) {
  var anim = this.controller.anim;
  var level = this.level;
    var oldY = actor.y;
    actor.y += actor.vy * anim.getTimeInterval();

    if (level.getZoneInfo(actor.getCenter()).inBounds) {
        actor.airborne = true;
    }
```

```
        else {
            actor.y = oldY;

            // handle case where player has fallen to the ground
            // if vy is less than zero, this means the player has just
            // hit the ceiling, in which case we can simply leave
            // this.y as oldY to prevent the player from going
            // past the ceiling
            if (actor.vy > 0) {
                while (level.getZoneInfo(actor.getCenter()).inBounds)
                {
                    actor.y++;
                }
                actor.y--;
                actor.vy = 0;
                actor.airborne = false;
            }
        }
    };
```

15. Define the `updateActorX()` method which updates the actor's x position:

```
Model.prototype.updateActorX = function(actor) {
  var anim = this.controller.anim;
  var level = this.level;
  var oldX = actor.x;
  var changeX = actor.playerSpeed * (anim.getTimeInterval() /
1000);
    if (actor.moving) {
        actor.facingRight ? actor.x += changeX : actor.x -=
changeX;
    }

    if (!level.getZoneInfo(actor.getCenter()).inBounds) {
        actor.x = oldX;

        while (level.getZoneInfo(actor.getCenter()).inBounds) {
            actor.facingRight ? actor.x++ : actor.x--;
        }

        // reposition to nearest placement in bounds
        actor.facingRight ? actor.x-- : actor.x++;
    }
};
```

16. Define the `nearby()` method which determines whether or not two actors are near each other:

```
Model.prototype.nearby = function(actor1, actor2){
    return (Math.abs(actor1.x - actor2.x) < actor1.attackRange)
    && Math.abs(actor1.y - actor2.y) < 30;
};
```

How it works...

In an MVC architecture, the model is considered to be the "meat" of the architecture, because it represents the data layer. As Canvas Hero is a game, our data consists of the hero, bad guys, the level, and the health bar objects. Each of these objects contain properties which must be updated and accessed during each animation frame.

The model for Canvas Hero has three key responsibilities:

- Initializing the game objects
- Updating the game objects
- Handling the bad guy AI

Quite arguably, the most interesting method in our model is the `moveBadGuys()` method. This method can be thought of as the "AI" for our game engine. I've put the "AI" in quotes because in all honesty, the bad guys in Canvas Hero are pretty dumb. The `moveBadGuys()` method loops through all of the bad guy objects, determines whether they are close to a wall using the `getZoneInfo()` method of the `Level` object, and then changes their direction if they're about to run into one.

There's more...

If you're wanting to create a more challenging game, you might consider beefing up the `moveBadGuys()` method by giving the bad guys an ability to jump or even use the levitation pods.

See also...

- *Creating an Animation class* in *Chapter 5*

Creating a View class

In this recipe, we'll create the View class, which is the simplest of the three MVC classes. The View class is responsible for drawing state screen images and also renders each animation frame by calling the `draw()` method for the level, each of the bad guys, the hero, and the health bar. In addition, the View class also renders a handy FPS display in the top-right corner of the screen so we can see how well the game is performing.

How to do it...

Follow these steps to create the view for Canvas Hero:

1. Define the `View` constructor:

```
/*
 * Game view
 *
 * The view has access to the canvas context
 * and is responsible for the drawing logic
 */
function View(controller){
    this.controller = controller;
    this.canvas = controller.anim.getCanvas();
    this.context = controller.anim.getContext();
}
```

2. Define the `drawScreen()` method which draws the loading, ready, game over, or win state screen:

```
View.prototype.drawScreen = function(screenImg){
    this.context.drawImage(screenImg, 0, 0, this.canvas.width,
this.canvas.height);
};
```

3. Define the `drawBadGuys()` method which draws the bad guys:

```
View.prototype.drawBadGuys = function() {
    var controller = this.controller;
    var model = controller.model;
  for (var n = 0; n < model.badGuys.length; n++) {
      var badGuy = model.badGuys[n];
    var offsetPos = {
      x: badGuy.x + model.level.x,
      y: badGuy.y + model.level.y
    };
      badGuy.draw(offsetPos);
  }
};
```

4. Define the `drawFps()` method which draws the FPS value of the game in the top-right corner of the screen so that we can see how well the game is performing:

```
View.prototype.drawFps = function() {
    var context = this.context;
    context.fillStyle = "black";
    context.fillRect(this.canvas.width - 100, 0, 100, 30);
```

```
        context.font = "18pt Calibri";
        context.fillStyle = "white";
        context.fillText("fps: " + this.controller.avgFps.toFixed(1),
    this.canvas.width - 93, 22);
    };
```

5. Define the `stage()` method which draws all of the objects on the screen:

```
    View.prototype.stage = function(){
        var controller = this.controller;
        var model = controller.model;
        if (controller.state == controller.states.PLAYING ||
    controller.state == controller.states.GAMEOVER || controller.state
    == controller.states.WON) {
            model.level.draw();
        this.drawBadGuys();
            model.hero.draw(model.heroCanvasPos);
            model.healthBar.draw();

            // draw screen overlay
            if (controller.state == controller.states.GAMEOVER) {
                this.drawScreen(controller.images.gameoverScreen);
            }
            else if (controller.state == controller.states.WON) {
                this.drawScreen(controller.images.winScreen);
            }

            this.drawFps();
        }
        else if (controller.state == controller.states.READY) {
            this.drawScreen(controller.images.readyScreen);
        }
    };
```

How it works...

As mentioned earlier, the main responsibility of the `View` class is to draw state screens and draw the game screen. Canvas Hero has four different state screens:

- Loading state
- Ready state
- Game over state
- Win state

Whenever the game state changes and a state screen is needed, the controller calls the `drawScreen()` method of the `View` object. Here's a screenshot for each of the game state screens:

Loading state:

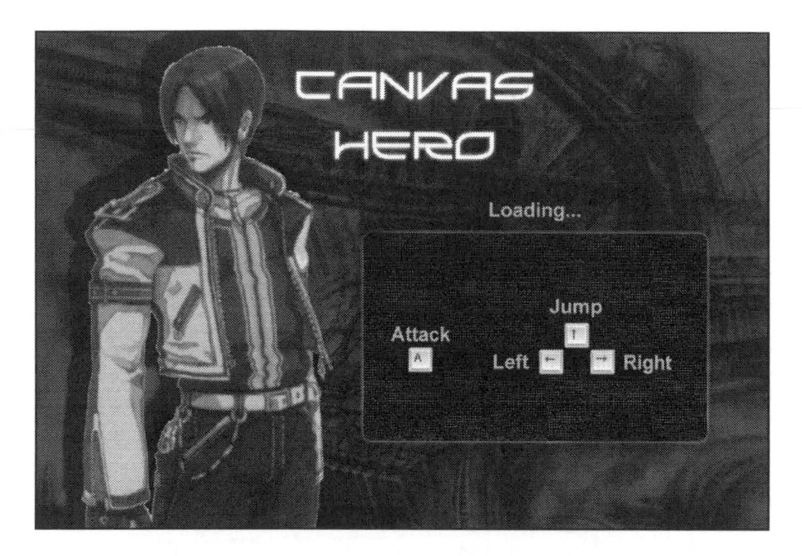

Ready state:

Game over state:

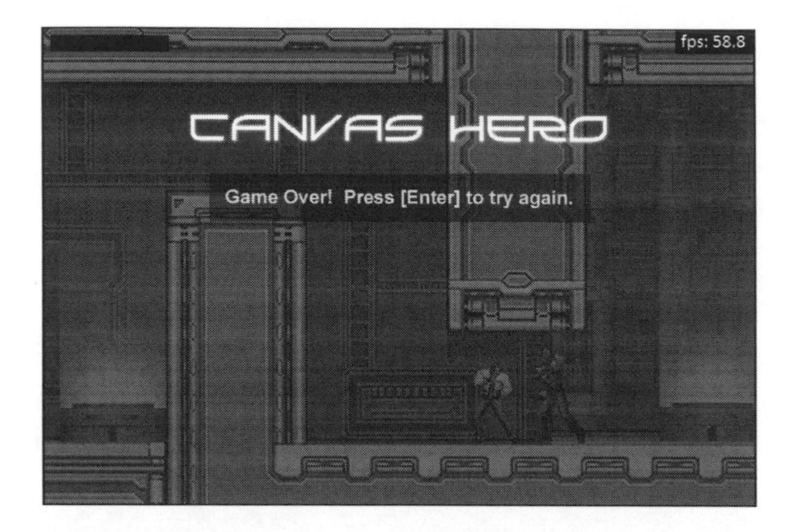

Win state:

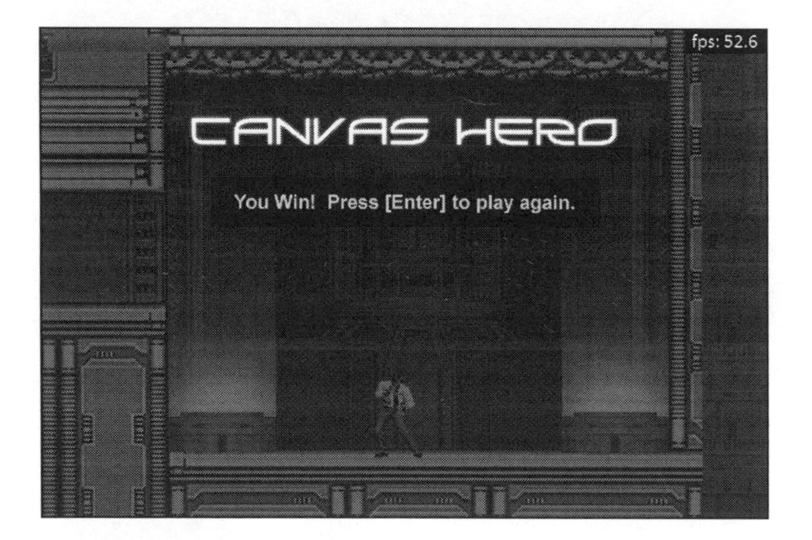

See also...

- *Stressing the canvas and displaying the FPS* in *Chapter 5*

Setting up the HTML document and starting the game

Now that we have all of the pieces for our game, including the graphics, the classes for the actors, the level, the health bar, and a completed game engine, it's time to tie it all together by setting up the HTML document and starting the game.

How to do it...

Follow these steps to set up the HTML document and start the game:

1. Link to the JavaScript files:

```
</style>
<script src="animation.js">
</script>
<script src="Controller.js">
</script>
<script src="Model.js">
</script>
<script src="View.js">
</script>
<script src="Level.js">
</script>
<script src="Actor.js">
</script>
<script src="HealthBar.js">
</script>
```

2. Initialize the controller:

```
<script>
    window.onload = function(){
        new Controller("myCanvas");
    };
</script>
```

3. Embed the canvas inside the body of the HTML document:

```
<canvas id="myCanvas" width="900" height="600">
</canvas>
```

How it works...

As you can see, the HTML markup is quite simple. It's purpose is purely to link to required JavaScript files, embed the canvas tag, and initialize the controller. The controller initializes the model and the view. The model initializes the hero, the bad guys, the level, and the health bar. Once the images have loaded and the game state is changed to the ready state, the player presses the enter key and the game begins.

There's more...

You're now ready to play the game and save the world! If you initialized the hero and the bad guys with a health of three units as defined in the model recipe, the hero can take up to three hits before game over, and each of the bad guys require three hits to be defeated. I've found that it's easiest to defeat the bad guys by jumping over them and repeatedly hitting them in the back until they're toast (cheap I know, but it works). It's also really fun to jump into the levitator pods and float in the air for a while, wait for just the right moment, and attack a bad guy from above like a ninja.

If you use this chapter as a foundation for your own side-scroller game, here are some other features that you might consider adding:

- Sound effects for jumping, landing, and punching using the HTML5 audio tag
- Pause feature that freezes the game until it's resumed
- Timer and top scores
- More levels, enemies, and bosses
- Power-ups
- An option to save the game state with HTML5 local storage or by saving the state in an online database
- Anything else you can imagine

See also...

- *Creating an Animation class* in *Chapter 5*

9

Introducing WebGL

In this chapter, we will cover:

- Creating a WebGL wrapper to simplify the WebGL API
- Creating a triangular plane
- Rotating a triangular plane in 3D space
- Creating a rotating cube
- Adding textures and lighting
- Creating a 3D world that you can explore

Introduction

Originally, when I first started writing this book, I had intended on only covering the 2D context of the HTML5 canvas (I strongly believe that most people who use canvas will be working with this context). I had also originally intended on covering techniques for rendering 3D shapes in the 2D context using 3D projection methods and vector operations. People were already busy creating some pretty incredible 3D JavaScript libraries for the 2D context, including Kevin Roast's K3D library (one of the reviewers of this book), and also Dean McNamee's Pre3d library.

As I neared writing this chapter, WebGL—a true 3D context—began to dominate 3D canvas demos across the Web. WebGL stands for **Web-Based Graphics Library**, and it's based on OpenGL ES 2.0 which provides an API for 3D graphics. Because WebGL leverages hardware acceleration by pushing buffers directly onto the graphics card to render 3D models, it performs much better than its 2D context, 3D projection library counterparts. Moreover, it exposes years of work already done with OpenGL. As you've probably already figured out by now, I decided to cover WebGL instead of covering 3D projection libraries with the 2D context because I very much believe that WebGL will be the standard for 3D applications in the near future. WebGL is of particular interest for people who want to create 3D games or 3D models on the Web.

This chapter will get you started with the basics of WebGL by covering concepts such as buffers, shaders, perspective and model-view matrices, normals, textures, lighting, camera handling, and much more. Let's get started!

Creating a WebGL wrapper to simplify the WebGL API

If you've already looked ahead and peeked at the code for this recipe, and you're not very familiar with OpenGL or WebGL, you're probably feeling pretty overwhelmed, and for good reason. WebGL, although extremely powerful, has quite a steep learning curve when diving into it for the first time. Frankly speaking, it takes many lines of code to perform simple tasks. Therefore, I've found it extremely convenient to work with a WebGL wrapper that essentially shrink wraps blocks of tedious code into simple methods. This recipe provides steps for creating a simple WebGL wrapper that will be used for all of the recipes in this chapter. Let's get started!

As the WebGL wrapper is quite complex, you might consider grabbing the WebGL wrapper code from the online resources for this book at `http://www.html5canvastutorials.com/cookbook/`.

How to do it...

Follow these steps to create a WebGL wrapper object to simplify the WebGL API, or go to `http://www.html5canvastutorials.com/cookbook` and download `WebGL.js` from the resources section:

1. Begin defining the WebGL constructor by initializing the canvas context and defining the animation properties:

```
var WebGL = function(canvasId){
    this.canvas = document.getElementById(canvasId);
    this.context = this.canvas.getContext("experimental-webgl");
    this.stage = undefined;

    // Animation
    this.t = 0;
    this.timeInterval = 0;
    this.startTime = 0;
    this.lastTime = 0;
    this.frame = 0;
    this.animating = false;
```

2. Use *Paul Irish*'s `requestAnimFrame` shim to create a cross-browser `requestAnimationFrame` function which enables the browser to handle the FPS for our animations:

```
// provided by Paul Irish
window.requestAnimFrame = (function(callback){
    return window.requestAnimationFrame ||
    window.webkitRequestAnimationFrame ||
    window.mozRequestAnimationFrame ||
    window.oRequestAnimationFrame ||
    window.msRequestAnimationFrame ||
    function(callback){
        window.setTimeout(callback, 1000 / 60);
    };
})();
```

3. As *Brandon Jones*'s `glMatrix` uses global variables, we can encapsulate them so that the variables can't be altered outside of the wrapper:

```
/*
* encapsulte mat3, mat4, and vec3 from
* glMatrix globals
*/
 this.mat3 = mat3;
 this.mat4 = mat4;
this.vec3 = vec3;
```

4. Define shader type constants and initialize the model-view matrix, the perspective matrix, and the viewport dimensions:

```
// shader type constants
this.BLUE_COLOR = "BLUE_COLOR";
this.VARYING_COLOR = "VARYING_COLOR";
this.TEXTURE = "TEXTURE";
this.TEXTURE_DIRECTIONAL_LIGHTING =
"TEXTURE_DIRECTIONAL_LIGHTING";

this.shaderProgram = null;
this.mvMatrix = this.mat4.create();
this.pMatrix = this.mat4.create();
this.mvMatrixStack = [];
this.context.viewportWidth = this.canvas.width;
this.context.viewportHeight = this.canvas.height;
```

5. Enable the depth test:

```
        // init depth test
        this.context.enable(this.context.DEPTH_TEST);
    };
```

6. Define getter methods for the context and canvas attributes:

```
WebGL.prototype.getContext = function(){
    return this.context;
};

WebGL.prototype.getCanvas = function(){
    return this.canvas;
};
```

7. Define a `clear()` method which clears the WebGL viewport:

```
WebGL.prototype.clear = function(){
    this.context.viewport(0, 0, this.context.viewportWidth, this.
context.viewportHeight);
    this.context.clear(this.context.COLOR_BUFFER_BIT | this.
context.DEPTH_BUFFER_BIT);
};
```

8. Define the `setStage()` method:

```
WebGL.prototype.setStage = function(func){
    this.stage = func;
};
```

9. Define the `isAnimating()` method which returns whether or not the animation is running:

```
WebGL.prototype.isAnimating = function(){
    return this.animating;
};
```

10. Define the `getFrame()` method which returns the current frame number:

```
WebGL.prototype.getFrame = function(){

    return this.frame;

};
```

11. Define the `start()` method which starts the animation:

```
WebGL.prototype.start = function(){
    this.animating = true;
    var date = new Date();
    this.startTime = date.getTime();
```

```
    this.lastTime = this.startTime;

    if (this.stage !== undefined) {
        this.stage();
    }

    this.animationLoop();
};
```

12. Define the `stopAnimation()` method which stops the animation:

```
WebGL.prototype.stopAnimation = function(){
    this.animating = false;
};
```

13. Define the `getTimeInterval()` method which returns the time in milliseconds that has passed since the last frame was rendered:

```
WebGL.prototype.getTimeInterval = function(){
    return this.timeInterval;
};
```

14. Define the `getTime()` method which returns the number of milliseconds that have passed since the animation was started:

```
WebGL.prototype.getTime = function(){
    return this.t;
};
```

15. Define the `getFps()` method which returns the current FPS value determined by the browser:

```
WebGL.prototype.getFps = function(){
    return this.timeInterval > 0 ? 1000 / this.timeInterval : 0;
};
```

16. Define the `animationLoop()` method which is responsible for updating the animation properties, drawing the stage, and requesting a new animation frame:

```
WebGL.prototype.animationLoop = function(){
    var that = this;

    this.frame++;
    var date = new Date();
    var thisTime = date.getTime();
    this.timeInterval = thisTime - this.lastTime;
    this.t += this.timeInterval;
    this.lastTime = thisTime;

    if (this.stage !== undefined) {
```

```
            this.stage();
        }

        if (this.animating) {
            requestAnimFrame(function(){
                that.animationLoop();
            });
        }
    };
```

17. Define the `save()` method which saves the model-view matrix state by pushing the current state onto the model-view matrix stack:

```
WebGL.prototype.save = function(){
    var copy = this.mat4.create();
    this.mat4.set(this.mvMatrix, copy);
    this.mvMatrixStack.push(copy);
};
```

18. Define the `restore()` method which restores the previous model-view state:

```
WebGL.prototype.restore = function(){
    if (this.mvMatrixStack.length == 0) {
        throw "Invalid popMatrix!";
    }
    this.mvMatrix = this.mvMatrixStack.pop();
};
```

19. Define the `getFragmentShaderGLSL()` method which gets **GLSL** (**GL Shader Language**) fragment code based on the shader type argument. Essentially, this method contains four different stand alone GLSL fragment shader programs that are selected with a `case` statement:

```
WebGL.prototype.getFragmentShaderGLSL = function(shaderType){
    switch (shaderType) {
        case this.BLUE_COLOR:
            return "#ifdef GL_ES\n" +
            "precision highp float;\n" +
            "#endif\n" +
            "void main(void) {\n" +
            "gl_FragColor = vec4(0.0, 0.0, 1.0, 1.0);\n" +
            "}";
        case this.VARYING_COLOR:
            return "#ifdef GL_ES\n" +
            "precision highp float;\n" +
            "#endif\n" +
            "varying vec4 vColor;\n" +
```

```
                "void main(void) {\n" +
                "gl_FragColor = vColor;\n" +
                "}";
            case this.TEXTURE:
                return "#ifdef GL_ES\n" +
                "precision highp float;\n" +
                "#endif\n" +
                "varying vec2 vTextureCoord;\n" +
                "uniform sampler2D uSampler;\n" +
                "void main(void) {\n" +
                "gl_FragColor = texture2D(uSampler,
                 vec2(vTextureCoord.s, vTextureCoord.t));\n" +
                "}";
            case this.TEXTURE_DIRECTIONAL_LIGHTING:
                return "#ifdef GL_ES\n" +
                "precision highp float;\n" +
                "#endif\n" +
                "varying vec2 vTextureCoord;\n" +
                "varying vec3 vLightWeighting;\n" +
                "uniform sampler2D uSampler;\n" +
                "void main(void) {\n" +
                "vec4 textureColor = texture2D(uSampler,
vec2(vTextureCoord.s, vTextureCoord.t));\n" +
                "gl_FragColor = vec4(textureColor.rgb *
vLightWeighting, textureColor.a);\n" +
                "}";
        }
    };
```

20. Define the `getVertexShaderGLSL()` method which gets GLSL vertex code based on the shader type argument:

```
WebGL.prototype.getVertexShaderGLSL = function(shaderType){
    switch (shaderType) {
        case this.BLUE_COLOR:
            return "attribute vec3 aVertexPosition;\n" +
            "uniform mat4 uMVMatrix;\n" +
            "uniform mat4 uPMatrix;\n" +
            "void main(void) {\n" +
            "gl_Position = uPMatrix * uMVMatrix *
            vec4(aVertexPosition, 1.0);\n" +
            "}";
        case this.VARYING_COLOR:
            return "attribute vec3 aVertexPosition;\n" +
            "attribute vec4 aVertexColor;\n" +
            "uniform mat4 uMVMatrix;\n" +
```

```
                "uniform mat4 uPMatrix;\n" +
                "varying vec4 vColor;\n" +
                "void main(void) {\n" +
                "gl_Position = uPMatrix * uMVMatrix *
                vec4(aVertexPosition, 1.0);\n" +
                "vColor = aVertexColor;\n" +
                "}";
            case this.TEXTURE:
                return "attribute vec3 aVertexPosition;\n" +
                "attribute vec2 aTextureCoord;\n" +
                "uniform mat4 uMVMatrix;\n" +
                "uniform mat4 uPMatrix;\n" +
                "varying vec2 vTextureCoord;\n" +
                "void main(void) {\n" +
                "gl_Position = uPMatrix * uMVMatrix *
                vec4(aVertexPosition, 1.0);\n" +
                "vTextureCoord = aTextureCoord;\n" +
                "}";
            case this.TEXTURE_DIRECTIONAL_LIGHTING:
                return "attribute vec3 aVertexPosition;\n" +
                "attribute vec3 aVertexNormal;\n" +
                "attribute vec2 aTextureCoord;\n" +
                "uniform mat4 uMVMatrix;\n" +
                "uniform mat4 uPMatrix;\n" +
                "uniform mat3 uNMatrix;\n" +
                "uniform vec3 uAmbientColor;\n" +
                "uniform vec3 uLightingDirection;\n" +
                "uniform vec3 uDirectionalColor;\n" +
                "uniform bool uUseLighting;\n" +
                "varying vec2 vTextureCoord;\n" +
                "varying vec3 vLightWeighting;\n" +
                "void main(void) {\n" +
                "gl_Position = uPMatrix * uMVMatrix *
                vec4(aVertexPosition, 1.0);\n" +
                "vTextureCoord = aTextureCoord;\n" +
                "if (!uUseLighting) {\n" +
                "vLightWeighting = vec3(1.0, 1.0, 1.0);\n" +
                "} else {\n" +
              "vec3 transformedNormal = uNMatrix * aVertexNormal;\n" +
                "float directionalLightWeighting =
max(dot(transformedNormal, uLightingDirection), 0.0);\n" +
                "vLightWeighting = uAmbientColor + uDirectionalColor *
directionalLightWeighting;\n" +
                "}\n" +
                "}";
        }
};
```

21. Define the `initShaders()` method which initializes the appropriate shaders based on the shader type argument:

```
WebGL.prototype.initShaders = function(shaderType){
    this.initPositionShader();

    switch (shaderType) {
        case this.VARYING_COLOR:
            this.initColorShader();
            break;
        case this.TEXTURE:
            this.initTextureShader();
            break;
        case this.TEXTURE_DIRECTIONAL_LIGHTING:
            this.initTextureShader();
            this.initNormalShader();
            this.initLightingShader();
            break;
    }
};
```

22. Define the `setShaderProgram()` method which sets the shader program based on the shader type argument:

```
WebGL.prototype.setShaderProgram = function(shaderType){
    var fragmentGLSL = this.getFragmentShaderGLSL(shaderType);
    var vertexGLSL = this.getVertexShaderGLSL(shaderType);

    var fragmentShader = this.context.createShader(this.context.
FRAGMENT_SHADER);
    this.context.shaderSource(fragmentShader, fragmentGLSL);
    this.context.compileShader(fragmentShader);

    var vertexShader = this.context.createShader(this.context.
VERTEX_SHADER);
    this.context.shaderSource(vertexShader, vertexGLSL);
    this.context.compileShader(vertexShader);

    this.shaderProgram = this.context.createProgram();
    this.context.attachShader(this.shaderProgram, vertexShader);
    this.context.attachShader(this.shaderProgram, fragmentShader);
    this.context.linkProgram(this.shaderProgram);

    if (!this.context.getProgramParameter(this.shaderProgram,
this.context.LINK_STATUS)) {
        alert("Could not initialize shaders");
```

```
        }

        this.context.useProgram(this.shaderProgram);

        // once shader program is loaded, it's time to init the
shaders
        this.initShaders(shaderType);
};
```

23. Define the `perspective()` method which wraps the glMatrix `perspective()` method that operates on the perspective matrix:

```
WebGL.prototype.perspective = function(viewAngle, minDist,
maxDist){
    this.mat4.perspective(viewAngle, this.context.viewportWidth /
this.context.viewportHeight, minDist, maxDist, this.pMatrix);
};
```

24. Define the `identity()` method which wraps the glMatrix `identity()` method that operates on the model-view matrix:

```
WebGL.prototype.identity = function(){
    this.mat4.identity(this.mvMatrix);
};
```

25. Define the `translate()` method which wraps the glMatrix `translate()` method that operates on the model-view matrix:

```
WebGL.prototype.translate = function(x, y, z){
    this.mat4.translate(this.mvMatrix, [x, y, z]);
};
```

26. Define the `rotate()` method which wraps the glMatrix `rotate()` method that operates on the model-view matrix:

```
WebGL.prototype.rotate = function(angle, x, y, z){
    this.mat4.rotate(this.mvMatrix, angle, [x, y, z]);
};
```

27. Define the `initPositionShader()` method which initializes the position shader to be used with position buffers:

```
WebGL.prototype.initPositionShader = function(){
    this.shaderProgram.vertexPositionAttribute = this.context.
getAttribLocation(this.shaderProgram, "aVertexPosition");
    this.context.enableVertexAttribArray(this.shaderProgram.
vertexPositionAttribute);
    this.shaderProgram.pMatrixUniform = this.context.
getUniformLocation(this.shaderProgram, "uPMatrix");
    this.shaderProgram.mvMatrixUniform = this.context.
getUniformLocation(this.shaderProgram, "uMVMatrix");
};
```

28. Define the `initColorShader()` method which initializes the color shader to be used with color buffers:

```
WebGL.prototype.initColorShader = function(){
    this.shaderProgram.vertexColorAttribute = this.context.
getAttribLocation(this.shaderProgram, "aVertexColor");
    this.context.enableVertexAttribArray(this.shaderProgram.
vertexColorAttribute);
};
```

29. Define the `initTextureShader()` method which initializes the texture shader to be used with texture buffers:

```
WebGL.prototype.initTextureShader = function(){
    this.shaderProgram.textureCoordAttribute = this.context.
getAttribLocation(this.shaderProgram, "aTextureCoord");
    this.context.enableVertexAttribArray(this.shaderProgram.
textureCoordAttribute);
    this.shaderProgram.samplerUniform = this.context.
getUniformLocation(this.shaderProgram, "uSampler");
};
```

30. Define the `initNormalShader()` method which initializes the normal shader to be used with normal buffers:

```
WebGL.prototype.initNormalShader = function(){
    this.shaderProgram.vertexNormalAttribute = this.context.
getAttribLocation(this.shaderProgram, "aVertexNormal");
    this.context.enableVertexAttribArray(this.shaderProgram.
vertexNormalAttribute);
    this.shaderProgram.nMatrixUniform = this.context.
getUniformLocation(this.shaderProgram, "uNMatrix");
};
```

31. Define the `initLightingShader()` method which initializes ambient and directional lighting shaders:

```
WebGL.prototype.initLightingShader = function(){
    this.shaderProgram.useLightingUniform = this.context.
getUniformLocation(this.shaderProgram, "uUseLighting");
    this.shaderProgram.ambientColorUniform = this.context.
getUniformLocation(this.shaderProgram, "uAmbientColor");
    this.shaderProgram.lightingDirectionUniform = this.context.
getUniformLocation(this.shaderProgram, "uLightingDirection");
    this.shaderProgram.directionalColorUniform = this.context.
getUniformLocation(this.shaderProgram, "uDirectionalColor");
};
```

32. Define the `initTexture()` method which wraps the WebGL API code necessary to initialize a WebGL texture object:

```
WebGL.prototype.initTexture = function(texture){
    this.context.pixelStorei(this.context.UNPACK_FLIP_Y_WEBGL,
true);
    this.context.bindTexture(this.context.TEXTURE_2D, texture);
    this.context.texImage2D(this.context.TEXTURE_2D, 0, this.
context.RGBA, this.context.RGBA, this.context.UNSIGNED_BYTE,
texture.image);
    this.context.texParameteri(this.context.TEXTURE_2D, this.
context.TEXTURE_MAG_FILTER, this.context.NEAREST);
    this.context.texParameteri(this.context.TEXTURE_2D, this.
context.TEXTURE_MIN_FILTER, this.context.LINEAR_MIPMAP_NEAREST);
    this.context.generateMipmap(this.context.TEXTURE_2D);
    this.context.bindTexture(this.context.TEXTURE_2D, null);
};
```

33. Define the `createArrayBuffer()` method which wraps the WebGL API code necessary to create an array buffer:

```
WebGL.prototype.createArrayBuffer = function(vertices){
    var buffer = this.context.createBuffer();
    buffer.numElements = vertices.length;
    this.context.bindBuffer(this.context.ARRAY_BUFFER, buffer);
    this.context.bufferData(this.context.ARRAY_BUFFER, new
    Float32Array(vertices), this.context.STATIC_DRAW);
    return buffer;
};
```

34. Define the `createElementArrayBuffer()` method which wraps the WebGL API code necessary to create an element array buffer:

```
WebGL.prototype.createElementArrayBuffer = function(vertices){
    var buffer = this.context.createBuffer();
    buffer.numElements = vertices.length;
    this.context.bindBuffer(this.context.ELEMENT_ARRAY_BUFFER,
    buffer);
    this.context.bufferData(this.context.ELEMENT_ARRAY_BUFFER, new
    Uint16Array(vertices), this.context.STATIC_DRAW);
    return buffer;
};
```

35. Define the `pushPositionBuffer()` method which pushes a position buffer onto the graphics card:

```
WebGL.prototype.pushPositionBuffer = function(buffers){
    this.context.bindBuffer(this.context.ARRAY_BUFFER,
    buffers.positionBuffer);
    this.context.vertexAttribPointer(this.shaderProgram.
vertexPositionAttribute, 3, this.context.FLOAT, false, 0, 0);
};
```

36. Define the `pushColorBuffer()` method which pushes a color buffer onto the graphics card:

```
WebGL.prototype.pushColorBuffer = function(buffers){
    this.context.bindBuffer(this.context.ARRAY_BUFFER,
    buffers.colorBuffer);
    this.context.vertexAttribPointer(this.shaderProgram.
vertexColorAttribute, 4, this.context.FLOAT, false, 0, 0);
};
```

37. Define the `pushTextureBuffer()` method which pushes a texture buffer onto the graphics card:

```
WebGL.prototype.pushTextureBuffer = function(buffers, texture){
    this.context.bindBuffer(this.context.ARRAY_BUFFER,
    buffers.textureBuffer);
    this.context.vertexAttribPointer(this.shaderProgram.
textureCoordAttribute, 2, this.context.FLOAT, false, 0, 0);
    this.context.activeTexture(this.context.TEXTURE0);
    this.context.bindTexture(this.context.TEXTURE_2D, texture);
    this.context.uniform1i(this.shaderProgram.samplerUniform, 0);
};
```

38. Define the `pushIndexBuffer()` method which pushes an index buffer onto the graphics card:

```
WebGL.prototype.pushIndexBuffer = function(buffers){
    this.context.bindBuffer(this.context.ELEMENT_ARRAY_BUFFER,
buffers.indexBuffer);
};
```

39. Define the `pushNormalBuffer()` method which pushes a normal buffer onto the graphics card:

```
WebGL.prototype.pushNormalBuffer = function(buffers){
    this.context.bindBuffer(this.context.ARRAY_BUFFER, buffers.
normalBuffer);
    this.context.vertexAttribPointer(this.shaderProgram.
vertexNormalAttribute, 3, this.context.FLOAT, false, 0, 0);
};
```

40. Define the `setMatrixUniforms()` method which wraps the WebGL API code required to set the matrix uniforms:

```
WebGL.prototype.setMatrixUniforms = function(){
    this.context.uniformMatrix4fv(this.shaderProgram.
pMatrixUniform, false, this.pMatrix);
    this.context.uniformMatrix4fv(this.shaderProgram.
mvMatrixUniform, false, this.mvMatrix);

    var normalMatrix = this.mat3.create();
    this.mat4.toInverseMat3(this.mvMatrix, normalMatrix);
    this.mat3.transpose(normalMatrix);
    this.context.uniformMatrix3fv(this.shaderProgram.
nMatrixUniform, false, normalMatrix);
};
```

41. Define the `drawElements()` method which wraps the WebGL API code that draws non-triangular position buffers based on the index buffer:

```
WebGL.prototype.drawElements = function(buffers){
    this.setMatrixUniforms();

    // draw elements
    this.context.drawElements(this.context.TRIANGLES, buffers.
indexBuffer.numElements, this.context.UNSIGNED_SHORT, 0);
};
```

42. Define the `drawArrays()` method which wraps the WebGL API code required to draw triangular position buffers:

```
WebGL.prototype.drawArrays = function(buffers){
    this.setMatrixUniforms();

    // draw arrays
    this.context.drawArrays(this.context.TRIANGLES, 0, buffers.
positionBuffer.numElements / 3);
};
```

43. Define the `enableLighting()` method which wraps the WebGL API code required to enable lighting:

```
WebGL.prototype.enableLighting = function(){
    this.context.uniform1i(this.shaderProgram.useLightingUniform,
    true);
};
```

44. Define the `setAmbientLighting()` method which wraps the WebGL API code required for setting ambient lighting:

```
WebGL.prototype.setAmbientLighting = function(red, green, blue){
    this.context.uniform3f(this.shaderProgram.ambientColorUniform,
    parseFloat(red), parseFloat(green), parseFloat(blue));
};
```

45. Define the `setDirectionalLighting()` method which wraps the WebGL API code required for setting directional lighting:

```
WebGL.prototype.setDirectionalLighting = function(x, y, z, red,
green, blue){
    // directional lighting
    var lightingDirection = [x, y, z];
    var adjustedLD = this.vec3.create();
    this.vec3.normalize(lightingDirection, adjustedLD);
    this.vec3.scale(adjustedLD, -1);
    this.context.uniform3fv(this.shaderProgram.
lightingDirectionUniform, adjustedLD);

    // directional color
    this.context.uniform3f(this.shaderProgram.
directionalColorUniform, parseFloat(red), parseFloat(green),
parseFloat(blue));
};
```

How it works...

The idea of the WebGL wrapper object is to handle some of the things that the WebGL API doesn't provide and to wrap tedious blocks of code that are required to do straightforward things.

There are two major components of WebGL that aren't built into the API—matrix transformation math and shader programs. In this chapter, we'll be using a handy matrix library built specifically for WebGL by *Brandon Jones*, called glMatrix, to handle all of the vector operations. As for the missing support for shader programs, our WebGL wrapper object includes pre-built GLSL shader programs. Shader programs are written in GLSL, which is short for OpenGL Shading Language, and is used to programmatically define how vertices and fragments should be rendered. Vertex shaders operate on every vertex that makes up the shape of our 3D models, and fragment shaders operate on every fragment which is produced by rasterization. To use shader programs , we'll actually have to pass in strings of GLSL code into the WebGL API.

In addition to the wrapper methods, the WebGL wrapper object also includes the animation methods that we put together in *Chapter 5, Bringing the Canvas to Life with Animation*.

The majority of the remaining methods in our WebGL wrapper object simply wrap blocks of code necessary to push buffers onto the graphics card and then draw the result. In the next five recipes, we'll dive deeper into each of these buffer types, including position buffers, color buffers, index buffers, texture buffers, and normal buffers.

There's more...

For a more in-depth exploration of WebGL and OpenGL, check out these two awesome resources:

- `http://learningwebgl.com/`
- `http://nehe.gamedev.net/`

See also...

- *Appendix A, Detecting Canvas Support*

Creating a triangular plane

Now that we have our WebGL wrapper set up, let's create our first WebGL application by drawing a simple triangle on the screen. It will serve as a good foundation for the typical steps that are required to create more complex 3D models. In this recipe, we'll introduce the concept of position buffers, which are simply arrays of vertices used to define the position and shape of a 3D model.

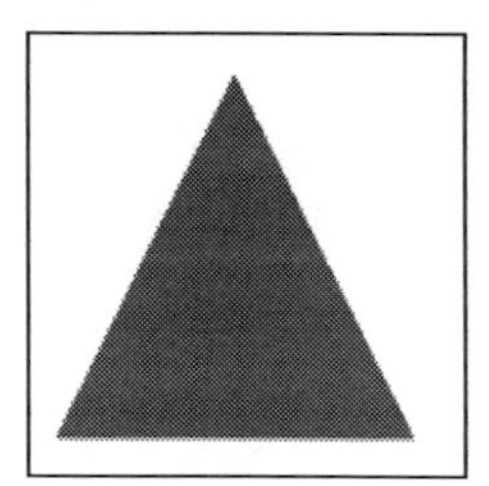

How to do it...

Follow these steps to render a 2D triangle with WebGL:

1. Link to the `glMatrix` library and the WebGL wrapper:

```
<script type="text/javascript" src="glMatrix-1.0.1.min.js">
</script>
<script type="text/javascript" src="WebGL.js">
</script>
```

2. Define the `initBuffers()` function which initializes the position buffers for our triangle:

```
function initBuffers(gl){
    var triangleBuffers = {};
    triangleBuffers.positionBuffer = gl.createArrayBuffer([
        0, 1, 0,
        -1, -1, 0,
        1, -1, 0
    ]);
    return triangleBuffers;
}
```

3. Define the `stage()` function which sets the perspective matrix, sets the model-view matrix to the identity matrix, translates the model-view matrix back -5 units in the z direction, pushes the position buffer onto the graphics card, and then draws the triangle using `drawArrays()`:

```
function stage(gl, triangleBuffers){
    gl.clear();
    // set field of view at 45 degrees
    // set viewing range between 0.1 and 100.0 units away.
    gl.perspective(45, 0.1, 100.0);
    gl.identity();

    // translate model-view matrix
    gl.translate(0, 0, -5);

    gl.pushPositionBuffer(triangleBuffers);
    gl.drawArrays(triangleBuffers);
}
```

4. When the page loads, create a new instance of the WebGL wrapper object, set the shader program to `"BLUE_COLOR"`, initialize the triangle buffers, and then draw the stage:

```
window.onload = function(){
    var gl = new WebGL("myCanvas", "experimental-webgl");
    gl.setShaderProgram("BLUE_COLOR");
    var triangleBuffers = initBuffers(gl);
    stage(gl, triangleBuffers);
};
```

5. Embed the canvas tag inside the body of the HTML document:

```
<canvas id="myCanvas" width="600" height="250"
    style="border:1px solid black;"></canvas>
```

How it works...

When the loads, the first thing we need to do is to initialize the WebGL wrapper object using the `experimental-webgl` context. At the time of writing, the `experimental-webgl` context is the only canvas context that's supported across all of the major browsers that support WebGL, including Google Chrome, Firefox, and Safari.

Next, we can set the shader program to `"BLUE_COLOR"`, which will use a pre-built GLSL program to render blue vertices and fragments. Once the shader program is set, we need to initialize our buffers. Buffers are an array of vertices that are used to define our 3D models. For this recipe, we'll only be using a position buffer, which defines the vertex positions of our triangle. In future recipes, we'll introduce other buffer types, including index buffers, texture buffers, and normal buffers. For this recipe, the position buffer contains nine elements which represent three vertices (each vertex has an x, y, and z component).

Once the triangle buffers have been initialized, we can draw the stage. The `stage()` function first clears the canvas and then sets the perspective matrix. The `perspective()` method of our WebGL wrapper object takes in three parameters, a viewing angle, a minimum visible distance, and a maximum visible distance. In this recipe, we've set the minimum visible distance to 0.1 units, and the maximum visible distance to 100 units. Any objects closer than 0.1 units will be invisible, and any objects further than 100 units will also be invisible. If our stage were to contain a lot of complex models spread throughout space, then having a large maximum visible distance could potentially cause performance problems because too much is being rendered on the screen at once.

Next, we can set the model-view matrix to the identity matrix using the `identity()` function, and then translate the model-view matrix to (0, 0, -5). This means that we've simply moved our model -5 units in the z direction which is 5 units away from the user.

Finally, we can push the position buffer onto the graphics card using the `pushPositionBuffer()` method and then draw the triangle using `drawArrays()`.

Rotating a triangular plane in 3D space

Now that we can draw a 2D triangle in 3D space, let's try spinning it about the y-axis using the animation methods we added to the WebGL wrapper object.

How to do it...

Follow these steps to rotate a triangle about the y-axis with WebGL:

1. Link to the `glMatrix` library and the WebGL wrapper:

```
<script type="text/javascript" src="glMatrix-1.0.1.min.js">
</script>
<script type="text/javascript" src="WebGL.js">
</script>
```

2. Define the `initBuffers()` function which initializes the position buffers for our triangle:

```
function initBuffers(gl){
    var triangleBuffers = {};
    triangleBuffers.positionBuffer = gl.createArrayBuffer([
        0, 1, 0,
        -1, -1, 0,
        1, -1, 0
    ]);

    return triangleBuffers;
}
```

3. Define the `stage()` function which sets the perspective, sets the model-view matrix to the identity matrix, translates the triangle, rotates the triangle about the y-axis, pushes the position buffer onto the graphics card, and draws the triangle using `drawArrays()`:

```
function stage(gl, triangleBuffers, angle){
    // set field of view at 45 degrees
    // set viewing range between 0.1 and 100.0 units away.
    gl.perspective(45, 0.1, 100.0);
    gl.identity();

    // translate model-view matrix
    gl.translate(0, 0, -5);
    // rotate model-view matrix about y-axis
    gl.rotate(angle, 0, 1, 0);

    gl.pushPositionBuffer(triangleBuffers);
    gl.drawArrays(triangleBuffers);
}
```

4. When the page loads, initialize the WebGL wrapper object, set the shader program, initialize the buffers, set the `stage` function for the animation, and then start the animation:

```
window.onload = function(){
    var gl = new WebGL("myCanvas", "experimental-webgl");
    gl.setShaderProgram("BLUE_COLOR");
    var triangleBuffers = initBuffers(gl);
    var angle = 0;

    gl.setStage(function(){
        // update angle
        var angularVelocity = Math.PI / 2; // radians / second
        var angleEachFrame = angularVelocity *
gl.getTimeInterval() / 1000;
        angle += angleEachFrame;

        this.clear();

        stage(gl, triangleBuffers, angle);
    });
    gl.start();
};
```

5. Embed the canvas tag inside the body of the HTML document:

```
<canvas id="myCanvas" width="600" height="250"
    style="border:1px solid black;"></canvas>
```

How it works...

To rotate our triangle about the y-axis, we first need to set up an animation stage by setting the `stage()` function of the WebGL wrapper object (similar to what we did in *Chapter 5* with the `Animation` object), and then start the animation with `start()`. For each animation frame, we can increase the angle of the triangle about the y-axis by rotating the model-view matrix with the `rotate()` method.

See also...

- *Creating an Animation class* in *Chapter 5*

Creating a rotating cube

Okay, now the fun really begins. In this recipe, we'll create a rotating 3D cube with differently colored faces. To do so, we'll introduce two new kinds of buffers—color buffers and index buffers.

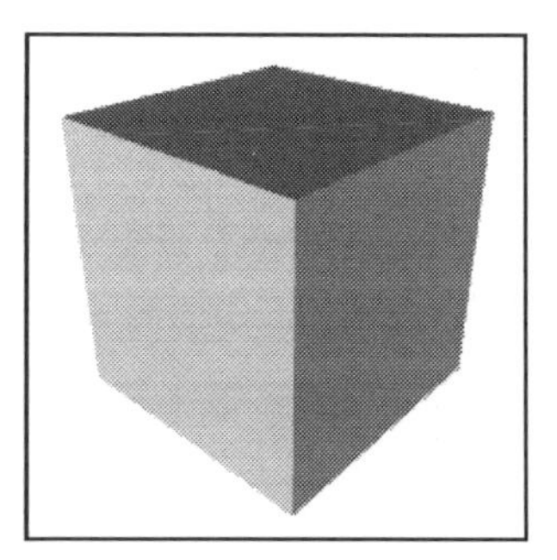

How to do it...

Follow these steps to create a rotating cube with WebGL:

1. Link to the `glMatrix` library and the WebGL wrapper:

```
<script type="text/javascript" src="glMatrix-1.0.1.min.js">
</script>
<script type="text/javascript" src="WebGL.js">
</script>
```

2. Define the `initBuffers()` function which initializes the position buffers, color buffers, and the index buffers for our cube:

```
    function initBuffers(gl){
        var cubeBuffers = {}
        cubeBuffers.positionBuffer = gl.createArrayBuffer([
            // Front face
            -1, -1,  1,
             1, -1,  1,
             1,  1,  1,
            -1,  1,  1,

            // Back face
            -1, -1, -1,
            -1,  1, -1,
             1,  1, -1,
             1, -1, -1,

            // Top face
            -1,  1, -1,
```

```
        -1,  1,  1,
         1,  1,  1,
         1,  1, -1,

        // Bottom face
        -1, -1, -1,
         1, -1, -1,
         1, -1,  1,
        -1, -1,  1,

        // Right face
         1, -1, -1,
         1,  1, -1,
         1,  1,  1,
         1, -1,  1,

        // Left face
        -1, -1, -1,
        -1, -1,  1,
        -1,  1,  1,
        -1,  1, -1
    ]);

    // build color Vertices
    var colors = [
        [1, 0, 1, 1], // Front face - Pink
        [0, 1, 0, 1], // Back face - Green
        [0, 0, 1, 1], // Top face - Blue
        [0, 1, 1, 1], // Bottom face - Turquoise
        [1, 1, 0, 1], // Right face - Yellow
        [1, 0, 0, 1]  // Left face - Red
    ];

    var colorVertices = [];

    for (var n in colors) {
        var color = colors[n];
        for (var i=0; i < 4; i++) {
            colorVertices = colorVertices.concat(color);
        }
    }

    cubeBuffers.colorBuffer = gl.createArrayBuffer(colorVertic
es);
```

```
        cubeBuffers.indexBuffer = gl.createElementArrayBuffer([
            0, 1, 2,        0, 2, 3,     // Front face
            4, 5, 6,        4, 6, 7,     // Back face
            8, 9, 10,       8, 10, 11,   // Top face
            12, 13, 14,     12, 14, 15,  // Bottom face
            16, 17, 18,     16, 18, 19,  // Right face
            20, 21, 22,     20, 22, 23   // Left face
        ]);

        return cubeBuffers;
    }
```

3. Define the `stage()` function which sets the perspective, sets the model-view matrix to the identity matrix, translates the cube, rotates the cube, pushes the position buffer, the color buffer, and the index buffer onto the graphics card, and finally draws the cube using `drawElements()` since the faces of our model aren't triangular:

```
    function stage(gl, cubeBuffers, angle){
        // set field of view at 45 degrees
        // set viewing range between 0.1 and 100.0 units away.
        gl.perspective(45, 0.1, 100);
        gl.identity();

        // translate model-view matrix
        gl.translate(0, 0, -5);
        // rotate model-view matrix about x-axis (tilt box
downwards)
        gl.rotate(Math.PI * 0.15, 1, 0, 0);
        // rotate model-view matrix about y-axis
        gl.rotate(angle, 0, 1, 0);

        gl.pushPositionBuffer(cubeBuffers);
        gl.pushColorBuffer(cubeBuffers);
        gl.pushIndexBuffer(cubeBuffers);
        gl.drawElements(cubeBuffers);
    }
```

4. When the page loads, initialize the WebGL wrapper object, set the shader program to `"VARYING_COLOR"` as the color of each face is variable and dependent on the color buffers, initialize the buffers, set the `stage` function for the animation, and then start the animation:

```
    window.onload = function(){
        var gl = new WebGL("myCanvas", "experimental-webgl");
        gl.setShaderProgram("VARYING_COLOR");
        var cubeBuffers = initBuffers(gl);
```

```
            var angle = 0;
            gl.setStage(function(){
                // update angle
                var angularVelocity = Math.PI / 4; // radians / second
                var angleEachFrame = angularVelocity * this.
    getTimeInterval() / 1000;
                angle += angleEachFrame;

                this.clear();

                stage(this, cubeBuffers, angle);
            });
            gl.start();
        };
```

5. Embed the canvas tag inside the body of the HTML document:

```
<canvas id="myCanvas" width="600" height="250"
    style="border:1px solid black;"></canvas>
```

How it works...

This recipe introduces the concept of index buffers and color buffers. In the previous two recipes, we created a triangular plane because models with triangular faces are the easiest to implement with WebGL because only one buffer is required—the position buffer. When we want to create a 3D model with non-triangular faces, such as a cube, it's a bit more complex because we need a way to represent the cube as a set of triangular faces. We can accomplish this by creating an index buffer that maps triangles to the vertices of the position buffer.

Take a look at the index buffer vertices in the proceeding code. You'll notice that the first six elements are `[0, 1, 2, 0, 2, 3]`. The first three elements, `[0, 1, 2]` refer to the 0th, 1st, and 2nd vertices of the position buffer, which form a triangle that covers half of the front face of the cube. The second set of elements, `[0, 2, 3]` correspond to the 0th, 2nd, and 3rd vertices of the position buffer and form a second triangle that covers the other half of the front face of the cube. Together, these two triangles form a solid face for the front face of the cube. When the index buffer is complete, it will contain a mapping of position buffer vertices that form triangular faces that cover the six faces of the cube.

In addition to index buffers, this recipe also requires the use of color buffers. Color buffers are used to define the colors of model faces. In this recipe, the color buffer will define six different colors for the six faces of our cube. Similar to index buffers, color buffers are used to map a color to each vertex in the position buffer. Each color is defined by four elements, [red, green, blue, alpha]. As defined by the position buffer, our cube is made up of six faces, each with four vertices. Therefore, our color buffer array should contain (6 faces) * (4 vertices per face) * (4 elements per color) = 96 elements.

Once we have our position buffer, color buffer, and index buffer defined, all that's left for us to do is to push each buffer onto the graphics card and render the model. Unlike the previous two recipes where we used the `drawArrays()` method to directly render the triangle, in this recipe we'll have to use the `drawElements()` method because our model is made up of non-triangular faces and requires an index buffer to map triangular faces to the square faces of our model.

See also...

- *Creating an Animation class* in *Chapter 5*

Adding textures and lighting

Now that we know how to create a simple 3D model using position buffers and index buffers, let's make a wooden crate by wrapping our model with a crate texture and then adding some ambient and directional lighting to create shaded surfaces. This recipe introduces texture buffers to create textures and normal buffers which are required to handle lighting effects.

How to do it...

Follow these steps to create a rotating crate with lighting in WebGL:

1. Link to the `glMatrix` library and the WebGL wrapper:

```
<script type="text/javascript" src="glMatrix-1.0.1.min.js">
</script>
<script type="text/javascript" src="WebGL.js">
</script>
```

2. Define the `initBuffers()` function which initializes the position buffer, normal buffer, texture buffer, and the index buffer for our cube:

```
function initBuffers(gl){
    var cubeBuffers = {};
    cubeBuffers.positionBuffer = gl.createArrayBuffer([
        // Front face
        -1, -1, 1,
        1, -1, 1,
        1, 1, 1,
        -1, 1, 1,

        // Back face
        -1, -1, -1,
        -1, 1, -1,
        1, 1, -1,
        1, -1, -1,

        // Top face
        -1, 1, -1,
        -1, 1, 1,
        1, 1, 1,
        1, 1, -1,

        // Bottom face
        -1, -1, -1,
        1, -1, -1,
        1, -1, 1,
        -1, -1, 1,

        // Right face
        1, -1, -1,
        1, 1, -1,
        1, 1, 1,
        1, -1, 1,

        // Left face
        -1, -1, -1,
        -1, -1, 1,
        -1, 1, 1,
        -1, 1, -1
    ]);

    cubeBuffers.normalBuffer = gl.createArrayBuffer([
        // Front face
```

```
         0,  0,  1,
         0,  0,  1,
         0,  0,  1,
         0,  0,  1,

        // Back face
         0,  0, -1,
         0,  0, -1,
         0,  0, -1,
         0,  0, -1,

        // Top face
         0,  1,  0,
         0,  1,  0,
         0,  1,  0,
         0,  1,  0,

        // Bottom face
         0, -1,  0,
         0, -1,  0,
         0, -1,  0,
         0, -1,  0,

        // Right face
         1,  0,  0,
         1,  0,  0,
         1,  0,  0,
         1,  0,  0,

        // Left face
        -1,  0,  0,
        -1,  0,  0,
        -1,  0,  0,
        -1,  0,  0
    ]);

    cubeBuffers.textureBuffer = gl.createArrayBuffer([
        // Front face
        0, 0,
        1, 0,
        1, 1,
        0, 1,
```

```
            // Back face
             1, 0,
            1, 1,
            0, 1,
            0, 0,

            // Top face
             0, 1,
            0, 0,
            1, 0,
            1, 1,

            // Bottom face
             1, 1,
            0, 1,
            0, 0,
            1, 0,

            // Right face
             1, 0,
            1, 1,
            0, 1,
            0, 0,

            // Left face
             0, 0,
            1, 0,
            1, 1,
            0, 1
        ]);

        cubeBuffers.indexBuffer = gl.createElementArrayBuffer([
             0, 1, 2,         0, 2, 3, // Front face
             4, 5, 6,         4, 6, 7, // Back face
             8, 9, 10,         8, 10, 11, // Top face
             12, 13, 14,     12, 14, 15, // Bottom face
             16, 17, 18,     16, 18, 19, // Right face
             20, 21, 22,     20, 22, 23 // Left face
        ]);

        return cubeBuffers;
    }
```

3. Define the `stage()` function which sets the perspective, sets the model-view matrix to the identity matrix, translates the cube, rotates the cube, enables lighting, sets the ambient lighting, sets the directional lighting, pushes the position buffer, the normal buffer, the texture buffer, and the index buffer onto the graphics card, and finally draws the cube using `drawElements()`:

```
function stage(gl, cubeBuffers, crateTexture, angle){
    // set field of view at 45 degrees
    // set viewing range between 0.1 and 100 units away.
    gl.perspective(45, 0.1, 100.0);
    gl.identity();

    // translate model-view matrix
    gl.translate(0, 0.0, -5);
    // rotate model-view matrix about x-axis (tilt box
    downwards)
    gl.rotate(Math.PI * 0.15, 1, 0, 0);
    // rotate model-view matrix about y-axis
    gl.rotate(angle, 0, 1, 0);

        // enable lighting
    gl.enableLighting();
    gl.setAmbientLighting(0.5, 0.5, 0.5);
    gl.setDirectionalLighting(-0.25, -0.25, -1, 0.8, 0.8,
    0.8);

    gl.pushPositionBuffer(cubeBuffers);
    gl.pushNormalBuffer(cubeBuffers);
    gl.pushTextureBuffer(cubeBuffers, crateTexture);
    gl.pushIndexBuffer(cubeBuffers);
    gl.drawElements(cubeBuffers);
}
```

4. Define the `init()` method which initializes the crate texture, sets the the `stage()` function, and starts the animation:

```
function init(gl, crateTexture){
    var cubeBuffers = initBuffers(gl);
    var angle = 0;
    gl.initTexture(crateTexture);
    gl.setStage(function(){
        // update angle
        var angularVelocity = Math.PI / 4; // radians / second
        var angleEachFrame = angularVelocity *
        this.getTimeInterval() / 1000;
        angle += angleEachFrame;
```

```
            this.clear();

            stage(this, cubeBuffers, crateTexture, angle);
        });
        gl.start();
    }
```

5. Define the `loadTexture()` function which creates a new texture object, creates a new image object, initializes the texture and starts the animation once the texture image has loaded:

```
    function loadTexture(gl){
        var crateTexture = gl.getContext().createTexture();
        crateTexture.image = new Image();

        crateTexture.image.onload = function(){
            init(gl, crateTexture);
        };
        crateTexture.image.src = "crate.jpg";
    }
```

6. When the page loads, initialize the WebGL wrapper object, set the shader program to `"TEXTURE_DIRECTIONAL_LIGHTING"`, and load the texture:

```
    window.onload = function(){
        var gl = new WebGL("myCanvas", "experimental-webgl");
        gl.setShaderProgram("TEXTURE_DIRECTIONAL_LIGHTING");
        loadTexture(gl);
    };
```

7. Embed the canvas tag inside the body of the HTML document:

```
        <canvas id="myCanvas" width="600" height="250"
            style="border:1px solid black;"></canvas>
```

How it works...

This recipe introduces the concept of texture buffers and normal buffers. Texture buffers allow us to define the orientation and scale of a texture image for each face of a 3D model. To define the texture buffer of our wooden crate, we need to map the four corners of the texture image to the four corners of each face of the cube.

In order to handle lighting effects with WebGL, we need to define the normals of the faces that make up our cube with normal buffers. Normals are vectors that are perpendicular to a surface. For example, the normal of a floor points straight up, and the normal of the ceiling points straight down. Once our normals have been defined, we are now in a position to set up ambient and directional lighting.

Although there are many other kinds of lighting effects that can be achieved with WebGL, this recipe focuses on the two most common—ambient and directional lighting, which can be used together or independently:

- **Ambient lighting** refers to the general lighting of a room or world, and is defined with RGB. A room with an ambient lighting value of `[0,0,0]` would be completely dark, and a room with an ambient lighting value of `[1,1,1]` would be completely lit. Also, if we had a room with an ambient lighting value of `[1,0,0]` for example, the room would be illuminated with a red light.
- **Directional lighting** causes the faces of 3D models that are facing towards the light to be lighter, and the faces of 3D models that are facing away from the light to be darker. Directional lighting is typically used to simulate very strong light sources that are far away, such as the sun.

To use both textures and directional lighting, we can set the shader program to `TEXTURE_DIRECTIONAL_LIGHTING` with the `setShaderProgram()` method and we can enable lighting with the `enableLighting()` method. Finally, we can set the ambient lighting of our world with the `setAmbientLighting()` method and set the directional lighting using the `setDirectionalLighting()` method.

See also...

- *Creating an Animation class* in *Chapter 5*

Creating a 3D world that you can explore

Now that we know how to create some basic 3D models with textures and lighting, we are now in a position to create our own 3D world. In this recipe, we'll create three sets of buffers—cube buffers, wall buffers, and floor buffers. We can use the cube buffers to render randomly placed crates throughout our world, the wall buffers to create four walls, and the floor buffers to create a floor and a ceiling (we can reuse the floor buffers for the ceiling buffers since they are the same shape). Next, we'll add keyboard event listeners to the document so that we can explore the world with the arrow keys and the mouse. Let's get started!

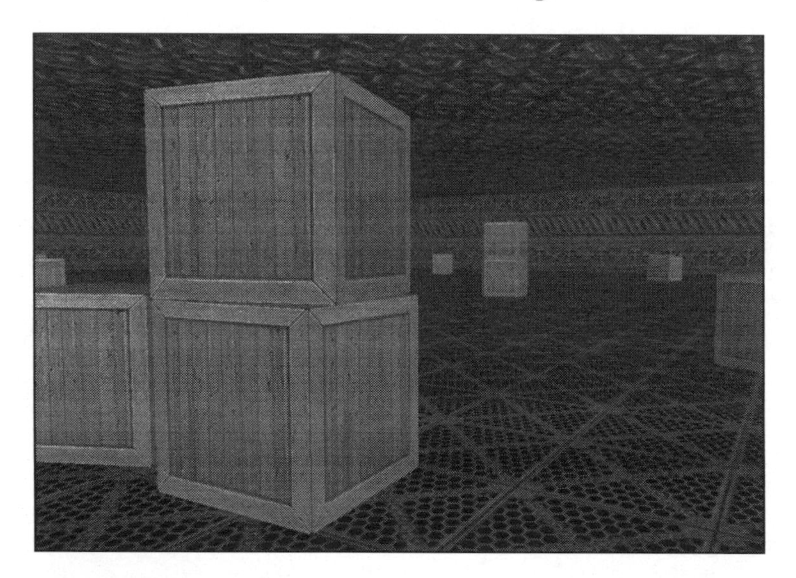

How to do it...

Follow these steps to create a 3D world full of randomly placed crates that you can explore with the keyboard and mouse in WebGL:

1. Link to the `glMatrix` library and the WebGL wrapper:

```
<script type="text/javascript" src="glMatrix-1.0.1.min.js">
</script>
<script type="text/javascript" src="WebGL.js">
</script>
```

2. Define the `Controller` constructor which initializes the view, the WebGL wrapper object, and the model, attaches keyboard event listeners, and loads the world textures:

```
/**************************************
 * Controller
 */
```

```
    function Controller(){
        this.view = new View(this);
        this.gl = new WebGL("myCanvas");
        this.gl.setShaderProgram("TEXTURE_DIRECTIONAL_LIGHTING");
        this.model = new Model(this);

        this.attachListeners();

        var sources = {
            crate: "crate.jpg",
            metalFloor: "metalFloor.jpg",
            metalWall: "metalWall.jpg",
            ceiling: "ceiling.jpg"
        };

        this.mouseDownPos = null;
        this.mouseDownPitch = 0;
        this.mouseDownYaw = 0;

        var that = this;
        this.loadTextures(sources, function(){
            that.gl.setStage(function(){
                that.view.stage();
            });

            that.gl.start();
        });
    }
```

3. Define the `loadTextures()` method which loads the world textures:

```
    Controller.prototype.loadTextures = function(sources,
callback){
        var gl = this.gl;
        var context = gl.getContext();
        var textures = this.model.textures;
        var loadedImages = 0;
        var numImages = 0;
        for (var src in sources) {
            // anonymous function to induce scope
            (function(){
                var key = src;
                numImages++;
                textures[key] = context.createTexture();
                textures[key].image = new Image();
```

```
                textures[key].image.onload = function(){
                    gl.initTexture(textures[key]);
                    if (++loadedImages >= numImages) {
                        callback();
                    }
                };

                textures[key].image.src = sources[key];
            })();
        }
    };
```

4. Define the `getMousePos()` method which gets the mouse position:

```
    Controller.prototype.getMousePos = function(evt){
        return {
            x: evt.clientX,
            y: evt.clientY
        };
    };
```

5. Define the `handleMouseDown()` method which captures the start mouse position, camera pitch, and camera yaw:

```
    Controller.prototype.handleMouseDown = function(evt){
        var camera = this.model.camera;
        this.mouseDownPos = this.getMousePos(evt);
        this.mouseDownPitch = camera.pitch;
        this.mouseDownYaw = camera.yaw;
    };
```

6. Define the `handleMouseMove()` method which updates the camera:

```
    Controller.prototype.handleMouseMove = function(evt){
        var mouseDownPos = this.mouseDownPos;
        var gl = this.gl;
        if (mouseDownPos !== null) {
            var mousePos = this.getMousePos(evt);

            // update pitch
            var yDiff = mousePos.y - mouseDownPos.y;
            this.model.camera.pitch = this.mouseDownPitch + yDiff
/ gl.getCanvas().height;

            // update yaw
            var xDiff = mousePos.x - mouseDownPos.x;
            this.model.camera.yaw = this.mouseDownYaw + xDiff /
gl.getCanvas().width;
        }
    };
```

7. Define the `handleKeyDown()` method which controls the user movement through the world:

```
Controller.prototype.handleKeyDown = function(evt){
    var keycode = ((evt.which) || (evt.keyCode));
    var model = this.model;
    switch (keycode) {
        case 37:
            // left key
            model.sideMovement = model.LEFT;
            break;
        case 38:
            // up key
            model.straightMovement = model.FORWARD;
            break;
        case 39:
            // right key
            model.sideMovement = model.RIGHT;
            break;
        case 40:
            // down key
            model.straightMovement = model.BACKWARD;
            break;
    }
};
```

8. Define the `handleKeyUp()` method which sets the user side movement to `STILL` if the left or right arrow key has been released, and sets the user straight movement to `STILL` if the up or down arrow key has been released:

```
Controller.prototype.handleKeyUp = function(evt){
    var keycode = ((evt.which) || (evt.keyCode));
    var model = this.model;
    switch (keycode) {
        case 37:
            // left key
            model.sideMovement = model.STILL;
            break;
        case 38:
            // up key
            model.straightMovement = model.STILL;
            break;
        case 39:
            // right key
            model.sideMovement = model.STILL;
            break;
```

```
            case 40:
                // down key
                model.straightMovement = model.STILL;
                break;
        }
    };
```

9. Define the `attachListeners()` method which attaches listeners to the canvas and document:

```
    Controller.prototype.attachListeners = function(){
        var gl = this.gl;
        var that = this;
        gl.getCanvas().addEventListener("mousedown", function(evt)
{
            that.handleMouseDown(evt);
        }, false);

        gl.getCanvas().addEventListener("mousemove", function(evt)
{
            that.handleMouseMove(evt);
        }, false);

        document.addEventListener("mouseup", function(evt){
            that.mouseDownPos = null;
        }, false);

        document.addEventListener("mouseout", function(evt){
            // same as mouseup functionality
            that.mouseDownPos = null;
        }, false);

        document.addEventListener("keydown", function(evt){
            that.handleKeyDown(evt);
        }, false);

        document.addEventListener("keyup", function(evt){
            that.handleKeyUp(evt);
        }, false);
    };
```

10. Define the `Model` constructor which initializes the camera and the buffers for the crates, the floor, and the wall:

```
    /*************************************
     * Model
     */
    function Model(controller){
```

```
        this.controller = controller;
        this.cubeBuffers = {};
        this.floorBuffers = {};
        this.wallBuffers = {};
        this.angle = 0;
        this.textures = {};
        this.cratePositions = [];

        // movements
        this.STILL = "STILL";
        this.FORWARD = "FORWARD";
        this.BACKWARD = "BACKWARD";
        this.LEFT = "LEFT";
        this.RIGHT = "RIGHT";

        // camera
        this.camera = {
            x: 0,
            y: 1.5,
            z: 5,
            pitch: 0,
            yaw: 0
        };

        this.straightMovement = this.STILL;
        this.sideMovement = this.STILL;
        this.speed = 8; // units per second
        this.initBuffers();
        this.initCratePositions();
    }
```

11. Define the `initCratePositions()` method which generates 20 crates with random positions in the world and also randomly stacks crates:

```
    Model.prototype.initCratePositions = function(){
        var crateRange = 45;
        // randomize 20 floor crates
        for (var n = 0; n < 20; n++) {
            var cratePos = {};
            cratePos.x = (Math.random() * crateRange * 2) -
            crateRange;
            cratePos.y = 0;
            cratePos.z = (Math.random() * crateRange * 2) -
            crateRange;
            cratePos.rotationY = Math.random() * Math.PI * 2;
```

```
                this.cratePositions.push(cratePos);

                if (Math.round(Math.random() * 3) == 3) {
                    var stackedCratePosition = {};
                    stackedCratePosition.x = cratePos.x;
                    stackedCratePosition.y = 2.01;
                    stackedCratePosition.z = cratePos.z;
                    stackedCratePosition.rotationY = cratePos.
rotationY + ((Math.random() * Math.PI / 8) - Math.PI / 16);
                    this.cratePositions.push(stackedCratePosition);
                }
            }
        };
```

12. Define the `initCubeBuffers()` method which initializes the cube buffers for the crates:

```
Model.prototype.initCubeBuffers = function(){
    var gl = this.controller.gl;
    this.cubeBuffers.positionBuffer = gl.createArrayBuffer([
        -1, -1, 1, 1, -1, 1, 1, 1, 1, -1, 1, 1, // Front face
        -1, -1, -1, -1, 1, -1, 1, 1, -1, 1, -1, -1, // Back
        face
        -1, 1, -1, -1, 1, 1, 1, 1, 1, 1, 1, -1, // Top face
        -1, -1, -1, 1, -1, -1, 1, -1, 1, -1, -1, 1, // Bottom
       face
        1, -1, -1, 1, 1, -1, 1, 1, 1, 1, -1, 1, // Right face
        -1, -1, -1, -1, -1, 1, -1, 1, 1, -1, 1, -1 // Left
        face
    ]);

    this.cubeBuffers.normalBuffer = gl.createArrayBuffer([
        0, 0, 1, 0, 0, 1, 0, 0, 1, 0, 0, 1, // Front face
        0, 0, -1, 0, 0, -1, 0, 0, -1, 0, 0, -1, // Back face
        0, 1, 0, 0, 1, 0, 0, 1, 0, 0, 1, 0, // Top face
        0, -1, 0, 0, -1, 0, 0, -1, 0, 0, -1, 0, // Bottom face
        1, 0, 0, 1, 0, 0, 1, 0, 0, 1, 0, 0, // Right face
        -1, 0, 0, -1, 0, 0, -1, 0, 0, -1, 0, 0 // Left face
    ]);

    this.cubeBuffers.textureBuffer = gl.createArrayBuffer([
        0, 0, 1, 0, 1, 1, 0, 1, // Front face
        1, 0, 1, 1, 0, 1, 0, 0, // Back face
        0, 1, 0, 0, 1, 0, 1, 1, // Top face
        1, 1, 0, 1, 0, 0, 1, 0, // Bottom face
        1, 0, 1, 1, 0, 1, 0, 0, // Right face
```

```
            0, 0, 1, 0, 1, 1, 0, 1 // Left face
        ]);

        this.cubeBuffers.indexBuffer =
gl.createElementArrayBuffer([
            0, 1, 2, 0, 2, 3, // Front face
             4, 5, 6, 4, 6, 7, // Back face
             8, 9, 10, 8, 10, 11, // Top face
             12, 13, 14, 12, 14, 15, // Bottom face
             16, 17, 18, 16, 18, 19, // Right face
             20, 21, 22, 20, 22, 23 // Left face
        ]);
    };
```

13. Define the `initFloorBuffers()` method which initializes the floor buffers (these buffers will be used for the ceiling as well):

```
    Model.prototype.initFloorBuffers = function(){
        var gl = this.controller.gl;
        this.floorBuffers.positionBuffer = gl.createArrayBuffer([
            -50, 0, -50, -50, 0, 50, 50, 0, 50, 50, 0, -50
        ]);

        this.floorBuffers.textureBuffer = gl.createArrayBuffer([
            0, 25, 0, 0, 25, 0, 25, 25
        ]);

        this.floorBuffers.indexBuffer =
gl.createElementArrayBuffer([
            0, 1, 2, 0, 2, 3
        ]);

        // floor normal points upwards
        this.floorBuffers.normalBuffer = gl.createArrayBuffer([
            0, 1, 0, 0, 1, 0, 0, 1, 0, 0, 1, 0
        ]);
    };
```

14. Define the `initWallBuffers()` method which initializes the wall buffers:

```
    Model.prototype.initWallBuffers = function(){
        var gl = this.controller.gl;
        this.wallBuffers.positionBuffer = gl.createArrayBuffer([
            -50, 5, 0, 50, 5, 0, 50, -5, 0, -50, -5, 0
        ]);

        this.wallBuffers.textureBuffer = gl.createArrayBuffer([
```

```
            0, 0, 25, 0, 25, 1.5, 0, 1.5
        ]);

        this.wallBuffers.indexBuffer =
gl.createElementArrayBuffer([
            0, 1, 2, 0, 2, 3
        ]);

        // floor normal points upwards
        this.wallBuffers.normalBuffer = gl.createArrayBuffer([
            0, 0, 1, 0, 0, 1, 0, 0, 1, 0, 0, 1
        ]);
    };
```

15. Define the `initBuffers()` method which initializes the cube, floor, and wall buffers:

```
    Model.prototype.initBuffers = function(){
        this.initCubeBuffers();
        this.initFloorBuffers();
        this.initWallBuffers();
    };
```

16. Define the `updateCameraPos()` method which is used to update the camera position for each animation frame:

```
    Model.prototype.updateCameraPos = function(){
        var gl = this.controller.gl;
        if (this.straightMovement != this.STILL) {
            var direction = this.straightMovement == this.FORWARD
? -1 : 1;
            var distEachFrame = direction * this.speed *
gl.getTimeInterval() / 1000;
            this.camera.z += distEachFrame * Math.cos(this.camera.
yaw);
            this.camera.x += distEachFrame * Math.sin(this.camera.
yaw);
        }

        if (this.sideMovement != this.STILL) {
            var direction = this.sideMovement == this.RIGHT ? 1 :
-1;
            var distEachFrame = direction * this.speed *
gl.getTimeInterval() / 1000;
            this.camera.z += distEachFrame * Math.cos(this.camera.
yaw + Math.PI / 2);
```

```
            this.camera.x += distEachFrame * Math.sin(this.camera.
yaw + Math.PI / 2);
        }
    };
```

17. Define the `View` constructor which sets the canvas dimensions:

```
/*************************************
 * View
 */
function View(controller){
    this.controller = controller;
    this.canvas = document.getElementById("myCanvas");
    this.canvas.width = window.innerWidth;
    this.canvas.height = window.innerHeight;
}
```

18. Define the `drawFloor()` method which draws the floor:

```
View.prototype.drawFloor = function(){
    var controller = this.controller;
    var gl = controller.gl;
    var model = controller.model;
    var floorBuffers = model.floorBuffers;

    gl.save();
    gl.translate(0, -1.1, 0);
    gl.pushPositionBuffer(floorBuffers);
    gl.pushNormalBuffer(floorBuffers);
    gl.pushTextureBuffer(floorBuffers,
    model.textures.metalFloor);
    gl.pushIndexBuffer(floorBuffers);
    gl.drawElements(floorBuffers);
    gl.restore();
};
```

19. Define the `drawCeiling()` method which draws the ceiling:

```
View.prototype.drawCeiling = function(){
    var controller = this.controller;
    var gl = controller.gl;
    var model = controller.model;
    var floorBuffers = model.floorBuffers;

    gl.save();
    gl.translate(0, 8.9, 0);
    // use floor buffers with ceiling texture
    gl.pushPositionBuffer(floorBuffers);
```

```
        gl.pushNormalBuffer(floorBuffers);
        gl.pushTextureBuffer(floorBuffers,
        model.textures.ceiling);
        gl.pushIndexBuffer(floorBuffers);
        gl.drawElements(floorBuffers);
        gl.restore();
    };
```

20. Define the `drawCrates()` method which draws the crates:

```
    View.prototype.drawCrates = function(){
        var controller = this.controller;
        var gl = controller.gl;
        var model = controller.model;
        var cubeBuffers = model.cubeBuffers;

        for (var n = 0; n < model.cratePositions.length; n++) {
            gl.save();
            var cratePos = model.cratePositions[n];
            gl.translate(cratePos.x, cratePos.y, cratePos.z);
            gl.rotate(cratePos.rotationY, 0, 1, 0);
            gl.pushPositionBuffer(cubeBuffers);
            gl.pushNormalBuffer(cubeBuffers);
            gl.pushTextureBuffer(cubeBuffers,
            model.textures.crate);
            gl.pushIndexBuffer(cubeBuffers);
            gl.drawElements(cubeBuffers);
            gl.restore();
        }
    };
```

21. Define the `drawWalls()` method which draws the walls:

```
    View.prototype.drawWalls = function(){
        var controller = this.controller;
        var gl = controller.gl;
        var model = controller.model;
        var wallBuffers = model.wallBuffers;
        var metalWallTexture = model.textures.metalWall;

        gl.save();
        gl.translate(0, 3.9, -50);
        gl.pushPositionBuffer(wallBuffers);
        gl.pushNormalBuffer(wallBuffers);
        gl.pushTextureBuffer(wallBuffers, metalWallTexture);
        gl.pushIndexBuffer(wallBuffers);
```

```
        gl.drawElements(wallBuffers);
        gl.restore();

        gl.save();
        gl.translate(0, 3.9, 50);
        gl.rotate(Math.PI, 0, 1, 0);
        gl.pushPositionBuffer(wallBuffers);
        gl.pushNormalBuffer(wallBuffers);
        gl.pushTextureBuffer(wallBuffers, metalWallTexture);
        gl.pushIndexBuffer(wallBuffers);
        gl.drawElements(wallBuffers);
        gl.restore();

        gl.save();
        gl.translate(50, 3.9, 0);
        gl.rotate(Math.PI * 1.5, 0, 1, 0);
        gl.pushPositionBuffer(wallBuffers);
        gl.pushNormalBuffer(wallBuffers);
        gl.pushTextureBuffer(wallBuffers, metalWallTexture);
        gl.pushIndexBuffer(wallBuffers);
        gl.drawElements(wallBuffers);
        gl.restore();

        gl.save();
        gl.translate(-50, 3.9, 0);
        gl.rotate(Math.PI / 2, 0, 1, 0);
        gl.pushPositionBuffer(wallBuffers);
        gl.pushNormalBuffer(wallBuffers);
        gl.pushTextureBuffer(wallBuffers, metalWallTexture);
        gl.pushIndexBuffer(wallBuffers);
        gl.drawElements(wallBuffers);
        gl.restore();
    };
```

22. Define the `stage()` method which updates the camera position, clears the canvas, positions the world relative to the camera position, and then draws the floor, the walls, the ceiling, and the crates:

```
    View.prototype.stage = function(){
        var controller = this.controller;
        var gl = controller.gl;
        var model = controller.model;
        var view = controller.view;
        var camera = model.camera;
        model.updateCameraPos();
```

```
        gl.clear();

        // set field of view at 45 degrees
        // set viewing range between 0.1 and 100 units away.
        gl.perspective(45, 0.1, 150.0);
        gl.identity();

        gl.rotate(-camera.pitch, 1, 0, 0);
        gl.rotate(-camera.yaw, 0, 1, 0);
        gl.translate(-camera.x, -camera.y, -camera.z);

        // enable lighting
        gl.enableLighting();
        gl.setAmbientLighting(0.5, 0.5, 0.5);
        gl.setDirectionalLighting(-0.25, -0.25, -1, 0.8, 0.8,
        0.8);

        view.drawFloor();
        view.drawWalls();
        view.drawCeiling();
        view.drawCrates();
    };
```

23. When the page loads, initialize the `Controller`:

```
    window.onload = function(){
        new Controller();
    };
```

24. Embed the canvas tag inside the body of the HTML document:

```
        <canvas id="myCanvas" width="" height="">
        </canvas>
```

How it works...

This recipe uses an MVC (model, view, controller) design pattern to separate the drawing logic from the data logic.

The `Controller` class is responsible for directing the model and the view, and also manages user actions. It handles arrow key events with the `handleKeyDown()` and `handleKeyUp()` methods, and it also handles screen dragging with the `handleMouseDown()` and `handleMouseMove()` methods. In addition, the controller is also responsible for pre-loading all of the textures before the simulation begins.

Next, the model is responsible for handling all of the data-setting logic. The data for our simulation includes the cube, floor, and wall buffers, the textures, the crate positions, the camera position, pitch, and yaw, and also the user movements. The crate positions are initialized with the `initCratePositions()` method, the buffers for the world are initialized with the `initCubeBuffers()`, `initFloorBuffers()`, and the `initWallBuffers()` methods, and the camera position, pitch, and yaw is updated with the `updateCameraPos()` method.

Finally, the view is responsible for rendering the 3D world using the model data. Buffers are pushed to the graphics card and rendered with the `drawFloor()`, `drawCeiling()`, `drawCrates()`, and the `drawWalls()` methods. For each animation frame, the `stage()` method is called which updates the camera position, clears the canvas, sets the lighting, and draws the scene with the aforementioned drawing methods.

There's more...

Here are some more ideas if you want to extend this recipe:

- Add boundary conditions so that the player can't run through crates and walls
- Enable the player to jump, and perhaps even jump on top of crates
- Create doorways to other rooms
- Create staircases so that the player can explore other floors
- Add walking sounds with the HTML5 canvas audio tag

Now that you're able to create 3D models with textures and lighting and put them together to form segments of a 3D world, the only thing standing between you and a real-life Tron is your own imagination. Have fun!

See also...

- *Creating an Animation class* in *Chapter 5*

Detecting Canvas Support

Canvas fallback content

As all the browsers do not support canvas, it's a good idea to provide fallback content so that the users know that something isn't working correctly in the event that their browser of choice does not support canvas. The simplest and most straightforward technique for handling browsers that don't support canvas is to add fallback content inside of the canvas tag. Typically, this content will be text or an image that tells the user that their outdated browser doesn't support canvas, followed by a suggestion for downloading a browser developed in this decade. Users who are using a browser that does support canvas will not see the inner content:

```
<canvas id="myCanvas" width="578" height="250">
            Yikes!  Your browser doesn't support canvas.  Try using
Google Chrome or Firefox instead.
</canvas>
```

Canvas fallback content isn't always the best solution. For example, if the browser doesn't support canvas, you might want to alert an error message, redirect the user to a different URL, or even use a Flash version of the application as a fallback. The easiest way to detect whether the browser supports canvas is to create a dummy canvas element and then check whether we can execute the `getContext` method:

```
function isCanvasSupported(){
            return !!document.createElement('canvas').getContext;
        }
```

When the page loads, we can call the `isCanvasSupported()` function to determine whether or not the browser supports canvas and then appropriately handle the result.

This function uses one of my favorite JavaScript tricks, the double-not trick (`!!`), which determines whether or not the `getContext` method successfully executes. The first not of the double-not coerces the data type into a Boolean. As the act of coercing the data type yields the opposite result that we want, we can add a second not (`!!`) to flip the result back. The double-not trick is a super convenient way of checking whether or not a piece of code successfully executes, and in my opinion is much more elegant than wrapping a line of code with a `try/catch` block.

Detecting available WebGL contexts

If your canvas application leverages WebGL, you might also want to know which contexts the browser supports so that you can successfully initialize a WebGL application.

At the time of writing, there are five major contexts:

- `2D`
- `webgl`
- `experimental-webgl`
- `moz-webgl`
- `webkit-3d`

All of the major browsers including Google Chrome, Firefox, Safari, Opera, and IE9 support the 2D context. However, when it comes to `WebGL` support, it's a completely different story. At the time of writing, Google Chrome and Safari support the `experimental-webgl` and the `webkit-3d` contexts, Firefox supports the `experimental-webgl` and the `moz-webgl` contexts, and IE9 does not support any form of WebGL.

To see this for yourself, you can create a function called `getCanvasSupport()` which loops through all of the possible contexts and uses the double-not trick to determine which contexts are available:

```
function getCanvasSupport(){
    // initialize return object
    var returnObj = {
        canvas: false,
        webgl: false,
        context_2d: false,
        context_webgl: false,
        context_experimental_webgl: false,
        context_moz_webgl: false,
        context_webkit_3d: false
    };
```

```
    // check if canvas is supported
    if (!!document.createElement('canvas').getContext) {
        returnObj.canvas = true;
    }

    // check if WebGL rendering context is supported
    if (window.WebGLRenderingContext) {
        returnObj.webgl = true;
    }

    // check specific contexts
    var contextMapping = {
        context_2d: "2d",
        context_webgl: "webgl",
        context_experimental_webgl: "experimental-webgl",
        context_moz_webgl: "moz-webgl",
        context_webkit_3d: "webkit-3d"
    };

    for (var key in contextMapping) {
        try {
            if (!!document.createElement('canvas').getContext(contextM
apping[key])) {
                returnObj[key] = true;
            }
        }
        catch (e) {
        }
    }

    return returnObj;
}

function showSupport(obj){
    var str = "";

    str += "-- General Support --<br>";
    str += "canvas: " + (obj.canvas ? "YES" : "NO") + "<br>";
    str += "webgl: " + (obj.webgl ? "YES" : "NO") + "<br>";

    str += "<br>-- Successfully Initialized Contexts --<br>";
    str += "2d: " + (obj.context_2d ? "YES" : "NO") + "<br>";
    str += "webgl: " + (obj.context_webgl ? "YES" : "NO") + "<br>";
```

```
    str += "experimental-webgl: " + (obj.context_experimental_webgl ?
"YES" : "NO") + "<br>";
    str += "moz-webgl: " + (obj.context_moz_webgl ? "YES" : "NO") +
"<br>";
    str += "webkit-3d: " + (obj.context_webkit_3d ? "YES" : "NO") +
"<br>";

    document.write(str);
}

window.onload = function(){
    showSupport(getCanvasSupport());
};
```

B

Canvas Security

In order to protect pixel data of images, videos, and canvases on your website, the HTML5 canvas specification has safeguards in place to prevent scripts from other domains from accessing these media, manipulating them, and then creating new images, videos, or canvases.

Before anything is drawn on the canvas, the canvas tag has an origin-clean flag that's set to true. This basically means that the canvas is "clean". If you draw an image onto the canvas that's hosted on the same domain as the code running it, the origin-clean flag remains true. If, however, you draw an image onto the canvas that's hosted on another domain, the origin-clean flag is set to false and the canvas is now "dirty".

According to the HTML5 canvas specification, the canvas is considered dirty the moment any of these actions occur:

- The element's 2D context's `drawImage()` method is called with an `HTMLImageElement` or an `HTMLVideoElement` whose origin is not the same as that of the Document object that owns the canvas element.
- The element's 2D context's `drawImage()` method is called with an `HTMLCanvasElement` whose origin-clean flag is false.
- The element's 2D context's `fillStyle` attribute is set to a `CanvasPattern` object that was created from an `HTMLImageElement` or an `HTMLVideoElement` whose origin was not the same as that of the Document object that owns the canvas element when the pattern was created.
- The element's 2D context's `fillStyle` attribute is set to a `CanvasPattern` object that was created from an `HTMLCanvasElement` whose origin-clean flag was false when the pattern was created.

- The element's 2D context's `strokeStyle` attribute is set to a `CanvasPattern` object that was created from an `HTMLImageElement` or an `HTMLVideoElement` whose origin was not the same as that of the Document object that owns the canvas element when the pattern was created.
- The element's 2D context's `strokeStyle` attribute is set to a `CanvasPattern` object that was created from an `HTMLCanvasElement` whose origin-clean flag was false when the pattern was created.
- The element's 2D context's `fillText()` or `strokeText()` methods are invoked and consider using a font that has an origin that is not the same as that of the Document object that owns the canvas element. (The font doesn't even have to be used; all that matters is whether the font was considered for any of the glyphs drawn.)

In addition, if you perform any of these actions on your local computer (not a web server), the origin-clean flag will automatically be set to false because the resources will be perceived to have come from a different origin.

Next, according to the specification, a `SECURITY_ERR` exception will be thrown if any of these actions occur with a dirty canvas:

- The `toDataURL()` method is called
- The `getImageData()` method is called
- The `measureText()` method is used with a font whose origin is not the same as the Document object

Although the canvas security specification was created with good intentions, it may cause us more of a headache than it's worth. As an example, let's say that you wanted to create a drawing application that hooks into the Flickr API to pull in images from the public domain to add to your drawings. If you wanted your application to be able to save that drawing as an image using the `toDataURL()` method, or if you wanted your application to have fancy pixel manipulation algorithms using the `getImageData()` method, you're in some trouble. Performing these actions on a dirty canvas will throw a JavaScript error and prevent your application from working correctly.

One way to circumvent this problem is by creating a proxy that obtains images from another domain and then passes it back to the client, making it look as if the image came from your domain. If you've ever worked with cross-domain AJAX applications, you'll feel right at home.

C

Additional Topics

Canvas vs. CSS3 transitions and animations

In addition to the canvas, the HTML5 specification has also introduced two exciting additions to the CSS3 specification—**Transitions** and **Animations**.

Transitions enable developers to create simple animations that can change DOM element styles over a defined period of time. For example, if you mouse over a button and you want it to gradually fade to a different color within one second, you could use a CSS3 transition.

Animations enable developers to create more complex animations by defining specified key frames which can be thought of as a series of linked transitions. For example, if you wanted to animate a `DIV` element by moving it up, then left, then down, then back to its original position, you could use a CSS3 animation and define a key frame for each point along the path.

So, here's where people get hung up. When should you use canvas and when should you use CSS3 for animations? If you're a seasoned developer, I'm sure you know that the correct answer is "it depends". As a general rule of thumb, it's good practice to use CSS3 transitions and animations if you're animating DOM nodes, or if the animations are simple and well defined. If, on the other hand, you're animating something more complex such as a physics simulator or an online game, it would probably make more sense to use canvas.

Canvas performance on mobile devices

As the mobile and tablet markets continue to eat away at the traditional desktop and laptop markets, it's important to address the role of canvas in the mobile space. At the time of writing, canvas animations perform very poorly on nearly all mobile devices simply because they don't have powerful enough CPUs to handle it. Tablets typically have much better performance. There's good news though. In addition to software improvements and more powerful CPUs, mobile devices and tablets are pushing harder than ever to better leverage hardware acceleration, helping animations to run more smoothly. If you're considering building a graphically intensive web application that makes heavy use of canvas animations, make sure that you do a little bit of research upfront to find out the current state of canvas animation performance on the leading mobile devices if you plan on making it mobile friendly.

Index

Symbols

A

B

C

G

H

I

N

O

T

U

V

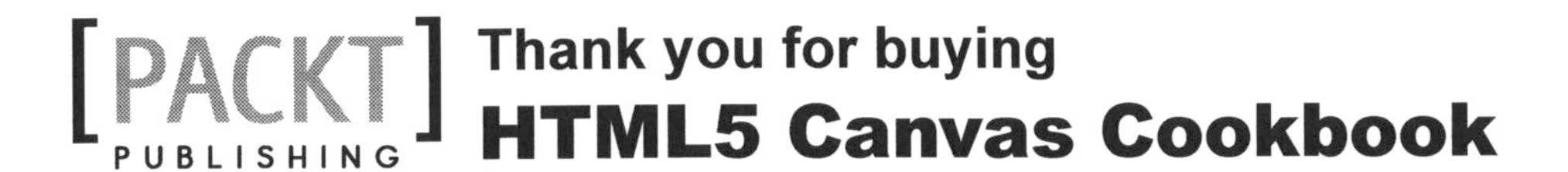

About Packt Publishing

Packt, pronounced 'packed', published its first book "*Mastering phpMyAdmin for Effective MySQL Management*" in April 2004 and subsequently continued to specialize in publishing highly focused books on specific technologies and solutions.

Our books and publications share the experiences of your fellow IT professionals in adapting and customizing today's systems, applications, and frameworks. Our solution based books give you the knowledge and power to customize the software and technologies you're using to get the job done. Packt books are more specific and less general than the IT books you have seen in the past. Our unique business model allows us to bring you more focused information, giving you more of what you need to know, and less of what you don't.

Packt is a modern, yet unique publishing company, which focuses on producing quality, cutting-edge books for communities of developers, administrators, and newbies alike. For more information, please visit our website: `www.packtpub.com`.

Writing for Packt

We welcome all inquiries from people who are interested in authoring. Book proposals should be sent to `author@packtpub.com`. If your book idea is still at an early stage and you would like to discuss it first before writing a formal book proposal, contact us; one of our commissioning editors will get in touch with you.

We're not just looking for published authors; if you have strong technical skills but no writing experience, our experienced editors can help you develop a writing career, or simply get some additional reward for your expertise.

HTML5 Mobile Development Cookbook

ISBN: 978-1-84969-196-3 Paperback: 358 pages

Recipes for building fast, responsive HTML5 mobile websites for iPhone 5, Android, Windows Phone and Blackberry

1. Solve your cross platform development issues by implementing device and content adaptation recipes

2. Maximum action, minimum theory allowing you to dive straight into HTML5 mobile web development

3. Incorporate HTML5-rich media and geo-location into your mobile websites

---

Dreamweaver CS5.5 Mobile and Web Development with HTML5, CSS3, and jQuery

ISBN: 978-1-84969-158-1 Paperback: 284 pages

Harness the cutting edge features of Dreamweaver for mobile and web development

1. Create web pages in Dreamweaver using the latest technology and approach

2. Add multimedia and interactivity to your websites

3. Optimize your websites for a wide range of platforms and build mobile apps with Dreamweaver

4. A practical guide filled with many examples for making the best use of Dreamweaver's latest features

Please check **www.PacktPub.com** for information on our titles

Made in the USA
Lexington, KY
21 June 2012